**contesting
postcolonialisms**

*to the tradition
of intellectual dissent and freedom*

contesting postcolonialisms

SECOND EDITION

edited by
jasbir jain
veena singh

Institute for Research in Interdisciplinary Studies

Rawat Publications
Jaipur and New Delhi

ISBN 81-7033-867-0
© Contributors, 2000

2nd Edition, 2004

No part of this book may be reproduced or transmitted in any form or by any means, electronic or mechanical, including photocopying, recording or by any information storage and for retrieval system, without permission in writing from the publishers.

Published by
Prem Rawat for *Rawat Publications*
Satyam Apts., Sector 3, Jawahar Nagar, Jaipur 302 004 (India)
Phone: 0141 265 1748 / 7006 Fax: 0141 265 1748
E-mail : info@rawatbooks.com
Website : www.rawatbooks.com

Delhi Office
4858/24, Ansari Road, Daryaganj, New Delhi 110 002
Phone: 011-23263290

Typeset by Rawat Computers, Jaipur
Printed at Nice Printing Press, New Delhi

Dear white fella,
Couple of things you should know
When I born, I black
When I grow up, I black
When I go in sun, I black
When I cold, I black
When I scared, I black
When I sick, I black
And when I die, I still black.

You white fella
When you born, you pink
When you grow up, you white
When you go in sun, you red
When you cold, you blue
When you scared, you yellow
When you sick, you green
And when you die, you grey.
And you have the cheek to call me coloured?

African Shakespeare

Hope you enjoy Indian perspectives
Jasmi

Contents

	Preface	9
	Introduction	12
1	Postcoloniality, Literature and Politics **Jasbir Jain**	20
2	Towards an Indian Theory of Postcolonialism **Avadhesh Kumar Singh**	40
3	Edward Said's *Orientalism* and Abbé Dubois **R.K. Kaul**	59
4	Gayatri Chakravorty Spivak: Problematising/Speaking the Margin **Santosh Gupta**	68
5	Decolonising the Indian Mind: Ahmad and Indian Literature **Seema Malik**	82
6	Ashis Nandy on Decolonisation **R.K. Kaul**	89
7	Destablising Meaning: *In Theory* and *Orientalism* **Jasbir Jain**	99
8	Redefining Tradition as Resistance: Raja Rao's *Kanthapura* **Veena Singh**	112
9	Mythologising Indian Freedom Movement in *Kanthapura* **Neelam Raisinghani**	122
10	Rhythms of Language in Raja Rao's *Kanthapura* **Jyoti Bhatia**	131
11	Judith Wright's Treatment of Love **Pradeep Trikha**	153

12	Race-retrieval in Chinua Achebe's *Things Fall Apart* **Amina Amin**	161
13	Proverbial Resistance to Authority: Chinua Achebe's *Things Fall Apart* **Supriya Agarwal**	168
14	Deconstruction of the Savage Myth in Chinua Achebe's *Things Fall Apart* **Veena Jain**	176
15	Too Close and Yet too Far: Naipaul's View of India as a Wounded Civilisation **Purabi Panwar**	185
16	A Technique of Stimulation: Naipaul's *India: A Wounded Civilization* **M.R. Khatri**	196
17	Thematic Perspectives of Culture in Wole Soyinka's *Death and the King's Horseman* **Meenu Bhambhani**	203
18	The Unfolding of a Text: Soyinka's *Death and the King's Horseman* **Jasbir Jain**	210
19	Arun Kolatkar's "Jejuri": A Spiritual Quest? **Tanuja Mathur**	222
20	Homecoming of an "Exile" after "Whoring after English Gods"? **Krishna Sharma**	228
21	The Divided Self in Parthasarthy's *Rough Passage* **Veena Jain**	238
22	*Midnight's Children*: A Fantasy **Urmil Talwar**	247
23	Overlapping Territories, Intertwined Histories: *A Passage to India* **Vijaya Singh**	261
24	Postcoloniality after 1947: The Split Identity of the Nation **Veena Singh**	289
25	Moving Beyond Postcolonial Frameworks: Home Concerns **Jasbir Jain**	299
	Contributors	313
	Index	316

Preface

The present volume brings together the proceedings of two seminars organised by the Institute for Research in Interdisciplinary Studies (IRIS) at Jaipur. The first of these took place in August 1998 and the second in February 1999. The main impulse behind these seminars was to understand and grapple with the much-bandied term postcolonialism, a term which is used to define writing according to geographical locations, political histories and economic contexts of its production and which focuses on thematic concerns related to oppression, opposition, rebellion and self-definition. But even these demarcators which appear to be so solidly identifiable are fluid and complex, and more than that they are extremely varied in their thrust and implication.

Postcolonialisms are many and the history of postcolonial literatures does not reflect any linear development. They do not fall into any easy periodisation. The thematic concerns are also not always governed by political oppression or subordination. They go beyond this to reflect aesthetic concerns. The relationship of postcolonial literatures with their past is even more complex—there are interruptions and disruptions, there are also connections which are deep and binding, which sustain and support. In fact the continuations in terms of aesthetics reveal a tradition which compels one to think all over again about the normative patterns of definition and periodisation, and about placements which make comparative value judgements. Just as political histories do not allow us to draw general conclusions, literary histories also present a varied relationship with aesthetic norms. Moreover there is no one definitive postcolonialism, there are many, each of which is strongly individualistic and assertive. And they contest among themselves even as they interrogate the so called "imperial" structures. Postcolonialisms are also contested from within as one attempts to open up these terms and establish an authentic relationship between their meanings and their realities. Rather than feel confined by this imposition from the west or treat it as a limiting condition, it is imperative to perceive the affirmative aspect which postcolonialism projects. The volume could well have been titled *The Other Side of Postcolonialism*. But for the present let it suffice to say that the word "contesting" in the title functions both as an adjective and as a verb.

The two seminars mentioned above were very focused seminars, the first on theory and fiction, and the second on theory and poetry. A concerted attempt was made to trace the plurality of origins through Fanon, Ashcroft, Griffiths and Tiffin, through Edward Said, Ashis Nandy, Aijaz Ahmad and Gandhi. In the second we focused more specifically on Aijaz Ahmad, Homi Bhabha and Gayatri Spivak. The intention was to juxtapose, understand, explicate and connect and, in the process, initiate the hitherto uninitiated while simultaneously allow space for fresh perspectives.

It has not been possible for us to include all the presentations made in the seminars as the revised versions failed to meet our constantly shifting deadline. We are missing out on the presentations on *The Empire Writes Back*, *The Wretched of the Earth*, on Nissim Ezekiel, Margaret Atwood, Keki Daruwalla, Homi Bhabha and Kamala Das. Both time and space imposed their limitations on us. Two of the papers in the volume were subsequently invited, one by Avadhesh Kumar Singh "Towards an Indian Theory of Postcolonialism" and the second by Amina Amin on Achebe's *Things Fall Apart*. Both Dr Amin and Professor Singh were prompt in their responses.

It is a pleasure to express our gratitude and thanks to all the contributors to this volume for being part of this exercise of critiquing, interpreting, and theorising. This book would not have been possible but for their consistent support, participation, encouragement and friendship.

A word of thanks also to all those agencies which made this happen—the Academic Staff College, Jaipur for facilities extended, the Department of English, University of Rajasthan for its cooperation, to the Institute for Research in Interdisciplinary Studies and to the publishers for their involved cooperation.

We warmly acknowledge the support of friends and colleagues. To end on a personal note, I would like specially to thank the co-editor of this volume, Dr. Veena Singh. The smoothness with which our roles have blended has made this a happy and an enjoyable experience.

* * *

Preface to the Second Edition

Nearly after four years, this volume is going in for a second edition. And though postcolonialism has been with us for nearly three decades, the time has now come to look at in a larger time frame, the before and the after, the seeds of dissent in the liberal tradition, the happenings of the mid-century which transformed us from colonised subjects to an independent nation and changed our focus form the external coloniser to the split nation, to explore the gradual transformation of our contemporary writers from postcolonial to 'Indian' subjects and the cessation of postcoloniality. These essays address the immediate contemporary and reflect the nature of intellectual dissent.

Jasbir Jain

Introduction

Postcolonialism is a much debated, discussed and deconstructed term. It is polysemic by its very nature and plural in its origins. Over the last two decades or more it has provoked a range of definitions and theories, even though the tendency is to use the singular form, specially when the word is used as an adjective. As for instance *Postcolonial Criticism* edited by Moore-Gilbert, Stanton and Maley, *Postcolonial Theory* by Bart Moore-Gilbert, *Postcolonial Theory* by Leela Gandhi, *The Postcolonial Studies Reader* edited by Ashcroft, Griffiths and Tiffin and a host of others books. It functions in the singular but when we try to bring together the diverse origins, political histories, cultures and people, it seeks to homogenise and undervalue, it creates inequalities and it discriminates. There are several postcolonialisms embedded in national histories and cultures each aspiring to be recognised. It is this recognition alone which can help us assess the significant changes which postcolonial attitudes have brought about and the shift these positions mark.

The term has evoked anger and resentment, it has provoked a range of analyses and critiques. It has compelled people to historicise, to relate culture and literary history with political happenings and to articulate the hitherto unarticulated positions. In the process the residual elements of new critical approaches have been washed away and a significant change has taken place in the relationship between writer and tradition and writer and reader/critic.

This change also marks power relations, questions the hegemonic structures of the west and posits alternatives by resurrecting traditions. There are no neutral positions just as there are no universally applicable aesthetic norms. Theory itself is not born out of sheer opposition or description. Instead it comes into being by establishing connections between the several disparate undercurrents which exist, but the connections were hitherto not visible. Theory attempts an explanation of historical trends, collective action, mass movements and of the nature of evolving methodologies. At this point of time if one were to draw a graph of the progress of postcolonial theory it would be a highly fluctuating one for it has resorted to a large number of strategies. There is an attempt at definition in *The Empire Writes Back*, an analyses of oppression, its nature and impact in *The Wretched of the Earth*, an explanation of the process of imperialism and the connection between knowledge and power in *Orientalism*, an exploration of the psychological formations of the self in psychological terms in Ashis Nandy's *The Intimate Enemy*. The above are only a few examples. There are many more and these are supplemented by the efforts of literary critics to categorise these histories and literatures, to define and describe terms and to facilitate classifications and application of methodologies.

Responses to the category of postcolonialism have been equally varied. While some critics consider it an enabling category which facilitates self-assertion, others are conscious of its limiting and controlling nature as it persists in exclusion rather than inclusion. There is a third response which bases itself on a refusal to be included. It looks upon postcolonialism as a position which emphasises difference. These responses are reflected in the present volume, but once the essential fluidity of the word postcolonialism is accepted, it becomes possible to identify certain dominant characteristics, words such as "resistance" and "retrieval" have a tendency to occur over and over again just as "confrontation" "transgression" and "opposition" surface repeatedly. These words are indicative of the conflict inherent in postcolonialism. There is always an awareness of an authority, of an imposition, of a hostility which needs to be combated, opposed or controlled. There is also a simultaneous awareness of a divided past and the inability to accept it as it has been presented, projected or interpreted. Further, there is consciousness of the need to confront—the past, the reality of one's inheritance and one's position, and the imposition of an external authority. Postcolonialism thus comes to represent a conflict within one's own self, a conflict through which the subject tries to step outside his colonial self, the western training, the history of the imperial phase and to approach his own past, history and reality from this position.

In most postcolonial literatures language is another category which needs to be examined and appropriated for one's own purposes which both the writer and the critic need to acknowledge. Thus at the heart of the postcolonial project is the need for the production of knowledge—knowledge of self, of context, of history, of tradition and of power relations. The production of this knowledge, however, is not and cannot be an immaculate process. Therein lies the paradox and the irony which besets the project of postcolonialism. To elaborate upon this, it becomes necessary to look a little more closely at the forces and agencies which facilitate and render this production of knowledge possible. These are the forces which have been born out of imperialism—language, education, training, methodology—all of which have been superimposed upon indigenous structures. Then come conferences, grants, scholarships, libraries, encounters and exposure to other alien cultures. Also take into account the publishing world, the universities, the agencies of recognition—all these are not indigenous and wherever they are, they are not necessarily valued accordingly. The other day when I complimented a mid-level academic on his presentation, he, while acknowledging the compliment, stated "I'm a western intellectual", thereby meaning that he owed it to his training. Stretching this example a little further, it would be natural to assume that authentic postcolonialism would mean stepping out of this acquired skin in order to know oneself. Primarily because this act is difficult, if not altogether impossible, the categories of mimicry and hybridity haunt us all along.

Of the twenty-two essays in this volume, seven are related to theory and aspects of theory, two to drama, two to nonfiction, four to poetry and seven to fiction. Divided along geographical categories five essays relate to African literature, one to Australian, one to a Palestinian American, and the rest to Indians both of the native and the diasporic variety. Cutting across the generic and geographical categories are a whole range of issues which are common to all of them.

Jasbir Jain's essay "Postcoloniality, Literature and Politics", is an attempt at tracing the articulate beginnings of postcolonialism and defining the cultural frameworks; it discusses the imposition of alien frameworks and the conscious need to resist these frameworks. The thrust of the paper is in the emphasis it lays on the recognition of agencies and the shift it insists should take place from language to ideas. Jain also focuses on Gandhi's *Hind Swaraj* as a major postcolonial text.

In "Towards an Indian Theory of Postcolonialism" Avadhesh K. Singh takes up the making of Kalidasa's *Abhigyanshakuntalam* from the narrative in Ved Vyas's *Mahabharata*. The deviations, he points out, are based on societal changes. Postcolonialism has an emotional dimension as well which has largely been ignored. The discourse is extended to include feminist perspectives and gender power relations. *Abhigyanshakuntalam* is a postcolonial text in the very same manner as *The Tempest*. Singh applies a deconstructive methodology and places his reading of *Abhigyanshakuntalam* within the practice of rewriting and appropriation of an earlier text in order to project the change in power relations.

R.K. Kaul's essay "*Orientalism* and Abbé Dubois" traces the motivation of Said's book to the anti-Vietnam movement, to a point of time when the immigrant intellectual was disillusioned with American political policies. Said's position is critiqued from within the Western constructs. Kaul examines Abbé Dubois's work on *Hindu Customs and Manners* (1806) in order to examine Said's statement that the Orientalists were selective in the formation of knowledge about the East. Kaul objects to any such generalisations which fail to examine the context related to the making of the text. In this he strikes a warning note to those of us who romanticise victimisation rather than subject it to a rational scrutiny.

The next essay is on Gayatri Chakravorty Spivak's privileging of the margins. Santosh Gupta builds up the connections between Spivak's earlier work, her training in deconstructive methodology and her later postcolonial and feminist positions and comments upon Spivak's critiquing of Kristeva. Spivak resists homogenisation and argues for heterogeneity, advocating a confrontational methodology.

The next three essays are concerned with specifically Indian positions as argued by Ashis Nandy and Aijaz Ahmad. Seema Malik taking up Ahmad's advocacy of Indian Literature and explores the need for comparative literature and the role which departments of English can play towards providing a forum. It is here that the language of the imperial rulers so different in its structure from Indian languages can play a significant role through translations.

Commenting upon Ashis Nandy's *The Intimate Enemy*, R.K. Kaul examines the rationalistic framework which enables logical connections. He perceives an unbridgeable dichotomy between the rational and the irrational. Reconstructions of national allegories, Kaul argues, need to be based on rational analysis. Kaul is critical of the role of imagination in the reconstruction of history and speculative explanations which seek to synthesize myth and history arouse his disbelief. In fact framed within rationalistic discourse, the hypothetical explanation offered by Nandy stresses the need for crossing the polarised divisions between East and West, and between reason and non-reason. Kaul is sceptical about the coloniser ever feeling guilty or the victim manipulating the oppressor, a disbelief which pushes one to a rigorous examination of Nandy's thesis which in its own right is an explanation of the national movement.

Raja Rao's 1938 novel *Kanthapura* is identified as a major postcolonial text both because of its appropriation of English language for its own use and the indigenous narrative structure which it employs. Veena Singh, Neelam Raisinghani and Jyoti Bhatia take up the dimensions of myth, of language and of structure placing them within postcolonial traditions. Veena Singh explores the strategies of decolonisation, resistance to authority and the appropriation of power through the strategy of *satyagraha*. Placing it within Gandhian ideology, she comments upon the social transformation. Jyoti Bhatia brings out the richness and flexibility of language, of the adjectives which evoke a culture and define value-structures, the rhythms which overlay a foreign language. Language also influences the narrative strategy. Neelam Raisinghani focuses on the process of mythologising which is so central to the novel and the combination of myth and legend which connects with history and reflects social transformation.

Pradeep Trikha's essay on Judith Wright allows us to see the multiple aspects of love in Wright's poetry. Wright depicts the desolation, the physicality, the aridity of love along with the pain and anguish inherent in it. Despite all this suffering and disillusion, love signifies the resumption of a humanistic force.

Things Fall Apart stands in the same relation to Nigerian literature as *Kanthapura* to Indian. Amina Amin, Supriya Agarwal and Veena Jain focus on the different aspects of *Things Fall Apart*. Amin views it as a task of a double retrieval one from the imperial deniers and the other from the alienated native intellectuals. It is viewed as a resistance novel. The intervention by outsiders interrupts the continuity of culture and creates a crisis of identity. Supriya Agarwal examines the use of language, of proverbs and idioms, the subtexts they create and the folklore they introduce. Strategic use of language resists the imposition of a foreign culture. Veena Jain comments upon deconstruction of the savage myth and the manner in which missionary intervention destabilises the counter-positing of native values.

There are two essays on Naipaul's *India: A Wounded Civilization*. While Purabi Panwar is interested in finding answers to questions regarding the writer's position (whether he is a western or an Indian writer), and the text's genre, and is the work a travelogue or not, Megh Raj Khatri is keen on examining Naipaul's technique which employs the method of provocation and alienation. Khatri looks at the relationship between the readers, the author, his material, and the cultural concepts. There is a need to recover lost vitality. Panwar stresses the absence of anxiety in *India: A Wounded Civilization*, an anxiety which is evident in *An Area of Darkness*. By the time he wrote the later work, Naipaul had accepted the fact that India is not-home and as such he stands outside it. Yet both religion and the concept of *dharma* are important concepts which influence cultural behaviour.

The two essays on Soyinka's *Death and the King's Horseman* bring out the dramatic element. Meenu Bhambhani focuses on the characters who reject westernisation, resist the denial of their culture and as such the fact of colonisation itself. Rituals acquire an added importance as they signify acts of resistance. Jasbir Jain in her analysis differentiates it from the other plays of Soyinka and foregrounds the performative aspects which bring about a reversal and thus effect a catharsis.

Tanuja Mathur in her essay on Arun Kolatkar relates his spiritual quest to a search for identity. The choice of pilgrimage as a central motif, the journeys and the encounters further emphasise this point. Parthasarthy's *Rough Passage* is the subject of both Krishna Sharma's paper and Veena Jain's exposition. Krishna Sharma is concerned with Parthasarthy's sense of dislocation and his desire to "find" his tongue, to rehabilitate himself in his native culture. Veena Jain centrestages his two different locations—India and England—and the sense of alienation which possesses him in both the places thus shifting the focus to a permanent dislocation.

Rushdie's *Midnight's Children* finds its place as a postcolonial narrative in Urmil Talwar's paper on the novel which explores Rushdie's use of fantasy as a subversive strategy. Fantasy questions reality, history and dismantles character. Fantasy brings together the personal and the public, emphasising their interrelatedness. Unreliability is common to both fantasy and postcoloniality, both lack reliable charts.

These essays explore and attempt to identify postcoloniality and its many dimensions. Even as some characteristics, attitudes and positions are identified, it is evident that no clear cut polarisations are possible, and that the production of knowledge itself works within a power structure. To question and to dislodge the imposed structures requires both consistency and perception. It requires the ability to separate and to stand outside defined frameworks. Postcolonialism itself needs to be constantly interrogated and defined in order to retain both its fluidity and dynamism.

* * *

We have added three essays to this second edition, each one of them opening out different issues. Between them they span a period of eighty years from Forster's *A Passage to India* (1924) to Nayantara Sahgal's *Lesser Breeds* (2003). They go on to relate imperialism and imperialistic interpretations, dislocations and affliations, power struggles and questioning of power structures with the issues both of the birth of postcoloniality and the gradual emergence from it. They reexamine the relationship between 'self' and the 'other' and reflect upon generic transformations with a sharp focus on Indian perspectives. Thus the journey goes on.

1
Postcoloniality, Literature and Politics

Jasbir Jain

The term postcoloniality describes for me an attitude of mind, a state of being, which even as it feeds into the project of postcolonialism and postcolonial studies, expresses a distinct ontology. Its formation is not rooted so much in intellectual debate as in the process of history, human psychology and the positioning within power relationships. The relationship of this postcoloniality with literature is born out of and reflects upon political conditions. When today I broach the subject, the idea is not to initiate a fresh debate, but instead to fill in some missing aspects of the narrative, to reflect upon some perspectives and positions from my location in India where there is increasingly a suspicion of the whole project, a growing dissatisfaction with the whole lexicon of the discourse on a part of some of us, and a felt need to review it afresh, and if necessary to redefine it. For me, India continues to be less visible than others both in debate and academics (despite the presence of theorists like Spivak and Bhabha), books on postcolonial criticism choose fewer examples from Indian writing, focus peripherally on some issues and then move on to other areas. The reasons for this may be several, India does not easily come within binary divisions—it counters binarism with its own multiplicity—and its dominant religion in itself becomes a distancing factor, what the European mind had perceived as the "multiheaded" monster, or we are simply not aggressive enough to assert ourselves, or it could be that our postcoloniality began much earlier than it did in Africa and Australia, or still more likely we theorise differently. Whatever be the reasons, our affiliations are hesitant and tentative. Harish Trivedi refers to postcolonialism as another form of metropolitan imposition (244), while Makarand Paranjape is of the view that "real postcoloniality is not contained in the discourse of postcolonialism" ("Coping with Postcolonialism" 37). Another critic Darshan Perusek picks up W.J.T Mitchell's observation (*Chronicle of Higher Education*, 1989) that the most important new literature is emerging from the colonies while the most provocative new literary criticism is emanating from the former imperial centres, reflecting a duplication of the earlier division of labour with the erstwhile colonies providing raw materials to the former imperial nations to be transformed into finished products, and Perusek then proceeds to analyse its implications as well as explore the possibilities of a truthful collaboration (*EPW* January 29, 1994). Colonial relations, he feels, have not ceased to exist. They are now "more concealed, more insidious, and on the surface, more 'clean' forms, like debt-dependencies of third world economies—and ... the draining of scarce resources in 'unfriendly' states through protracted 'low intensity warfare'."

The relevant question is are we "subjects" in the sense of having independent identities, ideas and views, or are we raw materials to be shaped and reformed into structures which are created? Where does it lead us—to a better understanding, a better self-assessment, reflection, decolonisation or to a perpetuation of power structures through seduction and semblance of recognition and authority—a place in the sun? Who is the patron? Who publishes? Who consumes? A whole lot of questions suddenly become relevant. A book, as Urvashi Butalia (co-founder of a women's publishing house, Kali for Women) has pointed out, is a highly mediated social activity. Political and economic conditions govern the choices publishers make (which in turn governs privileging of some texts over others, as well as the accessibility of knowledge). India ranks third in the world where English language publications are concerned, next only to UK and USA but has a reading public of a little more than 2%. The obvious question, is who reads the rest? To which the answer would be Indian scholars and India-baiters abroad.

Let me confess that my own relationship with the term postcolonial has passed through several different stages. Though perhaps first used with reference to India (in 1959), the term itself is a late arrival in India, arriving either in the late 70s or early 80s— till then we were quite content to use the word postindependence when suddenly critical discourse began to shift to postcolonial. I accepted it first as a conflictual intellectual phase, then as a mere marker, later as a forward-looking term, indicative of a wish to transcend the colonial experience to "step outside the influence and framework, to reclaim an autonomous and a free identity". This was in 1994 at an International Conference where, as Gareth Griffiths was also present, the discussion had a tendency to shift back to *The Empire Writes Back* every now and then. Many of us had sharp disagreements with some of the positions adopted in the book and even while it recognised some of the differences of the white settler colonies from other postcolonial societies, it did not go far enough in its appreciation of the differences[1] that existed in the different colonial situations and needed an in-depth analysis.

Later, in 1997, I tentatively used the word 'postnational' as a substitute for postcolonial, primarily because it helped to locate the beginning in our concerns, and it restored our subjectivity. The slant of the whole discourse towards the imperial centre is reinforced through terms, recurring images and nomenclatures which signify a colonial relationship. Words are not neutral. They have political memories: "postcolonial" marks the colonial as the dominant experience obliterating all earlier and simultaneous experiences, and when the "Empire" writes back, it is like getting even with a subordinate past. Contrast, for example, the positioning of a phrase like "the Empire writes back" (Rushdian rhetoric) with Tapan Ray Chaudhuri's fine assessment of nineteenth century intellectual history *Europe Reconsidered*. Words fix us in images, they define us[2]. While attempting to substitute it with postnational, the idea was to mark a shift from the concept of the nation-state to our plural composite culture as well as acknowledge a break with the dominantly nationalist discourse of the late nineteenth century. It would also signify a departure from the kind of nationalism which led to the Nazi persecution of the Jews, or the insular, myopic variety which divides people. It would help relocate us in our present and foreground the "self", enable our value-structures, tradition and aesthetics to be visible. The term also has its disadvantages, specially in the political game which is endless and unpredictable. On the other hand both the origin and the meaning of the word postcolonial are vague and contested. Has it come into use to define an aesthetics required to deal with non-western cultures and literatures? Or do we locate its birth in the multi-culturalism which migrancy has brought about? The process may have begun earlier; labelling is very often a retrospective act. But the positions which marked the consciousness of postcoloniality surfaced in the 50s and 60s[3], contemporaneous in time to the postwar world, the first time when it really became necessary for the superior "imperial" races to concede some kind of an equality to the erstwhile colonial cultures, and their enslaved populations. This was a period when the monolithic structures of western culture were threatened by refugees, immigrants and ideological splits. It is during this negotiation for equality that postcolonial discourse was born as the work of several writers testifies—Aimé Césaire, Frantz Fanon, Ngugi wa Thiang'o, Edward Said, Ashcroft et al. Gayatri Spivak, Homi Bhabha, Aijaz Ahmad—texts which force upon one the reality that geographical and cultural locations matter, that history and memory are important to any formulation of postcolonial theory. Meenakshi Mukherjee located in India, views it as an emancipatory concept particularly for students of literature outside the western world, thereby implying that it gave them both a visibility and an entry point into the western world (1996:3), while Arun Mukherjee, located in Canada views it as a constrictive framework which resulted in excessive homogenisation of the pluralities and diversities of the erstwhile colonies, obliterating all cultural and national differences (1996:13-15)[4]. She questions this attempt at encapsulating the postcolonial identity and comments:

> Anyway, the questions Indian readers must ask Indian literary texts, particularly in the context of struggling against fundamentalism, casteism, patriarchy, cannot be answered within the framing grid provided by postcolonial theory... I think I need another theory.

I recall that with the upsurge of African and Indian writing in the 50s and 60s, the dominant question became whether or not the literature of protest had any legitimacy. The dominant metaphor became that of Prospero and Caliban, mutually supported by criticism and creative writing. (As far I know, no Indian rewriting of the *Tempest* took place during this period—but we were also clubbed together with other colonial responses). Looking back I find this debate both irrelevant and humiliating for the normative structures were being defined purely by western aesthetics, which itself was in a state of revision.

This is also evident in the connection between postcolonialism and migrancy. Arif Dirlik perceives a "parallel between the ascendancy in cultural criticism of the idea of postcoloniality and an emergent consciousness of global capitalism in the 1980s", it marks the arrival of the Third World intellectuals in the First World academia (329). Fredric Jameson locates the beginnings of postcolonialism in a time when all these "natives" became human beings both within and without the First World (Jameson 128).

This is but a sampling of the contrary views which surround postcolonialism. Given the above uncertainties, where does one begin? What are the important issues in postcolonialism?

It becomes important to understand the nature of this hegemonic cultural encounter which in order to perpetuate itself worked through binary oppositions. As Ngugi wa Thiong'o has written in his Introduction to *Decolonising the Mind*:

> The effect of a cultural bomb is to annihilate a people's belief in their names, in their languages, in their environment, in their heritage of struggle, in their unity and ultimately in themselves.

With reference to India, Malcolm Muggeridge, himself an Englishman had written in *Chronicles of Wasted Time* as how the imperial imposition in India had drained the country of its life and creativity.

Thus any creative response to such an imposition needs to be engaged with a process of rehabilitation, of restoration of identity, vitality and creativity and moving from simple protest and resistance, go on to provide an alterity. The process needs to historicise as well as to mythicise. This the historical novel in the late nineteenth century began to do: it was a tentative move, but it was there. It could not, however, combat the several myths of the Empire, which facilitated hegemonic structures. One must not forget that the colonised countries were confronted not only by political power but a whole lot of ideological structures and anthropological research which fed into it. The theory of the "white man's burden" rested on categorising the conquered races as "primitive" and/or as fossilised survivals of earlier stages of evolution. Imperialism foisted itself on the theory of lack. Even psycho-analytical theory based its division into the normative and the deviant on racial categories. Though several critics like Elleke Boehmer, Henry Louis Gates and others have expanded upon this[5]: I quote at some length a passage from Sara Mills's work *Discourse* which brings out both the sinister and the comic aspects of this formation of knowledge. Mills's reference is mainly to Pratt's work on travel writing, *Imperial Eyes: Travel Writing and Transculturation* (1992). Mills writes:

> When nineteenth century botanists travelled to foreign countries to investigate non-European plant species, they carried with them a categorisation system originally developed by Linneaus to categorise European plants. As Mary Louise Pratt has shown, this meant that the plants which were 'discovered' by Europeans within India and Africa were categorised within a European system of classification which aimed to be a global system (Pratt 1992). The plants were extracted from the system of classification which indigenous subjects had developed to describe their properties, uses and habitats and they became part of a wider colonial project which aimed to demonstrate the 'civilising' force of colo-

nialism. The plants were thus no longer seen in terms of their original classification system, which often related to their use in medicine, their food-value, their relation to other elements within an eco-system and their position within a cosmological and symbolic system, but rather they were seen out of context in terms of the similarity or dissimilarity of their morphology to European plant species. (53)

Sara Mills goes on to comment that this process of globalisation based the colonial discourse on the annihilation of indigenous knowledge and knowledge-systems.

Resistance to such impositions is also concurrent in time to these comments in several different ways. One was the growth of a bilingual elite concerned with preserving their own languages, and incorporating indigenous models of writing, writing histories, and questioning the whole concept of modernity, resulting at times in a split in its application. The three main planks of the Enlightenment—objectivity, rationalism and universalism—also came to be gradually questioned in different ways.

Subjectivity, non-rationalism and difference were valuable constructs both at personal and cultural levels. The late nineteenth century in India is witness to a split at several levels,—not necessarily a two-way split, often a multiple one, the more significant ones, however, were the division into the "home" and the "world", the separation between "education" and "culture", and a little later even between the twin-concepts of culture and civilisation. It was almost an opting out of history, which Gandhi was later to define as a "narrative of interruptions". The Indian situation needs to be seen both in terms of linear developments and the conditions of simultaneity. Historically Indian's encounter with the British passed through several stages—interaction, military conflicts, partial acceptance, absorption of influence through education, imitation and conversion; the impact of rationalism and the spirit of scientific inquiry is also clearly visible in the events and responses of the third quarter of the nineteenth century. But then came a phase of nationalist upsurge which was an expression of disillusionment with western imperialism as well as a positing of a cultural model. The leading figures of this phase are Swami Dayanand Saraswati (1824-

1883), Vivekanand (1863-1903) and Aurobindo (1872-1950) men who spearheaded religious and social movements. But these even if they began as political gestures ended up as spiritual strategies, lacked a political methodology and were more religious than secular. Of the political leaders at the turn of the century, Dadabhai Naoroji, Bal Gangadhar Tilak, and the rest, it was Gandhi who was able to support his vision of a free society by an effective political strategy and later mass mobilisation. Gandhi recognised the simultaneity of other forms of resistance, and of other concerns than the merely spiritual. Gandhi's, *Hind Swaraj* or *Indian Home-Rule*, a slim volume of a hundred pages, originally written in Gujarati in 1909 first was published serially in the *Indian Opinion* in South Africa. He wrote it during his voyage from London, and in response to the Indian school of violence after Madanlal Dhingra had assassinated an Englishman in London. The book lacks a sophisticated literary style specially in the English translation, but follows the dialogic pattern of question and answer and addresses three major concerns: the opposition between culture and civilisation (the latter also includes industrialisation), political methodology and the role of the individual. Though Gandhi was later to revise his views on several issues or elaborate and clarify some of them, he did not detract from the main argument. In this essay, Gandhi rejected machinery and this was symbolic of an attempt to disassociate the idea of modernity from material and industrial progress[6]. Gandhi was critical of the idea of progress which enslaved men through its seductive comfort. In contrast to this true civilisation is "that mode of conduct which points out to man the path of duty... to observe morality is to attain mastery over our mind and our passions. So doing, we know ourselves" (55). Gandhi constructed a new subjectivity and in order to achieve this advised them to get out of the victim syndrome, to recognise their own role in perpetuating the British rule. He writes "the English have not taken India, we have given it to them.... To blame them is to perpetuate their power" (35-37). The two concepts which form the basis of selfhood are *karma*, that is both action and destiny, and *dharma* which is duty and conscience. Both *swaraj*, the idea of freedom, and *satyagraha*, holding fast to truth, are important concepts for the formulation of this new subjectivity. *Swaraj* is not viewed merely as political freedom or civil liberty but as personal will. "If man will only realize that it is unmanly to obey laws that are unjust, no man's tyranny will enslave him. This is the key to self-rule or home-rule" (72). The whole idea of freedom, of swaraj is founded on the individual's moral strength.

Hind Swaraj thus redefines the concept of freedom, of subjectivity, of civilisation, and projects soul-force as a necessary condition of sustaining a value system. It connects political well-being with individual well-being. The human being is central both to his political strategy and his utopian vision of *Ramrajya*. The fact that India's utopian imagination was directed towards the past is significant in itself: it was the natural outcome of a colonial situation, born out of the confrontational attitude towards the educational and cultural influences of the imperial culture, and it is also an exercise in retrieval. *Ramrajya*, for all practical and notional purposes, is the national myth of the golden age, a "collective fantasy embodying ideals and memories" (Levin: Preface). The *Ramayana* is a story of a man who sustains personal values in a world seemingly hostile to them, a world where attempts are constantly being made to dislocate order through power, temptation and ambition. It is the conduct of Rama which is central to the myth and this was the point which Gandhi emphasised.

It is amazing how Gandhi, located so firmly in family and community life, is able to perceive the strength of the individual self, and it is this self which is the source of the alternatives he projects. His apprenticeship, as Erik Erikson has observed, was "a naked... lonely confrontation with existential categories of sonhood, manhood, selfhood" (20). Others like Naipaul have also commented upon this sense of fierce self-concentration and absorption albeit critically viewing it as an inability to transcend the self (*India: A Wounded Civilization* 98). But Gandhi's introspective self-analysis led him to reject both Anglophilism and the nationalistic preoccupation with India's past glory, to step outside both imitation and nostalgia[7]. By concentrating on his personal past he internalised the concept of power and went to evolve a secular concept of nationhood. A nation was not merely a political entity, it was not synonymous with religion but was vested in cultural commonalty. India had a history of synthesis and assimilation, of an ability to accommodate different faiths and value-structures. His emphasis on the idea of self and the commonalty of culture together led to the concept of a secular nationhood. Gandhi at no stage projected the concept of a *Hindu Rashtra*. As Anil Nauriya has pointed out in a recent article (*Times of India*, 31 August 1998):

> Over emphasis, specially in Anglo-centric writings, on Gandhi's religiosity has sometimes blinded scholars to the fact that Gandhi's definition of nation is emphatically non-religious, non-denominational and secular in every sense of the term... and is shared by millions of Muslims, Hindus, Sikhs, Christians and others....

Gàndhi was not the only one to move away from the fierce nationalism of the nineteenth century thinkers and writers. As Ashis Nandy has pointed out in The *Illegitimacy of Nationalism*, Tagore (1861-1941) was also moving away from it, though he was not necessarily in agreement with Gandhi over several issues. *Gora* was written almost at the same time as *Hind Swaraj*, in 1909, and projects the strain of purist nationalism inspired by what Nandy terms the "nativism of Bankimchandra Chattopadhyay and Vivekananda..." which as it grew into a movement, "brazenly embraced Western concepts of the nation, state, statecraft, technology, and history as the unavoidable universals of contemporary politics" (Nandy 1994:36). Tagore's novel *Gora* is the story of a young man who is obsessed by his search for the authentic being and in this process follows all ritualistic observances, but confronts the limits of his narrow and parochial views when he discovers that he is an Irish orphan. This discovery marks a shift from the politics of exclusion to a more sensitive concept of the moral self. In 1916, Tagore also delivered some lectures on Nationalism wherein he viewed it as "a cruel epidemic of evil that is sweeping over the human world of the present age and eating into its moral validity"[8] (*Nationalism* 16, quoted by Dalton 69).

In many ways Gandhi and Tagore thought alike as one can assess from their work and actions—their rejection of a narrow, parochial, power-based concept of nationhood, their respect for the individual and the definition of civilisation as "code of conduct" [Gandhi defined it as such in 1909 referring to the Gujarati equivalent of the word civilization (*Hind Swaraj* 55) and Tagore referred to the Bengali equivalent "proper conduct" in his 1941 essay "Crisis in Civilization" (*Tagore for You* ed. Sisir Kumar Ghose, Viswa Bharti, Calcutta, 1984, 182)][9]. But there were differences in their background and their spheres of action. Tagore was a poet, member of a privileged aristocratic class, and more receptive than Gandhi to Western education and ideas, he could refer to the non-cooperation movement of 1919 as a "giant abstraction" (see Dalton 72). Gandhi on the other hand was from the middle class and had often experienced discrimination and been subjected to indignity; he was a trained lawyer and had honed the weapon of *satyagraha* through experience; for him the kind of universalism which Tagore projected could have been a giant abstraction. When Sarat Chandra Chatterjee's novel about a Bengali revolutionary *Pather Dabi* was banned, Tagore did not feel free to support him because of his faith in universal ideals of humanity. Similarly when Tagore delivered his lecture "Unity of Culture", Chatterjee responded with an essay on the "Conflict of Cultures" foregrounding the point of difference.

The two quotations which Dalton in his recent work uses to prove his point about Gandhi's narrow view of nationalism are "the interests of my country are identical with those of my religion" and "the attainment of national independence is to me a search after truth". These sentiments, to an Indian, do not hint at any extremism—instead they go on to define patriotism as *dharma* which leaves no scope for untruth, requiring the same sincerity in civil and political spheres as in personal and religious ones[10].

To disagree with Dalton is not to say that all critiquing of Gandhi is, or was, misplaced. In fact several of his contemporaries viewed his ideas with skepticism and both Gandhi and his critics were engaged in an ongoing process of questioning and reformulation. There was opposition, a sense of disillusionment, and at times a falling-off. The other simultaneities of violence, revolution, nationhood and imitation often submerged Gandhian views but for India there is no getting away from Gandhi. He, as Ashis Nandy has observed in *The Intimate Enemy*, was instrumental in turning the charge of the Indian culture being an effeminate culture to its advantage by projecting that "the essence of femininity was superior to that of masculinity"[11]. His ideological stance was in many ways also a disruption of the dominant Indian discourse as manifested in the nationalist tradition.

The current postcolonial discourse is being appropriated by the context of migrancy and is moving away, specially where India is concerned, from the Indian realities. The voices which articulate Indian reality are either relegated to the sidelines or have marginal visibility or are visible for the wrong reasons as compared to those who choose to work primarily within the western constructs[12].

Again, the rich tradition of the language literatures continues to be largely placed outside postcolonial discussion (though some of us stubbornly persist in bringing them in), or else when they are periodically highlighted as has happened with Gayatri Spivak's translation and comments on Mahasweta Devi's short stories, there is an inherent danger of their being assessed as symbolic representation.

Though postcolonialism began as an analysis of cultural formations within condition of unequal positions, and of the resistance offered there in, it is increasingly being confined to its relationship to the West, seeking accommodation and an audience there. It has at different times manifested strong affiliation with Marxism, cultural criticism, deconstruction and new historicism, and depending heavily on the concepts of Derrida, Foucault and Kristeva, has used them for interpreting texts from different cultures. This heavy affiliation with the West has led to an oppositional movement of 'nativism', which in India is being articulated by writers and critics who are either bilingual or write in Indian languages like Bhalchandra Nemade, Ashok Kelkar, and Ganesh Devy[13], a movement which apparently a pursuit for identity, conveys the feeling of being politically revivalist. This kind of polarisation in its move towards fundamentalism is frightening and compels one to rethink critically on cultural and literary issites, forcing upon one the need to forge an epistemology and an aesthetics which while making creative use of indigenous traditions can also help formulate independent positions in order to move outside the colonial experience.

In order to do this perhaps connections have to be made not only between the postcolonial past and the present, between the bhasha traditions and contemporary writing, but also a reworking of the concepts of "mimicry" and "hybridity" is required. They may have had their use as descriptive terms but now they encourage stereotyping. Any selfassessment which is continuously being based on selfmockery can become a second denigrated self. The perception is also through the western eye. Similarly "hybridity" fails to take note of the dialectical relationship and the conflictual tension which is inherent in this condition of "hybridity". It over simplifies and ignores all earlier hybridities and native multiplicities. It also does not accommodate any kind of reciprocal hybridity on part of the coloniser.

The relationship between literature and theory needs to be validated by social reality. This is pushing the departments of English to open out and enter other areas: Indian literatures in Translation, Translation Studies and to engage in interdisciplinary projects. There is also an attempt to extricate Indian literature from the "time-lag" theory by working out periodisation and modes on cultural and political grounds, not merely to look for a Proust or a Joyce or to trace the "outmoded stages" of the First World cultural development in the words of Fredric Jameson, but instead to identify Indian ways of telling stories, cultural expressions and aesthetics. The implication is to enter the postcolonial discourse through redefinition.

The 80s have been a period of engagement with history and historiography reflecting exploration of ordinary lives and personal concerns, Sahgal, Rushdie, Vikram Chandra, Amitava Ghosh, Mukul Kesavan, Shashi Tharoor, Krishna Sobti, Qurratulain Hyder, Phaneshwar Nath Renu, Bhisham Sahni, Kamleshwar, Rahi Masoom Raza, Khushwant Singh and a host of other writers have been part of this kind of historical reviewing—perhaps aimed at enhancing an Indian cultural identity, and projecting Indian cultural and historical heritage to enable an assertion of the Indian self.

Contemporary critiquing of the past is interrogating not only the several myths floated by the imperial rulers, but also the authenticity of narratives produced through their patronage. Alongside this there is a considerable amount of work which is aimed at the Western audience and engages primarily with Western theory written both by the expatriate and the stay at home writer. This is of varying degree, equality and authenticity, it is conflictual, experimental and also at times selectively exotic. Expatriate representation has often been questioned on several counts and a lot can be said both in favour and against. Distancing lends objectivity, but it can also lead to the ossification of cultural constructs; and even if memory is sharp and clear, the expatriate is not, as Sahgal has remarked, assailed by the raw winds of Indian reality. And always, as elsewhere, the market forces become dominant.

The postcolonial enterprise, legitimate and well-meaning in its recognition of the political nature of this discourse is now faced with the fact of stepping outside binarism, outside universalising generalisations and even outside the networking of English language discourse, if it really means to engage with postcoloniality. If we are to move away from colonial impact to finding ways of "resisting" and "countering" the "continued legacy of colonial domination", there is need to reflect upon the political implication of the present power relationships. The question finally at an existential level is as Rushdie has said "How are we to live in the world"? but more immediately it is also "how do we work for the acceptance of difference within the framework of equality,"—not doubt or disbelief, scepticism or wonder or ignorance—but equality? How do we not merely see the "other" but "know" the other? How in Foucauldian sense can this knowledge be an enabling one?

Notes

1. Ashis Nandy in *The Illegitimacy of Nationalism* comments upon the "idea of the modern nation-state" which came "riding piggyback on the Western ideology of nationalism" (ix). Late-nineteenth century writers and leaders, though in opposition to the British colonisation, adopted the idea of nationalism which was predominantly the construct of a Hindu nation. Bankim Chandra Chattopadhyay's patriotic novel *Anand Math* projects a militant Hindu nationalism. The social reform movements like Arya Samaj, the values of Swami Vivekanand and later Aurobindo were also predominantly similarly influenced.
2. There is a serious need to examine the terms and categories which are in use for some of them perpetually denigrate and subordinate. We have seen how the word 'Negro' has changed to 'Black' and to people of 'colour'. Most of the terms used for 'third world' literatures indicate subordination and dependence including the world 'third world' which even when used as an economic or a political term has the effect of distancing. Postcolonial is also one such term which relates the "self" to the colonial past rather than locate it in its own origins. Titles like *The Empire Writes Back* face the coloniser not the self. Words like 'subaltern' and 'sub-culture' also reveal a tendency towards recreating an hierarchy of control, origin and subordination.
3. Aimé Césaire's work appeared in the fifties but it is Frantz Fanon whose text has been privileged. Similarly on the Indian scene there are several thinkers and writers whose work has helped formulate resistance strategies and alternative structures, but the tradition has not been traced. Gandhi's *Hind Swaraj* is one such text.
4. It is symptomatic of the white attitude that Gareth Griffiths in his essay in the same anthology is dismissive of Arun Mukherjee's anxiety and writes that "rather than engage directly in such territorial disputes, I want to address the issue from a wider angle, since it seems to me that disputes over territoriality as a metaphor for the critical struggle for the postcolonial have their limitations.... The problems to which Mukherjee alludes in her paper may need to be addressed in more complicated ways then can be effected by the mere re-assertion of the archive of the local and

specific..." (22-23). Griffiths thus fails to recognise oppositional epistemologies or mind sets, or processes of thought formation and continues to focus on the concept of hybridity.
5. Refer *"Race", Writing and Difference* ed. by Henry Louis Gates, specifically the essay by Sander L. Gilman "Black Bodies, White Bodies" (223-261); also see Ronald Inden's *Imagining India*.
6. Mahadev Desai is his "Introduction" to *Hind Swaraj* comments upon this. Gandhi's rejection of machinery is on more grounds than one—it takes into cognizance the alienation which urbanisation forces on the individual, an alienation from the self, it also contextualised it in the imperial context and rightly perceived its association with progress as reinforcement of economic and political subordination. (He himself used the spinning wheel which was an acceptance of the concept of industrialisation). In this connection see Irfan Habib's *Essays on Indian History* [New Delhi: Tulika (1955) 1998], more specifically the essays "Potentialities of Capitalist Development in the Economy of Mughal India" and "Colonization of the Indian Economy" which together indicate the forces which interacted to force an identification of capitalism with imperialism.
7. The scene in the mid-nineteenth century presents a complex reality. While on the one hand the spirit of the Enlightenment and the ideas of the West seemed to overwhelm educated Indians, on the other it pushed them towards introspection forcing them to look within their own tradition for parallels and similarities. The results were often paradoxical and contradictory. The cultural encounter led to the nationalist movement which was one way of countering the onslaught of the imperial culture; it led to a separation between public and private life, the masculine and the feminine worlds. The historical novel became a very popular form during this period, partly as an attempt to evoke patriotic fervor and national pride by recounting acts of heroism of the past.
8. See Nandy, *The Illegitimacy of Nationalism*, 1994, 1-3 for his section on "Nationalism vs Patriotism". *Gora* is a very complex novel and though full of debates and arguments, in effect the novel is about the choices available to the Indian. Reformist activity is not in itself a solution for it alienates and binds as much as traditional Hinduism. Tagore and Gandhi both wanted to think

outside the narrow combines of religion and nation but in a colonial situation, universal aspirations could become another trap.

9. Rabindranath Tagore's views on culture are significant for three reasons—first they did not remain static; second, he recognised the need for a split between technological civilisational forces identified with the imperial mission, and the spiritual cultural traditions, but at another level he was not willing to accept the concept of difference. Universal or common world-wide culture was an ideal which he propounded. This was a development of humanist thought and is central to the beginning of colonial struggles. In order to emphasise their humanity, colonial societies accepted the idea of "universalism" which was also an argument which aided the expansion of imperialism and capitalism. See Tagore's essays "Unity of Culture" and "Crisis in Civilization".

10. Dalton's views are highly myopic and one-sided, his critiquing of Gandhi's concept of nationalism does not take into account Gandhi's definition of nation, nor does it take into account the distinction which was beginning to surface in the 'nationalist' and the 'patriotic' discourse. Gandhi's concept of nation did not base itself on race, religion or power: it based itself instead on the commonality of culture, the multi-lingual reality of India, and on the concept of self-respect. Religion in India was associated with right-doing, the meaning of the word *dharma* is not religion, it is rooted in a coherence between conscience and social code of conduct. I refer the reader to A.K. Saran's "Gandhi's Theory of Society and Our Times" (*Between Tradition and Modernity* ed. Dallmayr and Devy), wherein Saran writes that Gandhi not only bridged the schism between Gokhale and Tilak but also "radically changed the basis, the scope and the nature of the Indian freedom movement" by making it a mass movement and freeing it from a purely nationalist cause and by spiritualising it (203).

11. Ashis Nandy in *The Intimate Enemy* points out how Gandhi was instrumental in reviving the ordering of the values of the colonial culture which was *Purushatva* → *Naritva* → *Klibatva* [that is manliness is superior to womanliness, and womanliness to femininity in man). Gandhi substituted this with an ordering borrowed from the tradition of saintliness in India and went on to build on it to result in *Naritva* → *Purushatva* → *Kapurastava* (the essence of femininity is superior to that of masculinity, which in turn is bet-

ter than cowardice (Nandy 52-53)].

12. Indian theorists by and large, whether at home or abroad, use Western frameworks, or address Western critiquing. For instance the methods of approach which Gayatri Spivak adopts are Derridean deconstructionism, Bhabha goes on to build on Foucault's concept of heteroglossia, and Aijaz Ahmad is engaged in a Marxist critiquing of Said's *Orientalism*. The dialogue which needs to move horizontally in India becomes directed outwards.

13. "Nativism". In 1984 several critics and writers came together for a seminar to explore the concept of "nativism", i.e. to identify the aesthetics of language literatures with reference to the tradition of language literatures. This, though at one point signifies a systemic approach, at another becomes an exclusionist one. (Papers presented at the seminar have been published in *New Quest*, May 1984). Later G.N. Devy followed it up by *After Amnesia*. The Sahitya Akademi (National Academy of Literature) organised a seminar at Kanpur, and these proceedings have been published in a volume edited by Makarand Paranjape. "Nativism", though a valid literary statement cannot be isolated from the political conservatism of Hindu nationalism, the present ruling party, the Bhartiya Janta Party, and regional parties like the Shiv Sena.

References

Ashcroft, Bill, Gareth Griffiths and Helen Tiffin. *The Empire Writes Back: Theory and Practice in Postcolonial Literatures*. London: Routledge, 1989.

Boehmer, Elleke. *Colonial and Postcolonial Literature*. New York: O.U.P., 1995.

Butalia, Urvashi. "English Text, Indian Publisher", *Rethinking English*. Ed. Svati Joshi. New Delhi: Trianka, 1991.

Dalton, Dennis. *Gandhi's Power: Non-violence in Action*. Delhi: Oxford University Press, 1998.

Dirlik, Arif. "The Postcolonial Aura: Third World Criticism in the Age of Global Capitalism", *Critical Inquiry* Vol. 20, 1-3, 1993-94.

Gandhi, M.K. *Hind Swaraj or Indian Home Rule* (1909). Ahmedabad: Navajivan Publishing House (1938), 1996.

Gilman, Sander L. "Black Bodies, White Bodies": Toward an Iconography of Female sexuality in Late Nineteenth-century Art, Medicine and Literature" in *"Race", Writing and Difference*. Ed. Henry Louis Gates. Chicago: University of Chicago Press, 1986.

Inden, Ronald. *Imagining India*. Oxford: Blackwell, 1990.

Jameson, Fredric. "Periodizing the Sixties", *Postmodernism: A Reader*. Ed. Patricia Waugh. London: Edward Arnold, 1992.

Levin, Harry. *The Myth of the Golden Age in the Renaissance*. New York: Oxford University Press, 1969.

Mills, Sara. *Discourse*. London: Routledge, 1997.

Mukherjee, Arun Prabha. "Interrogating Postcolonialism: Some Uneasy Conjunctures", *Interrogating Post-colonialism: Theory, Text and Context*. Ed. Harish Trivedi and Meenakshi Mukherjee. Shimla: Indian Institute of Advanced Study, 1996.

Mukherjee, Meenakshi. "Interrogating Postcolonialism", *Interrogating Post-colonialism: Theory, Text and Context*. 1996.

Moore-Gilbert, Bart. *Postcolonial Theory*. London: Verso, 19997.

Naipaul, V.S. *India: A Wounded Civilization*. Penguin, 1977.

Nandy, Ashis. *The Illegitimacy of Nationalism*. Delhi: Oxford University Press (1994), 1996

—. *The Intimate Enemy: Loss and Recovery of Self Under Colonialism*. Delhi: Oxford University Press (1983), 1989.

Nauriya, Anil. "Notions of Nation: Gandhi's Composite Vision of India", *The Times of India* August 31, 1998, p. 12.

Paranjape, Makarand. "Coping with Postcolonialism" *Interrogating Postcolonialism: Theory, Text and Context*. 1996.

Perushek, Darshan. "Postcolonial Realities, Post-Structuralist Diversions: An Unamused Exchange", *Economic and Political Weekly*. January 29, 1994.

Said, Edward. *Orientalism*. New York: Random House, 1978.

Saran, A.K. "Gandhi's Theory of Society and Our Times", *Between Tradition and Modernity*. Ed. Fred Dallmayr and G.N. Devy. New Delhi: Sage Publications, 1998.

Tagore, Rabindranath. "The Religion of an Artist", *Tagore for You*. Ed. Sisir Kumar Ghose. Calcutta: Viswa Bharati, 1984.

Tagore, Rabindranath. *Gora*. Trans. Sujit Mukherjee. New Delhi: Sahitya Akademi (1997), 1998.

Thiong'o, Ngugi wa. *Decolonising the Mind: The Politics of Language in African Literature* (1986). Oxford: James Currey Ltd., 1997.

Trivedi, Harish. "India and Post-colonial Discourse", *Interrogating Post-colonialism: Theory, Text and Context*. 1996.

2

Towards an Indian Theory of Postcolonialism

Avadhesh Kumar Singh

Postcolonialism is one of the most "wanted" (Paranjape 1998: 48) 'isms' in the obtaining academic discourses. So much so that there is "a veritable scramble for postcolonialism" (Slemon 15). The unprecedented scramble for it and its 'wantedness' (wantonness) make it one of the greatest swindles in the history of twentieth century criticism, to be matched only by postmodernism. The reasons for this are not far to find. Like other 'isms' it comes to us by post or *poste* as part of the grand western project that treats the rest of the world as the data or guinea-pigs supplying the terms and criteria of measurement or evaluation of others. It is neither our category nor our agenda. It is given to us. It is our naivety that has persuaded us to accept it and, barring a few distinguished reputations, most of us seem to wallow in it without questioning it.

To begin with, the referent of postcolonialism is not fixed. Not necessary that it should ever be firmly fixed, for it is an 'ism' or *vaad* not a *shashtra*. Even then an 'ism', if suffixed to a term, demands that term to be surer or, more definite, less open-ended and anarchic than what postcolonialism is. That is why it means different things to different critics. They write it differently. For instance Vijay Mishra and Bob Hodge write it with hyphen with the justification for retaining it that if the hyphen is dropped, the term postcolonialism is used as "an always present tendency in any literature of subjugation marked by a systematic process of cultural domination through the imposition of imperial structures of power...." (Mishra & Hodge 1991:284). So do Peter Childs and R.J. Patrick Williams (1997). Others write it without a hyphen. Makarand Paranjape, one of our most perspicuous critics, in trying to cope with it writes it with a hyphen but drops the hyphen within a year (Paranjape 1996 and 1998). Before the discussion pertaining to the hyphen in postcolonialism becomes a bramble in one's throat, one feels tempted to write it as "Post(?) -(?) colonial(ism) ?" A question pops up here: is this exhibition of scepticism of some use to us or just another instance of our subscription to the still fashionable deconstructive methodology ?

Bill Ashcroft, Gareth Griffiths and Helen Tiffin use the term postcolonial "to cover all the culture affected by the imperial process from the moment of colonisation to the present day. This is because there is a continuity of preoccupations throughout the historical process initiated by European imperial aggression" (2). Stephen Slemon problematises the definition of postcolonial as forwarded in *The Empire Writes Back,* the so called Bible of postcolonialism, as he writes:

> Definitions of the 'post-colonial' of course vary widely, but for me the concept proves most useful not when it is used synonymously with a post-independence historical period in once-colonised nations, but rather when it locates a specifically anti- or *post*-colonial *discursive* purchase in culture, one which begins in the moment that colonial power inscribes itself the body and space of its Others and which continues as an often occulted tradition into the modern theatre of neocolonialist international relations.(3)

This formulation disentangles postcolonialism from political independence. In this case India becomes a postcolonial country not on 15 August, 1947 when it attained its independence but the day it started conceiving and constructing its various sets of discursive practices to resist colonialism, its ways, its ideologies and legacies. Then it becomes difficult to pin it to historical point, for Indian postcolonialism may be traced as far back as the discursive practices of different Indian writers like Bhartendu Harishchandra in Hindi, Narmad and Dalpat in Gujarati, Vishnu Shastri Chiplunkar in Marathi and Bankimchandra in Bengali among the different Indian writers who played multiple roles in the 19th century, and in the twentieth century the freedom fighters like Gandhiji whose *Hind Swaraj* may be called a poetics or manifesto of Indian postcolonialism.

Gayatri Chakravorty Spivak adds another dimension when she calls the term postcolonialism "just totally bogus" (Spivak 1991: 224) and she prefers the term postcoloniality to it, though she does not draw the demarcating line between the two terms. Later on she does throw some light on it as she says, "In postcoloniality, every metropolitical definition is dislodged. The general mode for the postcolonial is citation, reinscription, rerouting the historical" (Spivak 1993: 217). Anthony Appiah ungenerously calls it "a *comprador* intelligentsia" which stands for "a relatively small, Western-style, Western trained group of writers and thinkers who mediate the trade in cultural commodities of world capitalism at the periphery..."(348).

Whether postcolonialism is written with a hyphen or without one, whether it is fluid or fixed, bogus or genuine, and whatever it may be, it is to be accepted that it has attained an unsurpassable currency in our academic world whose questionings lend it greater strength. In reality it is continuation of colonialism, an avatar of colonialism and another name for neocolonialism whose culture is hyperconsumerism, and philosophy postmodernism, if the term philosophy is used a little loosely (cf. my 'Editorial Note', *Critical Practice*, Vol. IV, No 1, Jan. 1997, V-X). It is in currency and has come to stay in our critical and literary discourses. The cardinal question is: how should we respond to it ? And before that, "Can we ?"

In a fast changing and shrunken world it is neither possible nor advisable to insulate ourselves from what is happening around and also being done to us. Postcolonialism is still happening to us. Rather than regretting it what is needed is to understand it and its condition(s), its strategies and ways of operations. It cannot be wished away. We can respond to it and resist whatever is inimical to our interests with our own counter-strategies. We can respond to it in some of the following ways: (i) we can reject it and without taking note of it we can allow it to thrive around us, and get throttled in the end; (ii) we can accept its currency and supremacy, and surrender ourselves to it; (iii) we can celebrate it and commit intellectual and cultural suicide; and (iv) we can receive it pro-actively —understand it and resist and reject whatever is negative in it and accept pragmatically whatever may be of use to us in it, or redefine it or construct our theory or model from our own texts, though that may amount to complicit participation in it [See Harish Trivedi for his responses to 'postcolonialism' (231-247)]. In fact all postcolonial societies should do it though that may have political overlays in it, for by doing so they can resist the *singularity* of the term that "effects a re-centering of global history around the single rubric of European time" (McClintock 293), and also of resisting the homogenising project of the west or the "globalizing gesture of 'the post-colonial condition' or 'post-coloniality'" which "downplays multiplicities of location and temporality as well as the possible discursive and political linkages between 'post-colonial' theories and contemporary anti-colonial, or anti-colonial struggles and discourse" (Shohat 104).

The construction of a theory of postcolonialism is more easily said than done. Keeping my own prescription in mind my present endeavour is directed at nailing this term on the anvil of an Indian text and beat it along with the nail till it is turned to thin air so that it attains some Indian tinge by reading into Kalidasa's *Abhigyanshakuntalam* vis-à-vis William Shakespeare's *The Tempest* with focus on hitherto neglected emotional aspect of postcolonialism in particular, for political, sociological and economic[1] aspects have in comparison been discussed in greater detail.

II

Abhigyanshakuntalam is Kalidasa's crowning artistic achievement. This statement, though a resounding commonplace, seems less dangerous than the oft-quoted pronouncements sounding over praise "I name thee, O Shakuntala; and all at once is said", (Goethe) or patronizing statements ["Our illustrious poet, the Shakespeare of India" (Sir William Jones), "the Shakespeare of India" (Sir Monier Williams)]. Such proclamations as these still tickle us to such a measure that we oversee their not so innocent implications. Such distinguished reputations as Jones and Williams compared the incomparables and after doing that they did not specify the points of dissimilarities between the two. Kalidasa and Shakespeare between them do not share many similarities except for the terms drama, dramatic and dramatist. The comparison, however, is yet another instance of measuring the colonised from the standard of coloniser, however unconscious it may be. In the process they did injustice to Shakespeare as well. Further, it is interesting to note that if both of them have been equated, what has prevented all the Western critics in all these years and ages from calling Shakespeare, as the Kalidasa of England?

Kalidasa's achievement lies in breathing life, love and poetry into a bare lifeless unromantic epic tale. With his keen eyes of a genius 'in fine frenzy rolling', the poet-dramatist sublimated the story of sordid passion to the very quintessence of ideals of love and poetry. He picked up a rough stone and by chiselling it, he transformed it into a pure gem. It is no surprise then that Kalidasa's poetry, characterisation, plot construction, his diction, his treatment of nature and vision have attracted attention and adulation of critics from India and abroad. I would concentrate on a few hitherto oversighted or marginalised aspects of the play.

Abhigyanshakuntalam is a rich reservoir of multiple meanings fed by springs—large and small—flowing from every pore of the play. If examined beneath the surface of the play, the armature of the play, as furnished by the dramatist, seems to rest on various binary oppositions like nature-culture, rich-poor, folk-elite, village-city, man-woman, hunter-hunted, hermitage-palace of *gramya* and *aranyak* among others. The moment these binary oppositions are discovered, the play becomes a pregnant site hiding in it immense possibilities of interpretations from different perspectives.

III

Abhigyanshakuntalam bears in it enough ruptures which become evident when the play is viewed in the light of its source text. Kalidasa transformed the epic-tale into his play after appropriating the source text which represents the crude, simple and sordid realities as they were except for a few instances like the one in which the epic-poet strives to oversight the fatal flaw of Dushyanta in the original tale. The King rejects Shakuntala for the reasons far from convincing. His proposal of love, consummation and then his rejection give him the character of a lecher who would fain hide his debauchery of folly of his youth.

Kalidasa on more occasions than one represents Dushyanta as a bee that ever seeks fresh honey (Act V, shloka,1 & 19). His unwillingness to accept Shakuntala knowingly degrades his love into disgusting gross lust. Difficult it is to surmise the fate of the Shakuntalas who might have been exploited and then abandoned by this rake who could afford this and remained uncensured, for he was the king, the centre of power. It suggests that there is something wrong with Dushyanta, the man. If he can afford to forget or feign to do so in case of the celestial beauty like Shakuntala, then how many Shakuntalas might have been seduced and then rejected by him ?

Kalidasa made greater and effective use of the supernatural in the form of Durvasha's curse and its resolution through the fisherman's tale than the epic poet did to cloak the sins of the King. Ved Vyas was a poet historian, and related to Dushyanta however distant that relationship may be, and belonged to the family whose history he was narrating. So the compulsions of the centre of power and his association demanded that the narrator should either exclude the instances of royal 'omissions' which was not possible in this case, and if retained, then their gravity should be lessened through the introduction of supernatural like the celestial voice *(Mahabharata)* or the curse *(Abhigyanshakuntalam)*. The compulsions and situation of Kalidasa were different from Ved Vyas. He assumed the role of a poet-dramatist and that provided him more space to shuffle around and bring about the changes in the original story. Further, in Dushyanta he did not see the origin of the Kuru dynasty but a *dheerodatta nayaka* (a worthy hero) suitable as Shakuntala's paramour, and her husband, her *swami* (master) and her son Bharata's father. Kalidasa did achieve some measure of success in this, for in comparison the conduct of Kalidasa's Dushyanta is more acceptable than that of his counterpart in the epic. In Kalidasa, Shakuntala suffers and Dushyanta prospers at Shakuntala's expense, however exquisite her portrayal in the play may be. It had much to do with his age from whose octopusean tentacles he could not extricate himself on a few occasions particularly in treating his women on terms equal to men. In spite of this, Kalidasa (un)knowingly leaves enough 'blind' spots suggesting the real face of Dushyanta (man). For this we have to go a little close to both the texts and look at their margins.

IV

Let us stand at the threshold of the play and enjoy the pleasure of looking into the text. Our bid to centralise something marginal like the title may take us at least a few inches closer to the authorial intentions and compulsions, and sources and forces, however elusive they may be, which a literary work is made of.

Shakuntala goes through considerable transformation in *Abhigyanshakuntalam*. Kalidasa's Shakuntala is of different age, smeared as she is in the environs, dust and soil of Kalidasa's age. In the epic, if the title of the work can be a criterion to judge the centrality of a character, Shakuntala is the central character. Just as Section 1 (7b) 62-69 (B 68-74; C 2799-3125) of the "Adiparva" (The Origins) is sub-titled after her as "Shakuntaloupakhyan", similarly Kalidasa titles the play after her. But in fact it is not Shakuntala but her recognition which is central in Kalidasa. And in this recognition it is the recogniser, not the recognisee, who is central. The recognisee is at the receiving end. That Kalidasa wanted to centralize Dushyanta, for which he changed Dushyanta for the better, becomes evident from the title of the play.

Shakuntala in the epic is "Sri incarnate", "black-eyed girl" (65.1), "the sweetspoken girl" with "a flawless body" (65.5). Vaishampayana further appreciates her for her "beautiful hips, a lustrous appearance, and charming smile. She was radiant with beauty, with the sheen of austerities and the calm of self-restraint". The King also addresses her "as perfect of shape as of age", "fair-waisted girl", "such perfection of beauty" (65:10).

Ved Vyas's Shakuntala is the quintessence of the beauty of the Mahabharata age. She is simple, straightforward, innocent and though initially fearful but fearless and assertive when the King does not accept her. Sentimentality and emotional indulgence are foreign to her. With no qualms in her heart she coolly tells Dushyanta the story of her birth, and like a pragmatic mother she bargains the destiny of her offspring with the King for offering herself in the Gandharva marriage (67:15). She yields to Dushyanta's importunities but does not commit the mistake that Mir did:

Mir sahib hi chooke, ai bad-ahd,
Warna dena tha dil quasam lekar. (147)
(He gave his heart, but got no pledge,
A mistake, surely, Mir did make).

In the King's court when Dushyanta refuses to recognise her, she faces him quite courageously without being nervous. Her eyes turned copper red with indignant fury, her pursed lips began to tremble and from the corner of her eyes she looked at the King with the glances that seemed to burn him (1:7 68:20). She lectures to the King in the open court demanding justice for her son, and scolds him for "lying like a commoner". She says, "Why do you slight me in your assembly as though I were a commoner ? I am surely not baying in a desert—why don't you hear me?" (1:7:68:30) "My birth is higher than yours, Dushyanta!" (1:7:69:1). She is confidence incarnate. Even after her rejection she is sure of her son's future which is her prime concern. She tells Dushyanta:

There is no consorting with one like you. Even without you, Dushyanta, my son shall reign over four-cornered earth crowned by the king of mountains. (1:7:69:29)

Kalidasa's Shakuntala appears as an obedient daughter, beautiful beloved with bashfulness of a courtesan modelled after one from the court of the King Vikramaditya or the one in whose court he may have lived. She is a devoted wife and a loving mother. She is a modest, shy, coy, and submissive woman lacking in confidence of her counterpart in the *Mahabharata* suggesting change for the worse in the position and status of women in the age of Kalidasa.

Ved Vyas's Shakuntala is a product of the society that subscribed to the spirit of matriarchal society. Kalidasa's Shakuntala on the other hand is a product of a patriarchal society in which women are subservient to men. The tradition enunciated by patriarchy naturally found Kalidasa's Shakuntala more convenient to itself than Ved Vyas's. The acceptance of this tradition signalled prospective decline in the status and position of women in Indian society.

Kalidasa leaves quite a few evidences in the play regarding the position of women in the play. The imagery of the play reveals the subordinate position of the woman. The wife is referred to as creeper and husband its supporting tree (Act 1: 20: 15-6). In the conversation between Anusuya and Priyamvada, a woman (wife) is compared to a creeper, the *Vishakh*a star, and river; and a man (husband) is a tree, the Moon, and the sea (Act 3: 1 1-18). Further, a wife was not supposed to go against her husband, even if ill-treated by him, says Kashyap in his piece of advice to Shakuntala (Act IV, shloka 18). Moreover, in the court of the King (Act V) when Dushyanta does not accept Shakuntala, Sharadwata leaves Shakuntala at Dushyanta's mercy:

> *Tadesha bhavatah patni tyaj vaina gruhan va ? Uppanna hi daresh prabhuta sarvatomukhi.* (Act V, shloka 26)
> *(Here then is your wife. Abandon her or accept her. For husbands have all-extending authority over wives.*

Thereafter, Sharadwata! Sharangrava forsake pregnant Shakuntala. Gautami, seeing Shakuntala weeping piteously and following them, says to Sharangrava, "What possibly can a poor daughter do when her husband is harsh in repudiation ?" Hearing this Sharangrava turns to her, and says angrily, *"Kim purobhae, swatantryamavalembse"*. (Wanton girl, do you resort to independence ?) (Act V, 2,6,8).

He further says, *"Yadi yatha vadati kshitipastatha, Twamasi Kim piturutkulya twya, Ath tu vetsa shuchu vratmatmanah patikule tav dasyamapi kshamas"* (Act V, shloka 27).

(If you are as the king says, what has your father to do with you who have transgressed the family ? If, on the other hand, you know your own vow to be pure, even slavery in the family of your husband is sufficient for you).

This scene in a way comments on the subservient position of a wife in comparison to her husband in the age of Kalidasa. She was the husband's property to be mastered and abandoned if convenient for him. And in such a situation even her own people would not shelter her. The husband's (man's) was the ultimate verdict. But the conduct of the Kanva's disciples is deplorably unworthy of them—worse than Dushyanta's, as they leave poor Shakuntala quick with a child to her fate in a condition in which even an unknown woman should not be left unattended. Dushyanta the king and *gruhastha* may be excused but not Sharangrava and Sharadwata, for these Sanyasins were in the best position to defy the laws of the culture. Kalidasa misses an opportunity to express at least his dissatisfaction with the then insultingly inhuman treatment of women. It should however not be construed that the dramatist on his part subscribed to such an inhuman treatment of woman in his age. Moreover, the man-woman binary set informs us that polygamy, a barometer to measure the nature of women's position in a society because it indicates woman's economic and social dependence on man, was not uncommon in Kalidasa's days. Dushyanta has many wives in his palace breeding intrigues and rivalry among them to win the king's affections. Hanspadika cleverly censures the King through her song, for after enjoying her he has forgotten her, as his affection found new resort in the new queen Vasumati (Act V, shloka 1). Dushyanta himself accepts that he had many wives (Act III, shloka 19).

And Kashyap's piece of advice to Shakuntala is, "Act the part of a dear friend to co-wives" (Act IV, shloka 18) suggesting the existence of polygamous practices where it was affordable. In the next act Kalidasa introduces a minor story of Dhanmitra with the purpose of ennobling the character of the king. A leading merchant named Dhanmitra carrying on business by sea died in a ship disaster. "And childless, they say, is a poor man. His riches go to the king's treasure", is what has been written by the minister. The King comments on the report that since he had great riches, he must have had several wives. He was told that one of his wives, the daughter of a merchant of Saket, was soon to have a child. The King passed the judgement that the child would have inheritance rights (Act VI, 22-34-42). It means that the unborn child was entitled to the father's property but not the living widow suggesting once again the subordinate position of women. It would have been ideal if Kalidasa had provided some respectability to women by making his hero pass judgement at least in favour of the widow. Kalidasa contemporanised his characters and made them behave accordingly and in the process he could not rise above the prejudices of the age against women. His treatment of Shakuntala and of women in general is that of the Manu or the post-Manu period. Manu did not recognise women's right to inherit. Narada made provisions for her maintenance; and Brahaspati (1 century A.D. ?) and Yagyavalakya admitted her rights. Manu lip-serviced woman in principle but treated them disgracefully. Kalidasa depicted women in his play as he saw them around him. Though he does not express his dissatisfaction against their exploitation, and the poor and unequal treatment meted out to them in the course of the play, yet he provides a few small rents in the thick veil of the play through which we get an idea of their subjugation and subordination.

V

Kalidasa thinks in terms of pairs. He conceives and constructs his play accordingly by comparing and contrasting different genders, classes, worlds and views. He pairs Dushyanta and Shakuntala, two worlds within them, and compares them with another pair from another world of Kanva (the loving hermit) and Gautami (the motherly figure) further compared with the divine pair

Maricha and Aditi. Shakuntala is further compared with Hanspadika and Vasumati in the palace and in the hermitage with her two companions of almost contrasting nature Anusuya (grave and sensible) and Priyamvada (playful and vivacious). These female pupils of Kanva are balanced by another set of male pupils Sharangrava (proud, fearless and haughty) and Shardavata (reserved and calm). Dushyanta is given another companion in the form of Madhavyar, his *vidushak* or jester.

Apart from the man and woman binary opposition the play presents other prominent binary sets as nature and culture, *gramya* and *aranyak*, forest and city, palace and hermitage and the hunter and the hunted. In the play the *gramya* and *aranyak* represent the two opposite poles of the settlement—the wilderness and ordered peacefulness, of order and disorder, of nature and culture. The play contracts the two diverse backgrounds—of nature (forest) and culture (court). The forest knows no law or rule of the cultured court. The moods of nature—with teeth and claws red in blood on the one hand and on the other with help overbrimming with its bounties—rule the forest with no clear structures. The court on the other hand is a structured model after the patterns of manufactured culture with almost no intervention of the nature. The intervening laws of culture are alien to the forest.

The plot construction of the play presents this dichotomy quite clearly. Act I to IV depict the natural world. Even Dushyanta after seeing Shakuntala draws a demarcating line between the two worlds—between garden-creepers and forest creepers, between the beauties of his harem and the beauty of the forest. The subsequent acts unfold a different cultural world of the court marked with artificialities and crookedness—an altogether different world swarmed with men lapped in the flames of love, lust, moral obliquities and intrigues as opposed to the world of beautiful bounties of nature and living in harmony with them (Act IV, shloka 10 & 11). In the last act, Act VII, the dramatist again takes us away from the gross and stifling world of the court and the capital to a divine world of bliss different from Kanva's hermitage also. The consideration of the play on the lines of the binary oppositions of nature and culture becomes problematic because of

Kanva's hermitage. The hermitage defies being clearly categorised in any of the two. It is closer to nature but not absolutely unconnected with the life of the city. It is related to the culture, city and court in the way the *sanyasa is* to *gruhastha*. Further, there is the divine Immortal World of heaven that stands above all the three worlds—the nature city (cultural), hermitage (life in harmony with nature) and heaven (spiritual). The binary structures of nature and culture are suggested, spelt and scandalised simultaneously by Kalidasa in his play.

Lying otherwise separately, it is the hunt that connects the binary oppositions—nature and culture together. Culture, a cooked product of nature (raw), attacks its progenitor in the play and in the epic. The description of the hunt in the epic is more graphic and detailed than in the play. It is a war against nature (represented by the forest) animals, women (Shakuntala), led by Dushyanta representing culture, the court, city, and man. its catastrophic consequence is the dirty dance of death, destruction and havoc, all around. The hunt knows only two parties—the hunter and the hunted.

The hunting expedition led by Dushyanta, the master hunter, disturbed the atmosphere of the forest with its tumultuous noise. Not being content with it the king "stalked about killing wild game and fowl with javelin, sword, mace, bludgeon, halberd" (1:63:15). "Many families of tigers he laid low" (1:63:10). And a large number of deer was killed in the massive hunt. Kalidas also describes the hunting in the play. Dushyanta is in fact "addicted to the chase"; informs the Vidushak (Act 11, 13). The Senapati also considers the hunting a vice and wants the Vidushak to persuade the King against hunting.

Kalidasa voices his disapproval of hunting through his marginal characters like the Vidushak and the Senapati which is not the case with the epic suggesting change in the then society's attitude towards nature and animals—not to be merely mastered even if by killing, but to be with in harmony.

Notwithstanding this change in attitude towards nature, Dushyanta's hunting expedition is in no way less calamitous. He comes to the forest as a hunter of animals. But his deeper approach in the forest leads him to the hermitage of Kanva adding a new dimension to his hunting. The animals of the forest, and the inhabitants of the hermitage—animals and human beings all are vulnerable to alien (hunting) ways of the city and its people represented by Dushyanta and his people. The city, its palace, its court, its culture and people leave their dark disturbing shadows on forest, hermitage and its inhabitants. Shakuntala (means 'bird', named so because she was protected by birds when she was abandoned in the desolate wilderness by Menaka after her birth) symbolically represents the scar of that onslaught of the city. Vaikhanas, a pupil of Kanva's hermitage, who prevents the deer being killed by Dushyanta, says, "King, this is deer of the hermitage. He should not be killed" (Act 1, 9, 7). He further says: *Na khalu na khalu benah sannipathyoayamasmani. /Mridini mrugsharire pushprashvivagnih/Kwak harinkanam jeevitam chatilolam, /Kwach nishitinpatah vajrasarah sharaste. Tat sadhukrutsandhanam pratisamhar sayakam Atrtranay vah shahtram prahartumnagasi".* (Not indeed, not indeed, should this arrow be shot at the *delicate* body of a deer, like fire upon a heap of flowers. Where alas is the extremely *frail* life of a poor deer and where your arrows of sharp descent and adamantine strength ? Therefore, withhold your arrow which has been well aimed. Your weapon is for the protection of the distressed, not to strike at the innocent.) (Act I, shloka 10-11, emphasis added).

This statement covers not only the deer but also Shakuntala and all other innocent ones including societies. Ironically, in the play, the deer is spared but Shakuntala is not. The delicate innocent Shakuntala could not protect herself from the sharp and shrewd seductive ways of the man and the city, although hers is not a fully uncourted calamity. Here, Shakuntala in a way becomes a symbol of a colonised society.

VI

Imperialism "means the practice, the theory, and the attitudes of a dominating metropolitan centre ruling a distant territory; 'colonialism', which is always a consequence of imperialism, is the implanting of settlement on distant territory" (Said 1993:9). Further, imperialism and colonialism are not merely acts of accumulation and acquisition. They are sustained by and gain impetus from "impressive ideological formulations" including ideas that people of certain territories "requires and beseech" domination and also form of knowledge allied to it.

If we accept Edward Said's definition of imperialism and colonialism, than the play opens itself up to colonised and coloniser binary sets and also to its readings from that perspective. Dushyanta's hunting expedition is the city's invasion on nature and its societies for the sport of the former. Shakuntala's story contains in it the story of the city (the capital or metro) trying to control and rule over the distant territories. There may not be a clear cut instance of accumulation and acquisition in the play but it suggests that colonialism in his larger sense existed in one form or the other in all societies before they took it upon themselves either to colonise or be colonised.

Colonialism entails in it a loss of innocence on the parts of both the coloniser and the colonised as well. Dushyanta had already lost his innocence, and his advent into the hermitage spells Shakuntala's loss of innocence. Though the opposition between nature and culture, man and woman and coloniser and colonised seems to have been to good measure diluted by Kalidasa, yet Shakuntala at a level becomes a microcosm of the colonised societies. Shakuntala in a sense becomes a colony and Dushyanta a coloniser. Dushyanta exploits her, her innocence, her resources and her world like a coloniser (He is referred to as the *"bhoktar"* (the enjoyer) in the play" (Act II, shloka 10). Her colonisation, exploitation and then rejection are legitimised and sustained by diverse discourses of polygamy, social sanction or the supernatural produced by the culture. Colonisation leads to *abulia*---- lack of will, social prostration, loss of confidence and amnesia.

With the last point of amnesia the consideration of Shakuntala gets problematised. If the colonised society suffers from amnesia, then Shakuntala should. But it is Dushyanta who does. In the epic the amnesia is a feigned one—and in the play it is caused by the curse. Shakuntala escapes amnesia, for she is rooted in nature, and in her heritage and values. Her roots help her in sustaining herself and her confidence with which she challenges and even rebukes the king in the epic. Her roots have become a little weaker by the time she reappears in the play. In the play she does not lose her memory but she fails to assert herself like her counterpart of the epic even in the face of her imminent rejection. She says only this, *"Kathamanen Kitven vrpralabhdhasmi"* (Act V, 263). (How have I been deceived by this villain).

Taking this point a little further it can be said that societies like the Indian, that unfortunately suffered colonisation, could withstand the colonial ways and operations, for they were rooted in their past, heritage, values and culture. If Indian society has survived colonisation, it was because India did not lose her memory. The African societies could not sustain themselves, for they were either not so rooted as to withstand colonial pressures or so pragmatic as to turn around the ways of colonisers after understanding or assimilating them as, can be seen in the texts like *Things Fall Apart* or *A Grain of Wheat* among others. From the preceding discussion it can also be inferred that no singular or homogenising theory of colonialism or postcolonialism can speak for colonised or postcolonial societies, for the strategies and operations of colonial forces varied from country to country and continent to continent, and so did the resisting discursive practices.

Abhigyanshakuntalam contains in it not only the possibilities of seeking contours of colonial but also the postcolonial paradigm. At the end of the play Dushyanta repents and seeks Shakuntala's forgiveness. And she too obliges him gracefully. The reconciliation between Dushyanta and Shakuntala is the post-colonial period not in its traditional but in a new positive sense in which the erstwhile coloniser and colonised societies forgive each other for the way they treated each other—an otherwise explosive reality which they think they are condemned to remember—and work together closely for the betterment of their worlds leading to a new world for a new generation, not of reactionists, of the Bharatas (*abha* means 'light', and *rat* means 'engaged')—of those engaged in the pursuit of light. This condition of postcoloniality would be in consonance with the Indian spirit.

VII

William Shakespeare's *The Tempest* also offers itself to its consideration according to the coloniser and colonised paradigm. Even at the risk of repetition I must put it briefly that Prospero stands for the coloniser and Caliban for the colonised. To put it baldly, Prospero, the Providence of the play, is on a spree of 'happy making' as the beneficent character of his allegorical name may suggest. But in reality he makes only his daughter, his own self and his people 'happy', not Caliban for he had tried to un/outdo Prospero and thereby earned the coloniser's condemnation as "a devil, a born devil" *(The Tempest* IV, 162). In the last scene, the scene of reconciliation that marks the end of the colonial period at least for Caliban, the 'rarer action of virtue' is for Prospero's people and not for the colonised. Prospero's noble conscience feels no prick or repentance for whatever he did to Caliban, the colonised. On the contrary arrogance and condescension characterise his behaviour towards Caliban. Instead of repenting or seeking forgiveness from the colonised Prospero admonishingly says:

> He is as disproportioned in his manners
> As in his shape.
>
> (Act V, sc I, 200-201)

Caliban calls himself "a thrice-double ass" (295), promises "wise hereafter" and seeks for his grace, he responds with the words "Go to; away!" (237).

Can this be a suitable paradigm for the postcolonial condition? If we compare this with the scene in *Abhigyanshakuntalam*, we find that Kalidasa's text offers a more pro-active paradigm for postcoloniality. In *The Tempest* the seeds of that colonial arrogance which failed to inveigle upon the creative souls like T.S. Eliot and many of his ilk to say even a few words for the inglorious crimes committed by their colonising brethren. The virus still survives in the bones of the colonisers as was discernible during the visit of the Queen Elizabeth II in the golden jubilee year of India's Independence when she declined either to feel sorry or to apologise for the Jallianwala massacre.

Notes

1. The economic aspect has not earned the critical attention due to it. Terry Eagleton has rightly remarked that within 'postcolonial thought' one is allowed to talk about cultural differences, but not or not much about economic exploitation (Eagleton, "Goodbye to the Enlightenment", *The Guardian*, 5 May, 1994).
2. The hypocritical attitude of the patriarchal society towards woman is discernible in the *Manu Smriti*. He imposed severe restrictions on women and imposed harsh punishment in case of their violation, but garnished them with the few finest words glorifying woman in it: *"Yatranaryastu poojayante ramante tatradevatah. Yatrefa staknapoojyante sarsahstatraafald kriyah"* (Chapter III, shloka 56).

References

Appiah, Anthony. "Is the Post - in Postmodernism the Post - in Post colonial ?", *Critical Inquiry*, 17, Winter 1991.

Ashcroft, Bill, Gareth Griffiths & Helen Tiffin. *The Empire Writes Back*. London: Methuen, 1987.

Childs, Peter & R.J. Patrick Williams. *An Introduction to Post-Colonial Theory*. London: Prentice Hall, 1997.

Manu. *Manu Smriti*. Compiled with translation in Hindi by Srimat Raokrishna. Delhi: Mahmoodulamataba Mirza Alambeg Publishers, 1941.

McClintock, Anne. 'The Angel of Progress: Pitfalls of the term "Postcolonialism" ', *Social Text* 31/32, 1992.

Mishra, Vijay & Bob Hodge. "What is post(-)colonialism?", *Textual Practice* 5, 3, 1991.

Mir, Taqui Mir. *Mir Taqui Mir: Selected Poetry*. Trans. into English by K.C. Kanda. New Delhi: Sterling, 1997.

Paranjape, Makarand. "Coping with Post-colonialism," *Interrogating Post-colonialism: Theory, Text and Context*. Ed. Harish Trivedi and Meenakshi Mukherjee. Shimla: IIAS, 1996.

---. "Theorising Postcolonial Difference: Culture, Nation, Civilization", *SPAN. 47, October 1998.*

Said, Edward. *Culture and Imperialism.* New York: Alfred A. Knopf, 1993.

Shakespeare, William. *The Tempest.* Ed. A.W. Verity. London: Cambridge University Press, 1962.

Slemon Stephen. "The Scramble for Post-colonialism" in Tiffin and Lawson, pp. 15-32.

Spivak, Gayatri Chakravorty. "Neocolonialism and the Secret Agent of Knowledge", *Oxford Literary Review* 1 3,1 -2, 1991 .

----. *Outside in the Teaching Machine.* London: Routledge, 1996.

Shohat, Ella. "Notes on the "Post-Colonial". *Social Text* 31/32, 1992.

Tiffin, Chris and Alan Lawson. Eds. *De-scribing Empire: Post-colonialism and Textuality.* London: Routledge, 1994.

3
Edward Said's *Orientalism* and Abbé Dubois

R.K. Kaul

Said's *Orientalism* was published in 1978. Its thesis was tendentious. It was based on selective extracts from some western Orientalists. It ignored the more favourable representations of the Orient in the works of William Jones, Max Muller and others. Its overstatements, omissions and distortions have been exposed at the scholarly plane by specialists in Arab studies such as Bernard Lewis and its flawed logic by Aijaz Ahmad among others. While blaming the western Orientalists for their refusal to permit the Orient to speak for itself, Said has himself relied on the more up to date western scholars to refute the theses of their predecessors.

Since the publication of this book Said has revised and corrected his earlier statements in several books and articles. Of these the present writer is familiar with *The World, the Text and the Critic* (1983) and *Culture and Imperialism* (1993).

In spite of all its shortcomings Said's earlier book has proved to be so influential that it has given rise to a new subject of investigation: decolonisation.

Hippolyte Taine (1828-93) the French critic held that a writer's character is determined by the race, the milieu and the moment, Said's case proves that the impact of a book is determined by the milieu and the moment. The contemporary cultural climate caused the readers to overrate the book beyond its actual value. Although the book was provoked by the western injustice to the Palestinians its appeal was owing to the anti-Vietnam sentiment. After the American failure to exterminate the Vietnamese, a revulsion set in against the US arrogance towards the east, led by thinkers like Noam Chomsky and Susan Sontag. Of course this awakening began only after the American youths began to be killed. Still the reaction was widespread and led to what is known as Counter-Culture. In fairness to Said it must be stated that he did not abjure reason, the Enlightenment and humanism. He is in fact a teacher of Comparative Literature. He refused to concede to the west a monopoly of humanistic values.

The Indian intellectual, always avidly aping the latest trends of the western world, hailed *Orientalism* and proceeded to apply the thesis to Indian cultural history. They pointed out that English literature itself had been an instrument of British colonialism. A whole school of criticism emanated, promoting Said's ideology. Its centre is Delhi University but some of the more advanced centres outside Delhi have been equally enthusiastic.

Many Indian leaders during the rise of nationalism were inspired to fight for freedom by Byron and Shelley. Other western writers included Mazzini, Thoreau and Tolstoy. Except through the medium of English none of these writers would have been accessible to our leaders. (The Italian and Russian works were read in English translation). The constitutionalists learnt to define "Liberty" from John Stuart Mill since there is no native tradition of such a concept in India. The nearest Sanskrit equivalent to "independent" is *swatasa*, meaning "by oneself". The word *swatantra* must be a post British coinage. Perhaps the absence of the concept is related to the fact that there is no equivalent of the theological notion of free will in any religion other than Christianity.

Said's indictment of the western Orientalists is based on the assumption that the colonial powers were guided by them in their handling of the colonies:

> A text purporting to contain knowledge about something actual... (acquires prestige)
> Expertise is attributed to it. The authority of academics, institutions, and governments can accrue to it... such texts can *create* not only knowledge but also the very reality they appear to describe.

By way of illustration Said states that everything that Napoleon and de Lesseps knew about the Orient came from books written in the tradition of French Orientalism. He claims that "for them the Orient... was something to be encountered and dealt with to a certain extent *because* the texts made that Orient possible" (p. 94). The present writer would like to observe that the Arabs showed no such weakness when they captured Egypt in 639. No Egyptologists guided them in their imperial policy.

Since the history of the French invasion of Egypt and the building of the Suez canal is not so familiar to us a parallel from India would make the point more effectively. It would follow that if there had been no William Jones, Charles Wilkins and their like, there would have been no Robert Clive or Warren Hastings. In fact Clive (1725-74) preceded Jones (1746-94) and Wilkins (1749-1836), the English Orientalists, and not the other way round. Hastings's attitude to the Indians was to some extent guided by Jones and the Orientalists. But it was on the whole a beneficial influence. An attempt to understand the Hindu and Muslim codes of law helped them to administer justice in a manner that seemed fair to their subjects. Said's thesis could apply to the influence of Macaulay on the educational policy of the British government. It is still an open question whether the introduction of English was harmful to the country. Many of us do not think so. In any case Macaulay could hardly be accused of being an Orientalist. Perhaps the charge could justifiably be levelled against Mill's father, James Mill, whose *History of India* misrepresents India. But that appeared in 1817 while Cornwallis (1786-98) and Wellesley (1798-1805) had already conquered the best part of India.

II

According to Said the western Orientalist misrepresented the Orient in the following respects:
(i) It was assumed that the west is rational, developed, humane, superior; the Orient is aberrant, under-developed and inferior;
(ii) The Orientalist was guided by the classical texts in his attitude to the Orient rather than modern Oriental realities;
(iii) The Orient was considered to be unchanging and uniform;
(iv) Finally since the Orient is incapable of defining itself, an objective assessment of the east must be made by the western Orientalist.[1]

In an earlier study the present writer examined these charges in detail by analysing the works of William Jones.[2] In this paper I shall examine Abbé J.A. Dubois's *Hindu Manners Customs and Ceremonies* originally published in 1806[3] to see whether these charges are well founded. Abbé Dubois (born 1770) laboured for 31 years in India. He was attached to the Pondicherry Mission and he qualifies all his statements by reminding us that he never crossed the Vindhyas. He was familiar with Mysore during the reign of Tipu Sultan (died 1799). He lived like the natives, wearing their dress, associating with both the Brahmins and the peasants in the villages.

Abbé Dubois's observations appear to be quite accurate. He has an understandable abhorrence for polytheism and idolatry. He notes the Hindu resistance to social reform and conversion to Christianity. His view in fact is that there is not much hope of conversion on a large scale.

We now proceed to his analysis of Hindu society. he knows not only about the four castes but also of the sub-castes into which Hindu society is divided. He found that the Telugu speakers in Mysore observed their own practices and also that differences of customs and practices were tolerated in Hindu society. He describes the sub human treatment to which the Pariahs (from the Tamil *Paraiyan, Paraiyar*) are subjected, and adds that they possess a monopoly of artisan employment and manual labour (p.15).

After weighing the pros and cons of the caste system, the rigidity of the division and the lack of social mobility he concludes that its advantages more than outweigh its evils. That, however, is a matter of judgement. We must not forget that in the first place he left France because he wanted to run away from the "horrors of the Revolution" (p.x). He could not have been an egalitarian at heart. Very few would have been in 1792.

From this account does it follow that there is a polarity between the east and the west? There had been no attempt at the levelling of society in Europe before 1789 and universal suffrage was a long way off. Still there is substantial difference between the rigid stratification of Hindu society and the relative mobility of western society even in early 19th century.

Said accuses the western Orientalist of representing the east as unchanging and uniform. Let us consider one of the features of Hindu society which distinguishes it from all other societies, including the Muslim viz. the belief in pollution by contact and the necessity of purification. Once an upper caste Hindu is polluted he has to undergo purification. It may be added that pollution can take place owing to moral lapses, deviation from social norms and association with other communities and castes. Has there been any change in the Hindu concept or practice over the years in this respect?

It is laid down in *The Laws of Manu* that one of the ways by which "A twice born man so deluded that he has drunk liquor" can purify himself is by drinking boiling hot cow's urine, water, milk, clarified butter or liquid cow dung" till he dies (XI. 91-92).[4] The exact date of this book is not easy to determine but according to Monier Williams it can be placed not later than 250 B.C. It may be objected that the drinking of liquor lands a Muslim also in hell fire. The emphasis at present is on the mode of purification. In 1996 the distinguished Kannada Writer Anantha Murthy published a novel *Bharathipura* in which the father of the protagonist has to swallow *Pancha gavya* because he had visited the bhangi colony. It is true that the ceremony was not designed to kill him but the contents of what he had to swallow were the same as those prescribed by whoever compiled the *Dharma Sastra* which is ascribed to the mythical name of Manu.

It seems that the Orientalists were not far wrong in talking of the unchanging east. Indeed they did not anticipate the new wave of revivalism known as fundamentalism in the entire Muslim world.

Among other observations that the Abbé makes is that the first historians of India were in reality poets (p.2). This conforms to the claim of our Indologists and historiographers that ancient puranic literature is *itihas*.[5] In fact the distinction between fiction and fact was never made clearly. There was a general imprecision about dates and places. We still do not know Kalidasa's dates of birth and death, or the provenance of his works. One interesting illustration of the sheer delight of the ancient Hindus in multiplying number *ad lib* has been recorded by Abbé Dubois. There are according to the Hindu, 8,400,000 kinds of living creatures (p.144). No wonder it is claimed that every human has passed through 84 lakh incarnations before being elevated to humanity. This is part of our folklore.

Dubois records that the Indians "bow their head to oppression" (p.4), that "the wretched pariahs never complain of their estate" (p.50). They prostrate themselves before persons of high degree" (p.42). He does not appear to know the reason for the first viz. the doctrine of *karma*. As for submission to persons in authority it is common to all religious groups in India till today.

Having made these accurate observations he goes on to make an unacceptable moral judgement. He claims that the evil reputation of the Pariahs is well deserved. By way of proof he points to their unclean habits and willingness to eat carrion. The present writer is reminded of the European prejudice against the Jews. They were first condemned to live in ghettoes and then accused of possessing the ghetto mentality. The Jews were not allowed to practice any profession other than money-lending because it was not permitted to the Christians and then they were condemned as usurers.

The above, however, is not an instance of misrepresentation. It is an example of biased judgement. About the institution of family he makes very accurate observations. He notes that owing to the joint family system:

> A native's house is besieged as soon as he is known to be a wealthy man, and this is not only by his own relatives, but also by the indigent of his caste, and by a horde of parasites... (p.92).

He had no occasion to discover that Muslim families were afflicted by the same complaint.

He pays a very high tribute to the women of India when he asserts that no women are more faithful. It does not occur to him that the men do not observe any reciprocity in the matter. He also informs us that barren women are condemned (p.94). He does not seem to find anything wrong with the manner in which they are exploited. As a French man he must have found it odd that there was no freedom of association between the sexes in the early 19th century in India (p.131).

The Hindu faith in astrology does not escape his attention, nor their fear of the evil eye (p. 134). He was surprised at the accuracy of their almanacs, especially the precision of their forecast of solar and lunar eclipses (p.142).

With the eye of an economist he notes that there had been a rapid increase of population, leading to the increase of poverty (p.93). He also notes how industrialisation had deprived the weavers especially of their source of livelihood (pp. 93-94).

Dubois, as the head of a Roman Catholic monastery, was naturally interested in finding out the place of the priest in Hindu society. He found that the status of the *purohit* who attended to the funeral ceremonies of the lower castes was lower than that of the other Brahmins. The prestige of the *guru* was high, so was the fear of his curse. He notes their extortionist practices (p.126).

His final advice is one which many modern anthropologists would agree with, "let us leave them their cherished laws and prejudices". Indeed he warns the government against interfering with "their religious and civil usages" (p.94). The present writer does not accept the assumption that the character of a society is fixed forever. If the makers of revolutions had accepted this view Russia would still have slavery and serfdom, the Chinese would still be smoking opium. Society can be changed and reform should be introduced. These considerations, however, do not affect the accuracy of Dubois's observations.

To sum up, his over all conclusion is "our European ways, manners and customs are utterly different from theirs" (p.94). It confirms Said's thesis that the western Orientalists claim that there is a dichotomy between the east and the west. As compared to contemporary western society Hindu society was less rational, less progressive, and more superstitious. In his own way Dubois did attempt to improve things by introducing the small pox vaccine. But he knew perhaps that the "mother", as small pox is called in our language, would continue to be worshipped.

Said calls this view a dogma. In the case of Dubois and many other Orientalists such conclusions cannot be called dogmatic. They were arrived at after a patient and laborious study and observation. We may point to certain omissions. The present writer has himself been selective in choosing extracts for illustration.[6] Dubois has perhaps focused on the caste system and its ramifications, may be to the exclusion of other topics like marriage, the position of women and of the state of education. But no work of scholarship can be exhaustive. Every account must be selective. The only requirement is that there should be no distortion. The estimate of Max Muller is that it contains "the views of an eye witness, of a man singularly free from prejudice and of a scholar with sufficient knowledge, if not of Sanskrit, yet of Tamil, both literary and spoken, to be able to enter into the views of the natives to understand their manners and customs...."

Notes

1. A simplified version, partly in my words of what Said calls the *dogmas* of Orientalism. See *Orientalism*. Penguin, 1985, pp. 300-301.
2. See *Studies in William Jones*. Shimla: Institute of Advanced Study, 1995.

3. Trans. H.K. Beauchamp, Oxford : Clarendon Press (1897), 1928. Preface by F. Max Müller. Quotations from this book will be followed by page numbers within the text.
4. Trans. Wendy Deniger. New Delhi: Penguin, 1992.
5. See D.P. Chattopadhya, *JICPR*, June 1996. Many other essays in this number of the journal make the same point. See also T.N. Dhar. *History-Fiction Interface in Indian English Novel*. New Delhi : Prestige, 1999. p.63.
6. A large portion of the book describes the ceremonies and rituals. Those have been omitted in my account.

References

Dhar, T.N. *History-Fiction Interface in Indian English Novel*. New Delhi: Prestige, 1999.

Doniger, Wendy. Trans. *The Laws of Manu*. New Delhi: Penguin, 1992.

Dubois, J.A. Abbé. *Hindu Manners and Customs* (1806). Trans. H.E. Beauchamp. Oxford: Clarendon Press (1897), 1928.

Kaul, R.K. *Studies in William Jones*. Shimla: Institute of Advanced Study, 1995.

Max Müller. 'Preface'. *Hindu Manners and Customs* by Abbé J.A. Dubois.

Said, Edward. *Orientalism* (1978). Penguin, 1985.

4

Gayatri Chakravorty Spivak: Problematising/Speaking the Margin

Santosh Gupta

Gayatri Chakravorty Spivak uses her location as an immigrant Third World academic to problematise the postcolonial situation, and to understand continued Western domination. She uses her experience as a woman, an Asian and an immigrant in the west to build on the postcolonial feminist deconstructive analysis.

She calls herself a "Marxist - feminist - deconstructivist", a combination that makes her critical of west's predominant discourse in the 1970s and 80s. Her concern is with the imperialistic, neo-capitalist market strategies used by the west to control, manipulate and exploit the Third World population. The women are exploited and suppressed in a double bondage in the colonial and patriarchal system. Spivak relates the diverse aspects of the Third World population to analyse the causes and features of the conditions of exploitation. Spivak's essays and reflections on these different issues form a continuity of certain main ideas about suppression and objectification of the ex-colonised, Third World people, about the First World's unstated but commonly practised discriminations of race, gender and class. This paper attempts to analyse and state in a simplified manner some of her ideas, for Spivak's dense, multi-referential language becomes a deterrent to many interested scholars. She has made important contributions to the current debate on postcolonial theory, in taking a stance against imperialistic trends of Western discourse and to the issues of feminist struggle in the Third World.

As a Marxist-feminist Spivak emphasises the materialist grounding of all personal, emotional and aesthetic experience. The individual's experience is seen to be rooted in a specific historic, geographical and economic context. 'Materialist Feminists', as some of the Marxist Feminist, such as Judith Newton and Deborah Rosenfelt are called, relate the problems of women's oppression in patriarchal system with those of economic and political systems/interests and manipulations. Questions of aesthetic experience are seen to be related to the policies of market-value giving, economic conditions and labour surplus. The Materialist Feminists link race, gender and class politics with international market economy and emphasise plurality and diversity in feminist thought. She takes a deconstructivist approach to examine the Western intellectual discourse and the cultural institutions of the two worlds are interrogated within the framework of international capitalism, a methodology evolved through her close reading and translation *Of Grammatology* (1976).

In her experiences as a woman, Asian and an immigrant in the First World, Spivak found the experience of marginality to be a common factor. Inclusion in the mainstream, closeness to the centre was possible, on given conditions. However, whenever the margin considered itself close to the centre, the lines somehow shifted and marginality once again appeared. As a woman academic she could belong to the dominant male academic centre, and she would be treated (as Freud had suggested) to be 'better than other woman' ("French Feminism"), but this would lead to alienation from the other women. Looking upon her repeated experiences of marginality, Spivak tries to draw certain conclusions, and point out ways of dealing with these conditions. She would like to make her marginality a location, from which she can examine and deconstruct the hegemonic system of the west.

In her essay "Explanation and Culture: Marginalia" Spivak begins with her experience of marginality in a seminar called "Explanation and Culture". Her insistence upon questioning and examining the terms of discussion, rather than to indulge in using those terms for a discussion, she found herself being consistently ignored ("Explanation" 104). She was later offered token inclusion (105), and she realised that "The putative center welcomes selective inhabitants of the margin in order better to exclude the margin" ("Explanation" 107).

Spivak, however, insisted on deconstruction of the main terms, such as aesthetic, cognitive, culture and processes of explanation, to have clear assumptions. As a deconstructivist she wanted to, she says, "reverse and displace such hierarchies as cognitive-aesthetic" and to discover the expressed grounds of these assumptions. For she begins with the suspicion that "what is at the Center often hides a repression" ("Explanation" 104). She wanted to overturn and explore the commonly held assumptions of the liberal humanist discourse. Terms like 'culture' and 'explanation' need to be deconstructed to realise the hidden politics in the discourse.

Jacques Derrida's approach to the liberal humanist tradition has helped Spivak in realising how the old words would not resemble themselves anymore when one uses the new "tricks of re-reading" she learnt from Derrida. He "touches the texture language" and changes their meanings. The trick she says, is "to recognize that every textual production, in the production of every explanation, there is the itinerary of a constantly thwarted desire to make the text explain" ("Explanation" 105).

An attempt towards explanation reveals, Spivak writes, "a symptom, a desire to have a self and a world", for this presupposes an xplainable world and the explaining self. The world is assumed to be containable within our explanation, resolving the differences. So that, in "explaining" the other/world, "we exclude the possibility of the radically heterogeneous" ("Explanation" 105). Spivak perceives that the First World constructs explanations/ knowledge to "explain" the other. Humanities in the US academia have become a source of constructing explanation of Asia, East, the

Other, the postcolonial world. The constructed knowledge is a means of containing these diverse worlds into the systems. Spivak criticises the construction of knowledge in USA, the Western world and the use of technology in the dissemination of this product.

Within the universities, Spivak holds the gradual decline of humanities and social sciences to be the outcome of the capitalist control over most social, cultural, institutions, including education. High level technology has strengthened neo-capitalism, which controls production and dissemination of knowledge. The humanities have been entrusted with the role of producing the society's culture, but Spivak points out that the humanities are required to produce the culture that will describe and make neo-capitalism acceptable to the masses in the First and the Third Worlds. There is no neutrally created knowledge, universalist and morally guided. The production of knowledge has a sharp and clear political purpose, aiming to justify and popularise "explain" the culture of consumerism, high-fashion and advancing technology ("Explanation" 107).

The politicised construction of knowledge is responsible for power equation. Edward Said has argued that the construction of orientalism, was primarily directed by the west's colonial expansion during the 16th to 18th centuries. Spivak and other postcolonial critics maintain that the construction of knowledge in the metropolitan centers and the western universities produce a specific type of culture. Spivak finds that this culture then prescribes, defines and writes the scholars. By using interruptive perspectives of race, gender and nation in critiquing the First World's academic projects Spivak, Homi Bhabha and the other postcolonial critics argue for a rethinking of the concepts like selfhood, culture and national identity.

The "official explanations" become aligned with power and continually impose status of the 'Other' on those on the margin. These explanations, Spivak says, follow the requirements of the power "emphasizing continuity or discontinuity with past explanations, depending on a seemingly judicious choice permitted by the play of this power" ("Explanation" 108). In producing these officially sanctioned explanations (of culture) "we reproduce", she writes, "structures of possibility of a knowledge whose effect is that very structure" (108). "We" (the Third World scholars who study the knowledge produced by the First World academy "are a part of the records we keep", and "... we are written into the texts of technology. These effects upon us of the close adherence to the knowledge produced elsewhere, emphasize the "complicity" and the "surrender" to the controlling power of neo-capitalism" ("Explanation" 108). She states very emphatically that no individual writes these texts "with full control over the situation, but is rather an instrument in continuing the patterns desired by those in power. The view of a free individual thinker that liberal humanism had upheld—a "sovereign subject" is a grand illusion. Spivak, a deconstructionist, rejects the idea of a subject with a stable final awareness of selfhood, and deconstructs the terms and ideas that make this assumption. The crisis in the humanities is seen the world over: in the First World they are on a decline as they are being pushed by economic requirements from the society to become cost-effective, efficient. These pressures push the departments in universities to adopt courses that will bring financial security. The humanities are being "trashed" as they are being pushed into writing explanation literary aesthetic courses—using the practices that go on with the belief in the civilising effects of literature, philosophy and other subjects.

Looking at these pressures upon the humanities and the universities, Spivak makes a larger statement about the purposes and functioning of 'Theory(ies)'. The grand narrative of over-all synthesizing theory that comes up after every few years, in the west, is produced by a certain class and economic group. The purpose of Theory become self reproductive, for "the stability of a technocracy" depends upon this continued reproducing of the grand theory—running through diverse cultural social institutions ("Explanation" 113). The grand Theory checks any questioning, diversity or true multivocality. The main elements of Theory are "blind" to the "will to power through knowledge". It constantly tries to resolve contradictions, differences and regional diversity of interest, identity and goals.

Literary theories and criticism are also seen by Spivak as being subsumed within the grand narrative of capitalism. The theories of metaphor, modernism and postmodernism continue to function on the assumptions about the superiority of a particular class, group and race over the rest. These self centred practices that have had a continuity since romantic poetry privilege the Western concepts of its superiority over the rest of the world.

Gayatri Spivak's writing is a commentary on the First World's practice of imposing its political power over the Third World through indirect strategies. Its highly sophisticated system of production and dissemination of knowledge has strengthened its power through education, mass media and market forces. Spivak takes up these ideas again in her essay "Marginality in the Teaching Machine" (1996) and she discusses how the selection of a few texts valorises those as important sources of values and ideas. The selection leads to their importance in the canon. These texts create the mind set that perpetuate some specific ideological approaches.

Next to the selection is the impact of the teaching method. In both the essays "Explanation & Culture", and "Marginality in the Teaching Machine", Spivak discusses the need to evolve a confrontational methodology for Third World teachers. This is the method "that continually opens up texts"—the language, metaphors, form and deconstructs the repressed meanings. The critic must be on the lookout for heterogeneity, "heteroglossia" as Bakhtin calls it, rather than for final, grand truths. The teaching method of a postcolonial teacher, critic should be confrontational, opening out the implied assumptions of dominant discourse and should question them. Spivak refers to this strategy repeatedly in the different essays, and herself takes on a position of questioning major concepts, movements and ideas. She writes, "What I look for rather is a confrontational teaching in the humanities that would question the students" received disciplinary ideology (model of legitimate cultural explanations) even as it pushed into indefiniteness the most powerful ideology of the teaching of the humanities: the unquestioned explicating power of the theorizing mind and class, the need for intelligibility and the role of law" ("Explanation" 116).

Spivak examines the sudden popularity of postmodernism in the US literary circles, foregrounding Latin American narrative style of "magic realism", of terms like "Third World". Name giving is a source of power too. The name given to the ex-colonies as "Third World" in the USA reflects a clever dislocation of Britain's past of a great imperial power. It also creates the historical, present orientation in which the First World, mainly the US is ruling the world. A similar strategy makes Latin American literary style suddenly most important. Latin America's closeness to the US reflects their political and literary importance. Spivak notes that the Third World scholars accept the literary preferences from the US even though this technique may not reflect their cultural specificities. Pablo Neruda, Garcia Marquez have used this style to reflect their own cultural complexities. This style does not, Spivak says, "narrativise decolonisation" ("Marginality" 57) yet it is adopted in the countries, as a mark of being up to date in literary fashion.

Spivak also argues that the west uses Postmodernism to counter the important issues being raised by postcolonial writing. Many of the techniques that were part of the colonial world are, she says, taken over by the coloniser, appropriated and then given back to these countries, as if of Western origin. When the colonised people try to create their own systems of thought the west reclaims most of the important concepts. The language and concepts, such as "nationalism, constitutionality, citizenship, democracy, culturalism" are claimed to have been "written elsewhere". These concepts, when used in the postcolonial society become "catechresis", as their meaning changes in the new contexts. Spivak suggests that these catechresis may be used strategically, as a stock to begin with, to examine west's philosophical universalist concepts, to "peer, however blindly, into the constantly shifting and tangling network of techniques of knowledge and strategies of power through the question of value" ("Marginality" 61).

In questioning the west's continued hold over the Third World's labour market Spivak makes use of the Marxist analysis of "value" and "desire", capitalism's subtle manipulation of "desire" is, she argues, closely related to the wide spread consumerism and global marketing. The labour market of the poorer, postcolonial markets are still controlled by the rich and advanced countries' industrial system. The economic system spreads over other cultural institutions, including education. Spivak refers to the pressures of economic system on the universities where departments are being compelled into becoming more cost-effective, efficient and self financing. Areas of research, proposals for new studies and selection of texts are likewise considered.

Gender politics is as much under the networking of the market, for, Spivak finds the labour market determines gender value, which is "coding of the value-differential" ("Marginality" 63). She takes on the Feminist struggles in the Third World in their specific cultural and material contexts. Her criticism of the Western Feminist schools is based on her perception of difference and heterogeneity. Feminist theory is informed with postcolonial theoretical concerns. She applies deconstructive opening out of hegemonic images of the Third World Women as an important project of postcolonial feminism. This strategy lends weight to her sustained efforts to identify and criticise globalising relations of power/knowledge.

The postcolonial experience of a hybrid reality makes it difficult for Spivak to accept the notion of a unified self (male/female). In her examination of the First and Third World feminisms she brings in the considerations of race, gender and class. In distinguishing between the First and Third World Feminisms, one must, she agrees, take up an essentialist position, if only for the sake of argument,

"an assumption of an identity becomes necessary". Trinh Minh-ha, a Vietnamese postcolonial feminist, says in this context, "The reflexive question asked ... is no longer: who am I? But when, where, how, am I (so and so)? This is why I remain strategies skeptical of reversal when they are not intricately woven into strategies of displacement. Here the notion of displacement is also a notion of identity; there is no real me to return to, no whole self that synthesizes the woman, the woman of color and the writer"; there is rather, she further writes, "diverse recognition of self through differences and unfinished, contingent, arbitrary closures.... (quoted in Clough 114)[1]

This kind of identity is tentative and oppositional. Spivak admits that "it is not possible, within discourse, to escape essentializing somewhere". But this stance is taken for the discourse of the so-called "sub-altern" classes,, such as "subsistence farmers, unorganized peasant labor, the tribals and the communities of zero workers on the street or in the countryside." This is the position from where "history is narrativized into logic" ("Subaltern" 271).

The First World feminists' perceptions of the Third World women have not become free of the prevalent phallocentrism. As the First World women try to perceive and describe the Third World women there is a process of displacement (of the Third World women). She cautions the First World women (and scholars like herself located in the west, even if at its margin) to be careful not to 'romanticize' or patronize' them. The First World academic women should rather, she says, "learn to learn from them", to speak to them, and to overcome a sense of superiority ("French Feminism" 85). She tells the First World feminists to avoid taking intellectual short cuts in explaining/theorising the women of the Third World.

In her essay "French Feminism in an International Frame" (1981) Spivak emphasises the differences of social cultural and material background between the First and Third World women; the "immense heterogeneity of the field must be appreciated, and the First World feminist must learn to stop feeling privileged as a woman ("Feminism" 86). She uses as her reference book for discussing French Feminism, the book *New French Feminism: An Anthology* (ed. Elaine Marks and Isabelle de Courtivro Amherst: Univ. of Massachusetts Press, 1980).

Julia Kristeva's essay "About Chinese Women" (1977) was written after Kristeva's visit to China. Kristeva uses her observations as the starting point of analyses of the Chinese women's role in their society. This important essay, one of the few attempts of a First World feminist to analyse, Third World women, is taken by

Gayatri Spivak as a representative case. Its methodology is examined in detail, and the process of constructing an exotic, distant "Other" is decoded.

Kristeva builds up in her essay a theory about the continuity of matrilineal, materilocal social system in China, allowing the women access to a pre-patriarchal self awareness. Spivak questions the method, scholarship and the conclusions drawn by Kristeva. She is surprised at the casual inadequate scholarship; in some "seventy-odd pages, and always with no encroachment of archival evidence, speculation has become fact" ("Feminism" 88). This hastily drawn conclusion is made, Spivak says, because Kristeva "needs a way of valorizing the women of the countryside today over the woman of the cities". Spivak further says, Kristeva makes the "most stupendous generalizations about Chinese writing" (89) and women, and makes "wishful use of history". By linking some one detail, fact from Chinese history 1000 B.C. to the society in 1970s, Kristeva perceives continuities that could not be discovered without a prolonged and serious enquiry. In this approach the past, an almost pre-historical past, is pitted against the present. Spivak writers, "Kristeva prefers the misty past to the present" (89); she finds Kristeva's conclusions reflect a "colonialist benevolence" towards the Chinese society (89).

This attitude reflects, for Spivak, the tendency of the west to freeze select moment in the past, and ignore the living real present when it looks at the east; it is, she says, the "Construction of the "Classical" East treated with primitivistic reverence even as the "Contemporary" East is treated with realpolitikal contempt" ("Feminism" 89).

French Feminism is seen by Spivak to be caught within the politics of narrative forms, as it privileges avant-grade movement. The French Feminist try to base women's discourse on the experimental writing. But these experiments do not seem to benefit the reader. Quoting Derrida, Spivak argues that anti-humanist thinking of avant-grade movement has not provided Feminism a break-off from masculinist bias in Western discourse (91). She is emphatic that the French Feminists should first consider their own location, position and ideas before they assume the privilege to sum up to explain Chinese/Eastern women.

The essay then goes on to discuss the ideas that Feminism, especially of postcolonial countries should look into the construction of female identity that looks beyond woman's body to identify her as a subject. This part of the essay is an important statement of Spivak's perceptions about women's discourse. Here she takes into consideration the concepts of Cixous and Irigaray especially about women's relationships with other women, and on the construction of women's identity. Spivak finds Cixous' use of Derridean deconstructivist method useful in examining, "reversing and displacing hierarchized binary oppositions" ("Feminism" 96). Cixous in "Laugh of the Medusa", and "Sorties" talks of a dispersed and differential identity for woman. Talking of a complexity of identity formation that is unanalysable, Cixous says, "we can no more talk about 'woman' than about 'man' without being caught within an ideological theater where the multiplication of representations, images, reflections, myths, identifications constantly transforms, deforms, alters each person's imaginary order and in advance renders all conceptualization null and void" ("Laugh of the Medusa" 96). Woman constructed by the phallocentric Western discourse, which has an impact over most (Western) feminist theories. But to get out of these concepts, feminists should "cut through all the heavy layers of ideology that have borne down since the beginnings of the family and private property; feminists need to "change the imaginary in order to be able to act on the real, to change the very forms of language which by its structure and history has been subject to a law that is patrilinear, therefore masculine" ("Laugh of the Medusa" 130-131)[2].

Gayatri Spivak's views have invited criticism and discussion among other postcolonial, feminist writers. Benita Parry in her essay "Problems in Current Theories of Colonial Discourse" considers Spivak and Homi Bhabha to be engaged in "a purely negative task of deconstructing the texts of colonialism" (Maxwell 70). Parry disapproves of Spivak's "obliteration of the role of the native as a historical subject and competent possessor of another knowledge and producer of alternative traditions" (Parry 34). Further she criticises Spivak for her ideas about native subjects. Parry thinks that Spivak distrusts the native tradition, silences the subaltern, native, woman with her views. Spivak's discussion of the native, creole woman in Jean Rhys' *Wide Sargasso Sea*, regards Christophine to be as much bound by the imperialist discourse as the other women, and hence unable to speak independently. Parry however would like to treat Christophine as a speaking subject, and become an interpreter of her society (Parry 38).

Benita Parry takes on issue with Homi Bhabha and Spivak over their refusal to accept a Manichean discourse based on binary opposition. The purely deconstructivist nature of their approach is seen as a "weakness", for Parry regards this as a "narrowly textualist point of views, which does not allow for any position outside of discourse from which concrete forms of opposition can be marshalled" (Maxwell 71).

Anne Maxwell's discussion of this debate looks beyond Parry's criticism. She quotes Bhabha in his defence of theory. He argues that theory can be a revolutionary, subverting practice, when it is used to reveal and analyse the processes involved in the ideological production of representational images. He argues that the categorical distinction between practice and theory, politics and texts overlooks the metaphorical and rhetorical force of writing as "a productive matrix" (Bhabha 5). For Bhabha and Spivak textuality is more than a mere verbal symptom of a pre-given political subject. It can become a force for social change. As Maxwell puts it, "for Bhabha theory has more to offer in the way of hope for the oppressed than the sort of criticism which attempts to resurrect the rigid binary oppositions which inform 'identity'" (Maxwell 72).

Parry's view of a pure native voice is also, Maxwell argues, a reflection of the 19th century anthropological concept that encouraged the construction (and appropriative policies) of a native. For Spivak, Bhabha and Maxwell the colonial experience has left indelible impressions, creating hybrid, mimic selves, but it is not possible to reclaim a pure native now. Such hybrid natives are critics like Bhabha and Spivak, as Spivak claims in her essay.

Maxwell sums up Spivak's critical opinions and significance in the following words "Spivak alone endeavours to return postcolonial criticism to a Marxist notion of consciousness. Her aim here is merely to take the emphasis off an individualist concept of freedom so as to return anti-colonial struggle to its roots in collective as well as political and economic freedom" (Maxwell 81).

Notes

1. Trinh-Minh ha. 'An Interview', *Framers Framed*. New York: Routledge, 1992, 155, quoted in Patricia Vincento Clough, *Feminist Thought*, U.K., U.S.A., Blackwell, 1994, 114.
2. Cixous, Clement. 'La double seance', *La dissemination* (Paris, Senil, 1972) in Harold Bloom, et al., *Deconstruction and Criticism*. New York: Seabury Press, 1979, quoted by Spivak, "French Feminism in an International Frame", 97.

References

Bhabha, Homi. "The Commitment to Theory", *New Formations* 5 (1988).

Clough, Patricia Vincento. *Feminist Thought*. U.K.: Blackwell, 1994.

Kristeva, Julia. *About Chinese Women*. Trans. Anita Barrows. London: Marion Boyars, 1977.

Maxwell, Anne. "The Debate on Current Theories of Colonial Discourse", *Kunapipi* XIII, 3 1991, 70-84.

Parry, Benita. "Problems in Current Theories of Colonial Discourse" *Oxford Literary Review*, 9, 1-2, 1987, 27-58.

Spivak, Gayatri Chakravorty. "Explanation and Culture: Marginalia" (1979), *In Other Worlds: Essays in Cultural Politics*. New York: Routledge, 1988.

—. "French Feminism in An International Frame" *Yale French Studies* 62 (1981) 154-84. Reptd. in *Feminist Literary Criticism* edited and

introduced by Mary Eagleton. London: Longman, 1991, 83-109.
--- "Can the Subaltern Speak?" *Marxism and Interpretation of Culture.* Eds. Gary Nelson and Lawrence Grossberg. Urbana: Univ. of Illinois Press, 1988.
--- "Marginality in the Teaching Machine", *Outside in the Teaching Machine.* London: Routledge, 1996.

5

Decolonising the Indian Mind: Ahmad and Indian Literature

Seema Malik

The concept of Indian Literature is still at a nascent stage and its evolution not only demands some elucidation and concentrated thinking but also a reconditioning of the Indian mind. Unity in diversity is emphasised by the Sahitya Akademi in its propagation of the dictum—"Indian literature is one though written in many languages". But do we feel convinced about its veracity? This is possible only if Indian Literature is studied in its totality and a united, collective effort is made to understand deeper variations beneath the surface oneness.

In the seventh chapter of his book *In Theory* entitled "Indian Literature: Notes towards the Definition of a Category", Aijaz Ahmad explores some of the difficulties in constructing the conceptual category of "Indian Literature" and draws our attention to certain aspects which need immediate attention in order to validate the assertion that there is an "Indian Literature". There are suggestive pointers for the interested scholars, which might contribute towards establishing both the heterogeneity and the fundamental unity of "Indian Literature."

A literary history should not be a hurried categorisation of "a prolix and variegated archive" (243) with scant attempt to comprehend it and just a casual consideration of history. Rather, it should be a reflection of the culture as a whole, with due emphasis on the integral and the fundamental, along with a chronological and spatial account of the development and dominance of major generic forms and also an insight into the reasons of the subordination of other generic forms in the course of the historical development. And this implies venturing across languages, disciplines and state boundaries because "it is in these, rather than straight forward literary histories that one comes across some of the most profound insights about what we could generally designate as 'literary' " (245). Thus a theoretically unified or coherent concept of "Indian Literature" could be worked out on these lines.

Every book written by an Indian, in the country or abroad, forms a part of "Indian Literature". But an updated overview of this is rather rare because of the lack of systematised institutions that might give impetus to the efforts of individual scholars and assimilate the knowledge thus produced by the intelligentsia, thereby making it available to the people at large. No sustained efforts have been made to develop the tradition of studying different literatures in mutual relations through translations sans English resulting in limited accessibility of regional literatures. No comprehensive history of the development of the major languages and literatures is available either. The absence of a consolidated and reliable information about the texts, authors, genres, gradual "transition", modes of composition and transmission of various linguistic regions and the gaps in knowledge, specially of the earlier centuries, make the assertion of the existence of the 'Indian Literature' appear hollow.

Drawing attention to the fact that "multilinguality and polyglot fluidity" (248) were the characteristics of "Indian Literature" in the pre-modern phase because most of the poets of that period were multilingual the critic emphasises the need to capture the "linguistic fluidities" through comparative works and translations. However, in spite of individual efforts, the machinery of translations for the circulation of literary works within the various literary communities has not been properly developed because of the lack of institutionalised and systematic efforts. Ahmad's main concern and thrust is towards a "comparative scholarship, research and translation, aimed at a fuller understanding of the composite linguistic and cultural milieux.... " (250). And he feels that while tracing a literary history, merely enumerating the compositional forms, classifying their aesthetic effects and slotting the available works under different generic designations is most inadequate and quite often repetitive. In order to capture both the heterogeneity and the fundamental unity of "Indian Literature", besides enumeration of the compositional forms like the *pada* or the *doha*, the histories of their genesis, their usage, sociological influences and belief systems that account for their variations, popularity, decline and replacement, ought to be taken into consideration.

However, it is pertinent to point out here that Ahmad, while making an observation on the existing trends of translations, rightly points out that the largest archive of translations has been assembled in English. But he finds English "the most removed, in its structure and ambience, from all the other Indian languages, hence least able to bridge the cultural gap between the original and the translated text" (250). However, it is doubtful whether it would be wise to discourage translations in English simply because "English will become, in effect, the language in which the knowledge of 'Indian Literature' is produced" (250) as it would deprive the interested reader of what-so-ever meagre knowledge/information he gains of regional literatures and languages, through the medium of English. Also, whatever is available in English by way of translation, contributes significantly in presenting a general picture of the Indian Literature. By making use of these, we can at least come to an agreement that the unity of Indian Literature could be a reasonably sound hypothesis. Through the translations in English we can perceive the distinguishing commonness in the multifarious manifestations of regional literatures. At the same time, there is a point of agreement in Ahmad's above observation about the "cultural gap", hence parallel efforts should be made to create interest and give impetus to mutual translations in regional languages. Inter-literary exchanges on a national scale through translations should be encouraged so that discursive writings of great value, which seldom cross linguistic barriers, may become accessible. As Ahmad points out, "Literary study in our time and place... needs to be transgressive, and the very first transgressions need to be, in the most obvious and literal senses, against 'English' and against 'Literature' ". Thus the need is not only to cross linguistic but also disciplinary boundaries.

Further analysing the problems of historicising "Indian Literature", Aijaz Ahmad says that with the dominance of print capitalism, literature has been confined only to the printed text and the scope of the word 'literary' has been delimitised. Also, the pedagogy of 'New Criticism' that emphasises 'close reading' of the text tends to overlook the fact that the essential status of the literary products, even of the great constitutive products like the *Mahabharata* and the *Ramayana*, has been traditionally and fundamentally "performative". The "oral-performative" has been central to our literary tradition and undue emphasis on "print" ignores the dominance of these expressive arts in our culture. The "oral-performative" are pivotal because they are sensitive expressions representing the joys and sorrows, dreams and strivings of the common man. For a comprehensive picture of Indian Literature, the cultural values embedded in these expressive arts need to be emphasised. An insight into the "oral-performative" domain of literature would definitely throw light on the whole range of powers and meanings through the aesthetic densities of certain kinds of gestures, rituals, images, addresses and even expressions of grief or joy.

Because of print capitalism, the literary production has gradually become the domain of the literate class in a predominantly non-literate society. The incorporation of the 'oral-performative' would naturally result in the widening of the literary canvas including the life-process of the common man. Thus individual or collective efforts should be made to encompass the alternative modes of preservation and transmission which would naturally involve the rural and the popular along with the urban and the elite which belong to the print capitalism. Along with the linguistic, "civilisational moorings" and "cultural ethos" should also be taken into consideration for a wholesome view of "Indian literature".

The idea that the unity of "Indian Literature" resides in the common national origins of its authors and the common civilisational ethos of the Indian people, has been undisputedly accepted. And the gaps in our knowledge might be due to incomplete evidence and inadequately developed literary historiography. Such material conditions are acceptable. But Ahmad is critical of the notions that predominantly influence the approach of the researchers. They are governed by predetermined notions regarding the narrativisation of the Indian literary history There are two ways in which the "Indian Literature" is demarcated. First the traditional one of "Orientalist High Textuality" which privileges the classical texts, raising few texts to the level of canonicity through eclectic selection based on a preference for religion and metaphysics. It is governed by the view that the "essential Indianness" lies in the spiritual and the "otherworldliness" as oppose to "this-worldliness". The selection process based on this ideology enjoys complete authority and is rarely questioned. This approach thus privileges certain kinds of readings and tends to overlook other important texts. Sustained efforts should be made "to lift such fog" (262) and this is possible only when along with religion and metaphysics, the secular, familial and the material domains are also taken into consideration.

However, the second notion that the unity of 'Indian Literature' is based on is territoriality/geography of the existing nation state appears more reasonable. But the problem lies in that the process of selection is again very qualitative and aggregative. No doubt, a knowledge of the unity can be obtained through a comparatist method but the literature departments in our universities need to encourage and focus on Comparative Literature. In fact, the need for comprehensive and analytical history of 'Indian Literature' can be met not by merely assembling histories of different linguistic traditions, but by tracing the "dialectic of unity and difference" in the literatures of regional languages through the comparatist method.

Because of the residual effects of imperialist scholarship and colonially determined educational system in India, a conducive atmosphere could not be developed which could have given rise to a linguistic formation shared by all, thereby contributing to the emergence of an "Indian Literature". Although English was an imposition yet the Indian reformers wanted it, not as a literary language but as a window on the most advanced knowledges of the world. It is no use denying that English does have a rightful place in India and that the English Departments, in fact, are the only departments of literature which exist in the shape of a unified literary institution through the entire organisation of higher education in India. Also, the national literary intelligentsia in India is one that is well grounded in English and the only literature that is taught throughout India is English Literature.

But the thrust of the syllabi is not towards what gets written in India but outside it. With the increased professionalisation, the emphasis is on the acquisition of Ph.Ds from abroad, publication of articles in foreign journals and getting Indian literary products published abroad. The pressure of professionalisation force the English teacher away from bilinguality/multilinguality and consequently away from 'Indian Literature'. In "Literary Theory and Third World Literature", Ahmad calls it "disorientation of elite scholarship". He points out the intellectual dependence of the Indian University upon its metropolitan counterpart and says that the latter shape even the way we think of ourselves and it is most obvious in the teaching of English. The same is applicable to the literary productions which particularly keep the western market in mind.

We, the teachers of English, should rise from our slumber and re-orientate the direction of our study. It is high time we decolonised our minds and stopped taking pride in Fulbright and other similar scholarships. Without any sense of social superiority, we should adopt a utilitarian attitude towards English as it is the dominant expressive medium of discursive thought and emphasise a comparatist manner in relation to other Indian languages and literatures. It is only "by connecting the knowledge of that (English) literature with literatures of own, that we can begin to break that colonial grid..." (283). English should be taught not as a primary subject but in a comparatist manner, in relation to other Indian languages and literature.

"Indian Literature" still remains compartmentalised, without substantial interflow from other Indian languages. It is for us, the faculty of English department to inculcate among our students, an interest in "Indian Literature" and encourage them to take up research projects in this field. With the meagre information available, a plunge into the unfathomable depth of "Indian Literature" would demand exceptional industry and devotion. However, one can afford to be optimistic because the efforts in this direction have already begun—"Indian Literature" has been made a recognised subject in the curriculum of some universities. This is indeed a conscious step towards the promotion of literary nationalism.

Reference

Ahmad, Aijaz. *In Theory*. Delhi: Oxford University Press, 1992.

6
Ashis Nandy on Decolonisation

R.K. Kaul

Edward Said, a Palestinian Arab, settled in New York, published his very influential book *Orientalism* (1978) to demonstrate how the western specialists of the 19th century had misrepresented the Arabs and Islam. Said's allusions to the misrepresentation of India and the Hindus are incidental. Many intellectuals in India were stimulated to apply his thesis to India.

Ashis Nandy's essays, "The Intimate Enemy" and "Loss and Recovery of Self under Colonialism" are two such attempts. Nandy's thesis, however, develops along somewhat different lines. The one thing common is that the west is the enemy. By the west only the imperial powers are meant.

Said's complaint was that western orientalism had created a binary opposition between the east and the west. While the west is rational, humane, and superior; the east is aberrant, underdeveloped and inferior. He pointed out that the east, and especially the Arabs had contributed to the so-called western civilisation. It had a tradition of rationality, science and medicine which the west considered to be their exclusive domain.

Nandy agrees with Said in rejecting the polarity between the east and the west but he also claims that India has an alternative civilisation. To begin with he characterises the Indians as "innocent". They have the vulnerability of a child. He disapproves of those Indians who organised armed resistance to the British rulers, he is even mildly critical of those who offered constitutional opposition because both these forms of protest were borrowed from the west. Instead Nandy admires the "savage outsider" (p.xiii) who is neither willing to be a player nor a counter player. Instead of demanding universal suffrage, the savage refuses even to adopt the language of the rulers.

Nandy does not take this view to its logical conclusion. It would appear to follow that his ideal is the Maoris of New Zealand, the Red Indians of North America, and the Bhils and other tribes of India. "These essays", he states, "are a paean to the non-players" (p. xiv). The non-players, or savages, resist the loving embrace of the west's dominant self.

Nandy is opposed to the values of history and rationality. Even more emphatically he rejects secularism, progress, science and technology as the foundations of civil society.

By way of a mock apology he disowns English. Logically he should have written in Bengali, without sending his MS. to the press and without resorting to the use of paper—all these are the gifts of the colonisers who enslaved the Indian mind.

One example of the alternative to science and rationality is the sage Sri Aurobindo's "claim that his yoga was determining the course of the war in Europe and deciding the fate of Japan". Fortunately Nandy is rational enough to dismiss such claims.

In the first essay, "The Psychology of Colonialism; Sex, Age and Ideology in British India", he sets out to establish the thesis that economic gains and political power were not the primary motives of the colonial power. Nandy argues on the contrary that colonialism is a state of mind in the colonisers and the colonised (p.2). The proof, according to him, lies in the fact that even 35 years after the formal ending of the Raj (it should read 50 years now), the ideology of colonialism is still triumphant in many sectors of life.

The story of how the British used their superior military machine to wipe out every trace of native power in India and how they systematically promoted the interests of their commerce and industry at the expense of India's economy has been told by every historian.

The second part of his thesis is certainly worth examining. Even 50 years after the end of foreign rule, the colonial mentality is still in evidence. The most important evidence of it is the continued use of English by Nandy himself, the national newspapers, the television channels, the radio and above all the parliamentary debates and the higher courts.

Parents send their children to English medium schools not out of loyalty to the British but because of the employment market. Not only in India, but in Japan, in Germany, in Russia and other countries which have no background of colonial rule English is an essential requirement for a job in any prestigious firm. It is American monopoly capitalism, the so-called globalisation of the economy that is responsible.

Nandy approaches his subject via sex, age and ideology. The sexual impact of colonial rule is described in terms of masculinity, femininity and hermaphroditism. He blames the dominant British culture for upholding the values of masculinity and dividing it sharply from femininity. His own preference is for hermaphroditism or androgyny, the term used by Coleridge.

Politically its implication is that those who organised military rebellion against British rule had been tainted by the colonial mentality. Nandy ascribes a sense of guilt to the British rulers which would have been aggravated if the Indians, had demonstrated their moral superiority.

Such over-subtle formulations can neither be proved nor disproved. So far as the present writer is aware, no conqueror from Attila the Hun and Timur to Nadir Shah and Hitler has felt any compunction over the brutality of his conquests. Neither Mao nor Deng Xiaoping gave any evidence of guilt over the conquest of Tibet in spite of the moral authority of the Dalai Lama. Such refined sensibility cannot be expected from any predator whether Clive or Curzon.

After propounding an unconvincing theory about the superiority of androgyny over masculinity Nandy proceeds to examine the western attitude to childhood. There are enough documents available on the past of Europe for any system-maker to erect a theory of his choice. One has to select judiciously and ignore the contradictory evidence. That the child was seen as an inferior version of the adult (p.14) or that its mind was seen as a blank slate or that children had to be redeemed from reprobate sinfulness can all be documented. The theory sounds weighty until we remind ourselves of Rousseau, Wordsworth and above all Jesus Christ who declared that, "Except ye be converted, and become as little children, ye shall not enter the kingdom of heaven" (Matthew, 18: 3). That "Child is father of the man" is at least as influential as the views stated by Nandy.

The relevance of this discussion to the essay is that the colonised people were regarded as children who had to mature under the tutelage of the ruling power.

After the orientalists discovered the ancient civilisations of China and India it became difficult to think of the oriental way of life as child-like or childish. The difficulty was resolved by drawing a sharp dichotomy between ancient and contemporary Indians. It was believed that India's later degradation was "due to aspects of traditional culture" (p.18). Nandy disagrees with the view. Unfortunately the entire history of 17th and 18th century India is there to support this view.

We may point out here that like many other exponents of Indian culture Nandy equates Indians with the Hindus. Only on p.103 of the second essay, "The Uncolonized Mind" does he come out in the open. This unstated equation, however, causes a lot of confusion. So far as the Hindus are concerned, their decline set in quite early i.e. from the 11th century perhaps. There were attempts to reform them during the Bhakti movement and the rise of Sikhism in the 16th and 17th centuries but in the end the python which had encircled and crushed the Buddhist reform movement in ancient India also wiped out the influence of subsequent reform movements, including that of Ram Mohan Roy in the 19th century.

The curse of dividing society into castes and sub-castes, did not permit the Hindus to emerge as a united body. It is significant that the very word "community" changed its meaning in India. Instead of meaning "a body of persons leading a common life" it was used to differentiate persons professing different religious beliefs. Similarly the word "communal" was debased.

No western orientalist, however malicious, could make the picture worse than it is. At least two modern novels one in English the other in Kannada, namely *Untouchable* and *Samskara*, by M.R. Anand and Anantha Murthy respectively show that the evils are still alive.

But to return to Nandy. The best parts of the two essays are the detailed analyses of some of the leading 19th century thinkers, who were influenced by English education and who sought in different ways to reform Hindu society. But this story has been told by every historian so it is proposed to skip this part of the essays.

I have already stated that I do not have any tears to shed over the "long term cultural damage colonialism did to British society" (p.32). In an unusually clumsy sentence Nandy writes, "(British political culture) de-emphasised speculation, intellection and *caritas* as feminine". In fact he gets confused enough to mix up "ruthless social Darwinism" with colonialism. Confused language arises from confused thought.

His argument is more tangible but less tenable when he denounces the claim of science to liberate man from his daily drudgery. Only somebody who has compared the condition of the coal miner in India and in modern Europe can speak authoritatively about this. As expected he invokes the authority of an American post-modernist to assert that science and history are the two myths of the modern world. It follows that when Mr. Nandy travels by a Boeing jet plane to Boston or Berkeley (California) to denounce technology his flight is mythical. When vaccination eradicated smallpox from the world it was purely imaginary. No doubt it would have been better in Nandy's view to worship the goddess called *shitala mata* and eat stale food rather than cast out the mother goddess.

This assertion is followed by an analysis of the life and work of some Anglo-Indian writers like Kipling and Orwell and some English men and women like C.F. Andrews who adopted the Gandhian way of life

The most persuasive portion of this essay is the thesis that "some of the recessive elements of Christianity were perfectly congruent with elements of Hindu and Buddhist world views." There is no doubt that when Gandhi invoked the Sermon on the Mount in his non violent struggle the more sensitive English intellectuals felt guilty about the repressive policies of the British government. Gandhi sincerely believed that he was trying to liberate the English mind from its association with repression and the Indian mind of their hatred of the British.

This argument unfortunately gets blurred because of jargon picked up from American psycho-analysts with bogus theories about the superiority of androgyny to masculinity and femininity. Half-baked generalisations about the aggressive national character of the British and the Indians are equally unconvincing (it is ironic that Nandy quotes Nirad Chaudhuri in support of his view). One has to visit Afghanistan or Palestine to experience the aggressive mentality. Perhaps Nandy has not heard of Prussian or Japanese militarism. One should refresh his memory of Vietnam, Ayothullah Khomeini and Tiananmen Square to remind him about the meaning of ruthless aggression.

I now come to a controversial topic. Indologists and Indian historiographers have been at great pains to cover up the greatest omission of the ancient Hindus viz. the failure to record day to day events. The only notable exception is Kalhana who recorded genealogies on the lines of Kalidasa's *Raghuvansa*. Instead of acknowledging that there is no history (or geography) of ancient India ingenious explanations, subtle theories even metaphysical speculation about the two concepts of time—eastern and western—have been formulated. Nandy seeks the authority of Gandhi to evade the issue. He ascribes to Gandhi a view that Gandhi did not in fact state. According to Nandy, Gandhi "rejected history and affirmed the primacy of myths over historical chronicles" (p.55).

The fact is that Gandhi made a casual remark, disparaging the English "habit of writing history", in *Hind Swaraj* (1909) and went on to deflate the English pretensions "to study the manners and customs of all people" (p.3). May be he was thinking of the various Jesuit priests (not English in fact) who wrote about *Hindu Manners, Customs, and Ceremonies* like Abbé Dubois (1765-1848).

Gandhi did not offer mythology as a substitute for history. Nandy's pretentious jargon about the diachronic relationship of history as against the synchronic relationship of myths would have left the Mahatma gaping.

The assumption is that a people can either create myths or record facts. The truth is that most ancient civilisations including the Graeco-Roman not only wrote history, they also created elaborate myths. There is no incompatibility between the two activities. The ancient Hindus only transmitted their sacred books and epics by word of mouth. They invented the zero and felt free to add any number of zeros to any digit at random.

II

The second essay "The Uncolonized Mind" begins with a very perceptive analysis of Kipling's ambivalence towards India. He had to disown his Indianness as he grew up and learn not to identify himself with the victims (p.68). "He lived and died fighting his other self----a softer, more creative and happier self" (pp. 69-70). The other facet of Kipling's personality is that he was willing to respect only those Indians who were classified as members of the martial castes. This analysis is completely free of psychological jargon because Nandy owes his perception to one of the finest literary critics of our century, namely, Edmund Wilson.

Nandy's digression about the forgotten minority in the west which according to him has been fully subjugated by India need not detain us because it is a figment of his imagination. Another irrelevant digression is about the battle between the Apollonian and the Dionysiac within India and within the west. This leads him to state that westernised India is a sub-tradition of India (p.75).

There after Nandy dwells on the types that Kipling embodies in his stories and poems: the martial Indian, who represents the ideology of ksatriyahood, a type respected by Kipling and the brown sahib or the devious babu, of whom Kipling was most contemptuous. This, according to the author, illustrates Derrett's thesis that it was the British who were being manipulated by the Indians rather than the other way round (p.77). Consistency demands that he should have gone on to say that it was the Indians who conquered the British Isles and that the British empire was purely mythical.

The core of the second essay "The Uncolonized Mind" is section 3. There is a paradox about the Hindus staring us in the face. Are the Hindus spiritual as Ananda Coomaraswamy and Radhakrishnan claim or are they hypocritical and materialists as Nirad Chaudhuri and others assert? The historian D.D. Kosambi sums up the message of the *Gita* very candidly. It advises slippery opportunism on the one hand and on the other hand rejects material reality as a gross illusion (p.81). Nandy holds that the two Indias (he means the two streaks in the Hindu character) are both products of western intrusion. The modern gurus are "commodities in the western market place of spiritualism and instant salvation" (p.83). To the present speaker that seems to be an evasion. Nandy does not face the dilemma squarely.

In section 4 Nandy contrasts the visions of Kipling and Sri Aurobindo. While Kipling had to disown his Indianness in order to conform to his notion of the European, Aurobindo "did not have to disown the west within him to become his version of an Indian" (85-86). In fact one could say that some of the best Indians included elements of western civilisation within their version of India. This contrasted with the Anglo-Indians who looked upon India as the land of heat and dust.

It is a pity that Nandy chooses a cult figure Aurobindo to illustrate the eclecticism of Hindu culture. How can one take the sage seriously who "broke the monotony of prison life by levitating"? He accepted Mira, a French woman, as his *sakti*. He made "yogic attempts to bring down the supermind to the earth and to produce a new race of supermen" (p.95). A less pretentious figure like Nehru or R.K. Narayan would have been a far more acceptable example of how western values can be assimilated in our native culture.

Nandy's evaluation of Gandhi is unexceptionable when he states that Gandhi "transformed the debate on Indian hypocrisy into a simultaneous text on British self-doubt" (p.100). He "took the battle to Kipling's home ground by judging colonialism by Christian values". It is difficult, however, to disagree with the view that the immorality of colonialism was mitigated by its historical role as an instrument of progress. Nandy underrates the value of the science and technology which the British brought to India. Instead he mentions instances "endogenous scientific creativity" (102n). The *Alternative Sciences* of Nandy are a fiction. There is only one science which recognises no frontiers. The two examples of home-grown creativity which he mentions are Ramanujan and Jagdish Chandra Bose. They practised mainstream Mathematics and Botany respectively. Both found recognition at Cambridge University. A discipline which does not submit itself to logical analysis or empirical verification cannot be called a science. Perhaps Sociology itself is a pseudo-science because its conclusions are not verifiable.

The author concludes by summing up 4 sets of polarities with reference to colonialism. Some of these polarities have been created by the sociologists. They are pegs to hang their pet theories. Nandy's own preference is for the parochial, the spiritual, the non-performing and the insane as against the universal, the realistic, the performing and the rational. This formulation does not seem to be very valuable because it bears no relation to experience, which must be the ultimate criterion. At another place he states that the uniqueness of Indian culture lies in the permeability of boundaries and the fluidity of self-definition (p.107). That profound observation cancels all the unreal polarities which Nandy talks about. Human beings constantly contradict themselves, assimilating seemingly opposed, often contradictory qualities within themselves, unlike objects of scientific study like oxygen or plutonium.

References

Nandy, Ashis. *The Intimate Enemy*. Delhi: Oxford University Press (1983), 1989.

Gandhi, M.K. *Hind Swaraj or Indian Home Rule* (1909). Ahmedabad: Navjivan Publishing House, 1938.

7

Destablising Meaning:
In Theory and *Orientalism*

Jasbir Jain

Aijaz Ahmad's *In Theory* appeared in 1991, thirteen years after Edward Said's *Orientalism*, which is one of the texts which Ahmad critiques. There are a whole lot of postcolonial statements made and positions adopted not only in the intervening period but both before and after. Yet there is a sense of logic in putting the two texts together. Both the texts signify attempts at confronting the relationship between literature and power and between culture and politics and both are written by scholars who have their origin in the Orient. They are concerned with ideas and concepts and not necessarily with the condition of oppression or race as such.

The similarity, however, ends here; there are major differences, differences of location, context, methodology and purpose. They move in entirely different directions. While Said sets about to demystify the Orient and its literary and political construction, Ahmad's concern is with deconstructing the concepts which are in currency in the postcolonial discourse. Both concern themselves with historical processes but while Said takes a sweeping look in bits and pieces at the history of the last five hundred years, Ahmad moves back only as far as the nineteenth century to cover the period of British colonialism. These differences may not seem significant enough in themselves to mark any important shift but the difference in their approaches emphasises them. Said's main emphasis is on the text, the written text, which in itself represents a literary culture and is a lingual construct working within a system of semantics and philology, Ahmad's focus is on the context, on the processes which contribute to the making of the text. The text, for Ahmad, becomes a social text. *In Theory* has a subtitle "Classes, Nations, Literatures", a subtitle which not only identifies Ahmad's special concerns but also establishes their interconnection. Adopting a Marxist stance, he relates the making of cultural texts to the stage of capitalist development and the means of production. Working within this broad framework, he rejects the post-structuralist approach because it dissolves the categories of nation and nationalism which are important to his argument.

Poststructuralism is a direct descendant of new criticism; it is the close textual reading which has led to a perception of the absent word and the absent concept. The binary opposition between what is said and what is not, between the spoken and the silent, led to a recognition of structures—the surface and the deep. It was this concern with meaning which progressed towards a questioning of the 'sign' and became the basis for a semiotic approach bringing into play the interrelationships of signs and traces, the deferred meaning and the notion of difference.[1] Structuralism is a linguistic method, a rediscovering of the message of the code, a meaning "uncovered by an analysis of the immanent structures and not imposed from the outside by ideological prejudices" (Genette 66). This interplay between word and meaning and sign and signifier in its turn formed the basis of poststructuralism which as Robert Young has described "fractures the serene unity of the stable sign and the unified subject" (Young 8). Ahmad is interested in discussing the concept of 'nation', which is a unifying concept even if not a unified one. But despite his criticism of Said on these grounds and of his counter-reading of the 'canonical texts through the inventory of traces' (Ahmad 162), Ahmad is interested in deconstructing the categories used by Said.

Ahmad's take off point is Said's critiquing of Marxist approaches. He takes an extract from Said's *The World, The Text, The Critic* and uses it as an epigraph for his chapter "*Orientalism* and After", and proceeds to criticise Said's emphasis on canonical texts and "the privileging of literature and philology" (Ahmad 163), of master texts as it were. Ahmad views *Orientalism* as an attempt at creating a counter-history, as a system of knowledge, which employing the tools of scholarly training, questions the professed ideals of humanistic discourse in the Western literary tradition and exposes the "complicity" of humanism in the history of European colonialism. But that is evidently not enough; more important than the humanist stance are the "economic exploitation, political coercion, military conquest" (Ahmad 164) which accompanied the humanistic discourse.

Another ground on which Ahmad faults Said is his adoption of the Foucauldian concept of discourse, which being a rational category is not really applicable to the pre-Enlightenment literature, to the ancient and medieval systems of thought. Also the tracing of continuity and unity in the history of the West, the indifference on Said's part to the way "these textualities... have been received, accepted, modified, challenged, overthrown" by the colonised subjects are other grounds of disagreement. Said's exclusion of Marxist concerns renders his position an elitist one (even if Ahmad has not said so in so many words). Having critiqued Said on these grounds (and several others) Ahmad proceeds to question the stability of signs as well as of categories. He undertakes to destabilise the meaning of terms like third world, Indian literature, allegory and the Orient. This he does by locating them in socioeconomic and political contexts and by distinguishing between the manner in which these terms have been constructed and the manner in which they are used or imposed. (This is an important distinction and needs to be worked out at some length).

It is against this background that I want briefly to look at the structure and argument of *In Theory*. There are eight chapters in all. Of these one is in the nature of an introduction, one about class, two are in the form of responses to other critics, one on Jameson, and another on Said. A fifth chapter elucidates and defends Marx's views on India, one is on the expatriate writer of which Rushdie is an example. That leaves us with two significant chapters, in fact the only two which make positive statements or suggest partial solutions and are not in the nature of defence or explanation and these chapters are the ones on Indian literature and Third World Theory. Both these chapters stress the need for comparative studies and a deconstruction of the category of the Third World and these arguments run through the text. In fact, the chapter on Jameson engages with Jameson's interpretation of Third World literature and the one on Said is about the impossibility of shaking off western hegemony unless we are willing to shed western perspectives. Despite this common thread which runs through the body of the work it is not of a piece, for while his main aim appears to be to examine the Indian situation and project Indian theoretical and conceptual categories, a great part of his energy is devoted to disengaging himself from west-imposed and west-generated theories, or theories floated by 'third world' scholars in the west, leaving him limited space to project explanations, ideas or theories.

Methodology again is divided in itself. Having rejected Said's poststructuralist methods, he himself proceeds to adopt deconstructive strategies by opening out the terms employed in the postcolonial debate for discussion and then attempting a re-formation. The strength of the work lies in its socio-economic framework, in the connections he establishes between literature and politics, in his attempt to indicate the direction of culture formation and in the periodisation he projects.

The fact of decolonisation is linked with political independence but the process itself is linked with class revolution. Political freedom does not in itself decolonise the mind. The nature of national projects has to change. The truth of this need to be sensed at multiple levels—at the level of the ruling class, the educated intelligentsia and the disadvantaged categories of society.[2] Pawan Verma's *The Great Indian Middle Class* (1998) offers an analysis of this (49-63). Independence in 1947 did not in itself bring the desired change. It merely signified the passing of authority from one hegemonic structure to another, from the British to the bourgeois elite without effectively involving the common man in the process of change. The middle classes continued to pursue the earlier agenda of a socialist India but were unable to transcend their own limitations. The real shift of power began to be experienced only much later when the process of democratisation resulted in multiple social revolutions in different parts of the country.

Ahmad considers decolonisation in three phases: post 1945 when several colonies gained their independence, post 1965 when socialist revolutions in different parts of the colonised world led to the re-formation of nationalist agendas, and post 1975 when Asian countries, not subjected to any earlier colonisation and hence protected from intrusive cultural influences, experienced revolution. The last phase also initiated a process of change in the USSR resulting in a collapse of the Communist block. Later he examines this from two other perspectives, one the centre of power—Britain, France or America—and second, the territories of influence. But by linking the process of decolonisation to social revolution he succeeds in shifting the debate from cultural encounters and the impact of Western ideas to one of internal societal changes which shake up existing relationships. He fails, however, to account for the increased orthodoxy in certain societies. Nowhere does he move into questions of religious fundamentalism vis-à-vis the processes of decolonisation. This apart, Ahmad's analysis of Marx's views about India (and Said's interpretation of these views), is significant at least on three grounds. First, he is in disagreement with the selection of Said's extracts from Marx, as they are being quoted out of context. In this connection it is the methodology which is important. The true significance of the meaning of a text lies not in its textual meaning alone but in its context. The conditions of the making of the text are in themselves important. Second, he approaches Marx from the Indian perspective and disagrees with the view that the entry of the British brought about a social revolution. "Colonialism", he states, "did not bring us a revolution" (Ahmad 224). What it brought us was "a non-revolutionary and retrograde resolution to a crisis of our own society, which had come to express itself, by the eighteenth century, in a real stagnation of technologies and productivities, as well as regional and dynastic wars so constant and ruinous as to make impossible a viable coalition against the encroaching colonial power" (224).[3] Third, Marx drew attention to the resistance to colonial power and this was a gain in terms of metropolitan centres being forced to recognise colonial presence and issues of race, gender and empire were foregrounded. But Marxist interpretations have not really been incorporated or transformed into a literary culture perhaps because literature absorbs radicalism into the bourgeois tradition.

Other concepts which are central to Ahmad's argument are language, agency and nation. Language in itself defines certain positions. There is the first the formation of an elite on the basis of the learning of English which has led to the marginalisation of Indian languages. There is also a sense of alienation from Indian values and cultural structures, a disaffection which is a fall out of the language question. This issue throws up the need for bilingualism and the necessity for an ever-increasing number of translations. This does not, however, do away with the difficulty of forming a canon on the basis of translations not only at the national level but also where comparative literatures are concerned. Further there is the continuation of western critical frameworks, evaluations and methodological approaches. The over-dependence on western recognition and appreciation remains. Ahmad asks whether given the above situation, it is possible to shift the centre with the agency of change—educated intelligentsia—itself being subjected to disaffection.

Suggested solutions to the above problem are through a structural change in the syllabuses being taught in the departments of English (for they have an inbuilt suitability for this change, and can take on this new role) and the positing of a counter canon through the process of increased translations. Ahmad is conscious of the need for a crucial change at the attitudinal level. There is need for the abandonment of passivity where acceptance of critical terms, terminologies and methodologies is concerned. They need to be questioned, deconstructed and relocated. Terms and methodologies have also come to represent power-structures, and their role as agencies of power itself contains the possibilities of change. When Ahmad uses the word 'agency' his reference is primarily to human agency which in turn is constituted by a number of elements and controlled by a whole range of cultural, ideological and political formulations.[4] Yet, human agency contains within it the possibility of change. He views it as a dynamic force which has its own ability to interrogate its location, to alter its circumstances and to consciously intervene in the process of change. The human agent need not be passive.

What is problematised both by Said and Ahmad is the system of knowledge. If language and literature are powerful means of constituting knowledge, they need to be constantly reviewed and the systems they generate or propagate examined. In fact, one of the significant methodologies Said uses is what he defines as *strategic location*, the author's position in the text, and another is *strategic formations* which is a way of analysing the relationship between texts (*Orientalism* 20). Ahmad moves outside the text to examine both the location and the formation. Both Said and Ahmad attach significance to language though in different ways. Said is aware of the way philological studies opened out the way for secularisation by disassociating language from divine origins (*Orientalism* 135). Histories of language have an uncanny way of revealing the hidden thrusts, discrepancies and misrepresentations. When Ahmad turns to language, he is conscious of its role in class formation. Language is central not only to literary formulations but also to socio-political and cultural ones. By drawing attention to the issue of language, Ahmad focuses simultaneously on the nature of literature (which is so complexly embedded in economic and political constructs), and on the need for a continued questioning of words which seek to impose patterns on our thought structures.

It is in this connection that he examines Fredric Jameson's use of the term "third world" as a descriptive category and of the term allegory with reference to the fiction of the erstwhile colonies. Ahmad's objection is primarily to the sweeping generalisation and the note of condescension and secondarily to the categories themselves. Ahmad argues that the term "third world" is not a political category as it has been made out to be by tracing its origins to the Bandung Conference (as critics like Viney Kirpal have accepted, see (*The Third World Novel of Expatriation*). It is also not an ideological specification signifying the ground between capitalism and communism or an association of non-aligned countries. The category may acquire some legitimacy if placed within the matrix of developmental economies but this is also a partial or an insufficient legitimacy because while it privileges the nation state with its socialist agenda of welfare activities, five year plans and the rest, it also bypasses and ignores the force of mass movements. The term "third world" has shifted attention from systems of production to the role of nation states, imposing a kind of uniformity which the term does not possess in itself.

Seen in the context of power, the term acquires another meaning. Capitalist countries like the United States and Communists countries like the USSR alike exercised an authority which placed them within similar power structures. Both the United States and the USSR exercised political power which is characteristic of the first world; the other industrialised/developed countries would fall in the category of the second world and the third world would consist of agricultural, under developed poor countries. As such the term is limiting, divisive and confining; it imposes a position of subordination and locates the "third world" within the concept of the "other", placing it outside the capitalist world. Such a categorisation is in itself a limitation because it completely ignores the historical differences in the journey towards capitalism and the manner in which colonialism was instrumental in furthering it. It also ignores the suppression of democratic rights and social processes in the colonies. Again how far does India have a capitalist structure or an under-developed economy is in itself a difficult question to address. No matter how one approaches this kind of lumping together, it is an exercise in diminishing the importance of nationalist discourses and of subordinating them to western influences. Ahmad asserts that the world projects one reality, and both the colonisers and the colonised, the powerful and the powerless belong to the same world, and where knowledge is interrelated and has to be contested on its own grounds (not by pre determined structures). He writes that we live "not in three worlds, but in one,... this world includes the experience of colonialism and imperialism on both sides of the global divide" (Ahmad 103). This is not merely an emotional statement, it has a relevance beyond that at least in two significant ways. First it places the responsibility for the kind of world we have squarely on everyone, not merely parceling it off into small measures; secondly it seeks to get out of the structuralist approach of binary oppositions. More importantly, to my mind, it takes the argument back to the nineteenth century civilisational discourse of liberal humanism which after having been used for exploitative reasons and as a strategy of inferiorisation has now been abandoned giving way to divisions of humanity along the categories of race, power relations and economic development.

When Fredric Jameson makes the statement about third world novels being national allegories, Ahmad opposes it on several grounds. It imposes a homogenisation on the so-called third world, and on the writing of the developing countries; it refers primarily to the literature written in English, excluding the writing in other languages (as well as oral traditions), it pushes the "Third World" literatures into a quasi-religious pre-modernistic situation. The first two grounds of homogenisation and exclusion of language literatures are very valid objections, but the term 'allegory' in itself need not push us into a defensive position. Here by accepting the narrowness of meaning implied by the term as used by Jameson forces one to accept the same norms and parameters which Jameson is applying. Allegory is not necessarily medieval, it also does not necessarily specify a particular stage in the evolution of literary categories. Instead it encompasses a wide range of modes and meanings; it is modern in the sense that writers like Joyce, Kafka and Borges have all employed it. It is also modern in the sense that it acknowledges the multiplicity of meaning (and not merely one to one correspondence between two contexts). The polysemic quality of language and the cultural pulls in the readership would render most writing allegorical. New Historicism as a method of critical evaluation does in some measure privilege allegory. The meaning of allegory includes metaphorical strategies. While Rosamund Tuve defines it as "a metaphor",[5] Angus Fletcher in his work *Allegory: The Theory of a Symbolic Mode* describes it as "a protean device, omnipresent in western literature from the earlier times to the modern era" (1). Allegory destroys the normal expectations from language and creates space for several levels of meanings. Northrop Frye also does not treat allegory merely as a quasi-religious medieval approach.

Moreover we need not fight shy of the fact that Indian literary and philosophical imagination does not devalue allegory. Religious texts, views of good and evil and the recognition of the centrality of ritual all facilitate allegorical interpretations. There is nothing wrong or inferior if a people are engaged in writing "national allegories", for it indicates a constant need to review the existing reality in terms of histories, genealogies and continuities. Allegories do not always remain the same. The mode has ample provision for initiating subversion, inversion, expansion, alterity and accommodating other socio-political shifts. Where Jameson goes wrong is in treating the colonial experience as the single determining experience, and in the dismissive attitude he adopts. Ahmad, by not challenging the narrow meaning which Jameson imposes on the term 'allegory', accepts his definition.

The issues related to periodisation of literary movements and to the multi-lingual character of Indian literature are issues which have been subjected to endless debate and discussion by several scholars.[6] The relationship with other literatures of the developing and under-developed countries through the intervention of western critical categories has long been a matter of concern for those of us who seek to interact with the literatures of Asian and African people. By drawing attention to these problems here Ahmad is emphasising the complexity of the role which English language is performing in the multilingual societies of the erstwhile colonies. It is not merely a lingual construct. It becomes a means of constructing our meanings not only of our ourselves but also of the multiple 'other'. This task also it does not perform as a neutral agent, but as an active one which introduces terms and categories into the discourse which pre-determine its direction.[7]

In Theory raises a large number of issues which have been part of an ongoing debate on the national scene and has foregrounded the issue of language and raised the question of the justification and legitimacy of the departments of English literature. The last is an important point because it acknowledges the role of pedagogical structures and by placing it within a theoretical position, there is a conscious attempt at a collective effort at intervening in the formation of theory. That brings me to the title. Why *In Theory?* The "in" could signify a variety of meanings. One, in theory several desirables can be perceived, and several patterns discerned, but how and where are these to be effected becomes the main issue. Another, it is an exercise at an intervention in the process of theorising. At yet another level the title can be perceived as the dialogic relationship between 'text' and 'context', the text being the ground for theorisation but the context has worked its way into the text. In the introduction, Aijaz Ahmad admits to linking up various perspectives, questionings, disagreements through "theoretical and thematic" unity (1). Finally in theory one can perceive where one is heading for theorising is a rational act of explanation, while in practice the chaotic elements at work are hard to control and the individual need for self respect, dignity and a wholeness is oddly at disagreement with the processes of history as set into momentum by the west. *In Theory* is an attack both on hegemonic and homogenising structures and expresses a need for fluid and dynamic concepts and categories which can accommodate change and difference. It is in this that its significance lies.

Notes

1. The seeds of structuralist thought can be discerned in Coleridge's *Biographia Literaria* when he reflects upon the language of poetry and writes "The best part of human language, properly so called, is derived from reflection on the acts of the mind itself. It is formed by a voluntary appropriation of fixed symbols to internal acts, to processes and results of imagination... by imitation and passive remembrance... (chap. xvii 11. 320-330).
2. The literature in Indian languages gives abundant proof of this. While English language writing was engaged in reflecting middle class realities, and in the rhetoric of the freedom struggle, writers like Gopinath Mohanty and Thakazi Shiva Shankar Pillai were reflecting upon the revolution which was gradually taking form

amongst the dalits and the disadvantaged. See for instance Pillai's novel *Do Ser Dhan* and Mohanty's *Paraja*. A similar statement would be applicable to the women's movement. But one must realise at the same time that these position became possible only as democratic processes began to percolate down to the masses.

3. Ahmad is not the only one to think on these lines or to support Marxist thought. The thrust of Subaltern studies has been on this. Also historians like Irfan Habib have been engaged in researches which demonstrate that industrialisation was in the process of evolving and would have done so even without the British intervention. In this connection, I draw attention to Arif Dirlik's "The Postcolonial Aura: Third World Criticism in the Age of Global Capitalism," (*Critical Inquiry*, Vol. 20, Nos. 1-2, 1993-94) wherein Dirlik locates postcoloniality and the critical orientations of the postcolonial critics in the changing conceptual needs of the new world situation (330). He locates changes in the socialist countries also within the process of global capitalism (353-354). Ahmad does not consider this at any length but apparently the intellectual reinforcing and the desired attitudinal change are in the form of oppositional strategies.

4. He engages with the term right at the beginning of his work and points out that (a) the role of human agency has become circumscribed, (b) that class and institutional location etc. are important structures which shape the human mind, (c) possibility of change would lie in the strength (and ability) of the agent to be self-critical and ready for change hence the need to address the question of 'social determination of one's own practice' (6).

5. Rosamund Tuve in *Elizabethan and Metaphysical Imagery*, Chicago, 1947 quoted by Angus Fletcher in *Allegory: The Theory of a Symbolic Mode*: New York: Cornell University Press, 1964, p. 71.

6. The seminars organised by the Sahitya Akademi, the Indian Institute of Advanced Study and other similar centres have addressed these questions time and again. Some of the major scholars who have participated in them are V.K. Gokak, Niharranjan Ray, C.D. Narasimhaiah, Suniti Kumar Chatterjee, Amiya Deb, Sujit Mukherjee, Namvar Singh, Sisir Kumar Das and several others.

7. I am not quite sure that Ahmad goes this far, but I interpret it as such and have voiced this at several seminars including one held on African literature at the Jawaharlal Nehru University in the

early 90s and in my paper "The Need to Consciously Interrupt the Unconscious Formulation of Theory", presented at a Seminar in Jaipur in November 1997.

References

Ahmad, Aijaz. *In Theory: Classes, Nations Literatures.* Bombay: Oxford University Press, 1992.

Coleridge. *Biographia Literaria, English Critical Texts.* Eds. D.J. Enright and Ernst de Chickera. London: Oxford University Press, 1962.

Dirlik, Arif. "The Postcolonial Aura: Third World Criticism in the Age of Global Capitalism", *Critical Inquiry,* Vol. 20, Nos. 1-2, 1993-94.

Fletcher, Angus. *Allegory: The Theory of a Symbolic Mode.* New York: Cornell University Press, 1964.

Genette, Gerard. "Structuralism and Literary Criticism", *Modern Criticism and Theory: A Reader.* Ed. David Lodge. Longman Group, 1988.

Said, Edward W. *Orientalism* (1978). Harmondsworth: Penguin, 1991.

—. *The World, the Text and the Critic.* Massachusetts: Cambridge University Press, 1983.

Verma, Pavan K. *The Great Indian Middle Class.* New Delhi: Penguin, 1998.

Young, Robert, ed. *Untying the Text: A Post-Structuralist Reader* (1981). London: Routledge, 1987.

8

Redefining Tradition as Resistance: Raja Rao's *Kanthapura*

Veena Singh

Kanthapura, published in 1938, captures the psychology and the ideology of the Gandhian movement. By this time the bugle of freedom struggle had already been sounded: Gandhi's demand for the release of the people imprisoned during civil disobedience resulting in Gandhi-Irwin Pact 1931, followed by Government of India Act, 1935 introducing provincial autonomy in place of dyarchy and prior to these in 1929 at Lahore, the resolution of complete independence and the decision to observe 26 January as Purna Swaraj Day had been adopted.

Set against this political background, *Kanthapura* gives the reader an insight into the condition in rural India where the masses were oppressed both by caste hierarchy and the political power structures. It was in these conditions that Gandhi mobilised the masses, awakening them to a realisation of their own strength and to their latent aspirations for freedom and equality. *Kanthapura* is a post-colonial text, coming as it did in the wake of the Gandhian movement it focuses on the encounter of the two cultures and shows how while countering the imposing culture the weaker one redefines and reinterprets its tradition while it seeks its identity.

Ashcroft, Griffiths and Tiffin in *The Empire Writes Back*, while discussing post-colonial literatures state that they understand 'Post-colonial' as a term that "covers all the cultures affected by the imperial process from the moment of colonisation to the present day" (1-2). The same idea is reiterated in their book *The Post-Colonial Studies Reader*. They write, " 'Post-Colonial' as we define it does not mean post-independence or 'after colonialism' for this would be to falsely ascribe an end to the colonial process. Post-Colonialism, rather, begins from the very first moment of colonial contact. It is the discourse of oppositionality which colonisation brings into being" (117).

Going by this definition the process of colonisation in India began almost two centuries ago. Although the encounter with the British can be traced back to the early 17th century with the advent of the East India Company, the process of colonisation, however, began much later. The Battle of Plassey 1757, no doubt resulted in the British gaining a stronger and a more firm hold on India, particularly on Bengal, but the process of colonisation became more formalised as a policy with Macaulay's defence of the East India Company 1833 and his Minutes on Indian Education 1835, culminating in the Crown Act 1858, vesting all power with the queen. But the great Indian Mutiny of 1857 marks a significant turn of events for it is the first open revolt against the colonisers. By then several other voices of dissidence had began to surface. Swami Dayanand Saraswati (1824-83) gave the clarion call "Back to the Vedas" and propagated the idea of 'Swadeshi' but his insistence upon 'Shudhi' made it difficult for this sort of Hindu Nationalism to grow up into Indian Nationalism. Like Dayanand, Swami Vivekananda (1836-1907) also worked for the revival of Hinduism. No doubt he made a tremendously unique contribution in the religious history of mankind by rejuvenating and extolling religion but he could not involve and move the masses. This phase too came to an end with the coming of Gandhi. Gandhi was the first and the only leader of his kind to mobilise a mass movement by establishing a set of ethics, setting the moral tone and demonstrating the values like *ahimsa* and *satyagraha* in his own behaviour. Perhaps it is for these reasons that the masses lovingly revered him. To quote Subhas Bose:

> Gandhiji came to be looked upon by the mass of the people as a Mahatma before he became the undisputed political leader of India... the asceticism of Gandhiji, his simple life, his vegetarian diet, his adherence to truth and his consequent fearlessness—all combined to give him a halo of saintliness. His loin-cloth was reminiscent of Christ, while his sitting posture at the time of lecturing was reminiscent of Buddha. (125)

Kanthapura deconstructs the myth of the power of the foreign ruler, views resistance as an enabling strategy and examines in detail the meaning and practices of *satyagraha* and *ahimsa*. It also incorporates the Gandhian ideology of social justice both between castes and between genders. This position of resistance can also be viewed as the beginning of the process of decolonisation in the sense that it questions the cultural impositions along with the political authority. There is a conscious effort to resist Western ideas and values. This process can be perceived in the reformist movements like the Arya Samaj Movement as well as in Gandhi's rejection of modernisation in *Hind Swaraj*. "Decolonization", writes Fanon, "is a historical process... it cannot become intelligible nor clear to itself except in the exact measure that we can discern the movements which give it historical form and content"(27). In India the decolonisation process as stated earlier in the paper spreads over a little more than 175 years but with the coming of Gandhi it gained a new impetus.

The small village of Kanthapura is also shaken up by this process which has been going on in the rest of the country. In the novel the almost devotional rapturous shouts of "Mahatma Gandhi ki Jai" explicitly show the hypnotising power that Gandhi wielded over the masses. These shouts are also symbolic approval of the new gospel of non-violence and non-cooperation as practiced and taught by Gandhi. In other words the revolutionary consciousness of the masses creates new history. The credit for this attitudinal change in the masses goes to the transformative leadership of the protagonist Moorthy, a fellow villager, a seriously committed Gandhian.

Gandhi's method of dissent did not come from the west. In fact his ideas had their basis in religion and ethical ideologies, in values as well as in the tradition of his own people. He was able to create a new audience for he was able to alter the shape of understanding by passing on information in such a manner that it fixed and secured tradition. Emphasising this aspect Dalton writes:

> ...his ability to use symbols and images in a language for and of the Indian people. Like a poet, Gandhi treated his past with affection, drawing from the Indian classics old words Ahimsa, Karamayoga, Ram Raj, Tapasya, Moksha—and charging them with fresh meaning, until they became symbols of both past and future. (32)

Moorthy—an image of Gandhi—also organises 'Bhajans', 'Satyanarayana Puja' and exploits indigenous tradition of 'Harikatha' in which symbols and images are in a language comprehended and used by the people. The strength of the Hindu symbols draws the crowds and has an appeal for the masses. The Harikatha, used as a strategy to mobilise the villagers, apparently religious has a political connotation. In the words of the narrator it was a katha in which:

> Parvati in penance becomes the country and Siva becomes heaven knows what! 'Siva is the three eyed' he says 'and Swaraj too is three eyed. Self-purification, Hindu-Moslem unity, Khaddar' and he talks of... and every where there is something about our country and something about Swaraj.(16)

The Harikatha man Jayaramachar then recalls the rich cultural and religious heritage of India and goes on to enumerate names like Ashoka, Chandragupta, Vikramaditya, Akbar, Krishna to Buddha, Sankara to Ramanuja and immediately juxtaposes it against the contemporary times:

> ...men have come from across the seas and the oceans to trample... they have come to bind us and to whip us, to make our women

die milkless and our men die ignorant. (17)

The shastri then convincingly states that in such times the only bright light that can dispel darkness of ignorance and bring relief to people is "our Mohandas", who is then compared to the mythological Krishna crushing the serpent Kali and killing the demons. After having drawn comparisons and analogies from the Indian mythology, history and religion the shastri elaborates upon the Gandhian ideology—harm no soul, love all, not love riches as riches create passions. He finally appeals to the villagers, "spin and weave every day, for our Mother is in tattered weeds and a poor Mother needs clothes to cover her sores" (18). In addition to this emotional and nationalistic appeal Moorthy logically explains how spinning yarn would change the economic structure of the society and consequently their plight. He, like Gandhi, stresses the need for swadeshi. These appeals convince and energise the villagers and they are set to fight at one level the prevailing casteism, the village power structure and the sahib of the Skeffington Coffee Estate and on the national level imperialism.

Moorthy the acknowledged leader of the villagers is for them the "Small Mountain" and Gandhi the "Big Mountain"(127). Moorthy like Gandhi adopts the principles of *satyagraha* and *ahimsa* in life. When Bade Khan whips, kicks and drives away Rachanna and his wife, Moorthy is of-course saddened and like the Mahatma he resolves to "fast for 3 days in the temple" as he holds himself responsible for it(87). The fasting is aimed at self-purification and not for a personal gain. In fact this fast is in the nature of prayer for purity, strength and power from God to fight the tyrants. Following the example set by Gandhi, Moorthy also resolves to love his enemies (90). When the police pounces upon the volunteers the reaction is "Monsters, monsters, yes they may be, but we are out to convert them, the Mahatma says we should convert them, and we shall convert them; our hearts shall convert them. Our will and our love will convert them... send out our love that no hatred may live within our breasts" (164). When the police comes to arrest Moorthy, Moorthy's appeal is to live up to the spirit of the *satyagrahi*.

The concept of *ahimsa* is based on the religious faith that life is sacred and therefore killing is sacrilegious. For Gandhi *ahimsa* meant more then not killing. For him every evil thought, telling lies, hatred, wishing ill of others was against the principle of *ahimsa*. He firmly believed that it was impossible to seek and find truth without *ahimsa*: the two were intertwined. Moorthy also urges the people to vow to speak the truth. When in jail, Moorthy does not employ an advocate to defend himself for he is sure "I shall speak that which Truth prompteth and Truth needeth no defence"(92).

Both *ahimsa* and the doctrine of *satyagraha* have been derived essentially from the *Gita*. But Gandhi's practical application of it in the social and political sphere was entirely his own. *Satyagraha* in the political sphere assumes the form of civil disobedience. It is for this form of *satyagraha* that Gandhi is mostly known. Gandhi gave the call for civil disobedience—mass resistance—against the government when constitutional methods failed. It was civil because it was non-violent. It was disobedience to laws that hurt the people's dignity and deprived them of the basic rights. *Dandi March* or *Salt Satyagraha* was an unprecedented act of mass civil disobedience. It was a resistance to Imperialism. Moorthy, in the novel, conveys to the villagers the daily progress of Gandhi's nation-wide movement and in turn leads the men and women of Kanthapura to picket toddy booths, for according to him the toddy trees are governments and the toddy booths "exploit the poor and the unhappy" (129).

According to Gandhi the method of non-cooperation was a process of touching the heart and appealing to reason and not one of frightening others by rowdyism. Moorthy also explains to his villagers not to be harsh or wicked even in the face of violence. He explains, "Brothers and sisters, remember we are not out to fight the white man or the white man's slave, the Police and the Revenue officials but against the demoniac corruption that has entered their hearts, and the purer we are the greater will be our victory, for the victory we seek is the victory of the heart" (129). He reiterates that they are not warriors but "soldier saints" and that they ought to add "to the harmony of the world" (180). The non-violence which overcomes evil in this manner is not the passive resistance of the weak but unflinching stand of the brave. Gandhi was that brave son of India.

Gandhi took deep offence at the segregation of the depressed classes from the rest of the Hindu community. He firmly believed that untouchability is the greatest blot on Hinduism and that if untouchability continued Hinduism would die. Moorthy, a brahmin, crosses the threshold of the Pariah house and becomes an out caste in his own house. He sits "by the kitchen threshold and eats like a servant"(48). His mother cannot bear the thought of her son being excommunicated. She ultimately dies a sad woman. For Moorthy there are no socially superior people and the barriers of caste and class are transcended. Resistance to the British coloniser and living Gandhian ideology can even demand the price of severing ties with one's own family. For Moorthy the village is the entire family.

Similarly the gender difference also does not exist for Moorthy as it did not for Gandhi. Subash Bose also refers to Gandhi's appeal to the women to devote their free time to spinning with a "view to stimulating the production of Khadi". This appeal was "transmitted all over the country and it had a magic effect" (*The Indian Struggle* 204). Moorthy also asserts, "We need a woman in the Committee for the Congress is for the weak and the lowly"(81). His appeal is, "Sisters from today onwards I want your help... everybody who will become a member of that panchayat will spin and practice *Ahimsa* and speak the truth"(81). The women of India found a considerable champion in Gandhi, similarly women of Kanthapura look up to Moorthy. Moorthy sensitises them to their social obligation. In the novel itself there is a very close parallel to Harikatha: Ratna reading out the vedantic texts and the discussion on philosophy following it. Rangamma's interpretation of the text is the same strategy as that of the Harikatha man. She asks the women to "...'for the thorny pit the illusioned fall into you put the foreign government, and for the soul that searchers for liberation, you put our India, everything is clear', and this way and that she would always bring the British Government into every page and line." She also urges them on to fight cruelty by narrating tales of Rani Laxmi Bai and the Rajput women who fought along with their husbands (109). Like men's organisations, the women of Kanthapura get together and become 'Volunteers', form 'Sevika Sangha' and call themselves "Sevis". They exercise and prepare themselves physically, mentally and morally to face 'the lathi' of the ruler.

The importance of the role of women in the process of decolonisation is further explicitly conveyed by the fact that the narrator in the novel is an old brahmin woman, Achakka, who is not just a narrator or a commentator or a mere observer but one who had actively participated in the freedom struggle. Her narration reminds the reader of the old traditional katha style. Raja Rao in his preface to *Kanthapura* expresses that the tempo of Indian life, spirit, the thought-movement could only be best conveyed in this style and language. The reader realises that, the texture, sound, rhythm and words used in the novel are not used in the manner they are used in standard English, and this is what makes the language and the style characteristically Indian. Ashcroft in "Replacing language" uses the term 'english' for this sort of "language variant cultural fidelity" (54). Thus Raja Rao's deliberate use of the oral tradition and violation of the standard English usage is a statement of resistance and rejection of English—the language of power and superiority—and also a devise signifying the cultural distinctiveness that exists between the two cultures.

As is evident from the above discussion, Raja Rao has created a postcolonial text in *Kanthapura*. The novel questions the very form of the western novel. It questions its time frame and appropriating an alien language uses it for purposes of expressing a native myth. What begins as a tale told by an old woman soon transforms itself into a political narrative. He makes abundant use of the oral narrative discourse which depends heavily on a sense of community. His audience is literally collected in one place allowing for a collective response to be built. Gradually, right under our eyes, religious space is converted into secular space with the religious Kathas giving place to the Gandhi katha, the tale of his birth. Simultaneously Gandhi is absorbed into their consciousness as a saviour, a breath of fresh breeze. This portrayal, however, is not allowed to go unquestioned. There are disbelievers and dissidents, for many Gandhi's advocacy of equal rights for all irrespective of caste position is unacceptable. There are others who are opposed to him both inside and outside the village. But then every Ram has had his Ravana. Opposition and dissidence both have their place in the Hindu religion. The myths are transformed into a living legend and this is made possible by the narrative mode itself. The opening passage tells us that once upon a time there was a village, Kanthapura which, however, no longer exists having been destroyed by a fire. Although in the novel the dates are not mentioned (except 1921 mentioned on page 93), yet it is possible for the reader to evolve a time frame with the help of the history of the freedom struggle for instance the non-operation movement, Dandi March etc.

Again, one is aware of the force of this living legend as Moorthy sits outside his house as a true Gandhian follower, as the widowed Rangamma takes up the leadership, as the women read scriptures, as the young girl, Ratna, dons the mantle which falls on her. The empowerment of women fills them with confidence. They march on in sun and in shower, face "bang-bang of the lathis" and court arrest. The seven months pregnant Radhamma has her baby in these adverse circumstances but the women can manage and take care of themselves (151-159).

Furthermore, words like 'excommunication' cease to have any importance. On the contrary a new. vocabulary is introduced. People are addressed as 'brothers' and 'sisters' the concept of "I" or the "individual's identity" which is purely a western concept is nonexistent. The form of address, in fact is in keeping with the Indian notion of community.

The novel ends on a realistic note. Moorthy writes to Ratna, "Jawaharlal will change it... he, too, is for non-violence and he, too, is a *Satyagrahi*, but he says, "in Swaraj there shall be neither the rich nor the poor. And he calls himself an 'equal-distributionist', and I am with him and his men" (133). This is very significant in this context as it captures the prevalent mood of the contemporary Indian people. By the late 30s the political debate about modernisation and socialism had began and Nehruvian policies held greater attraction for the youth, who were impatient for change. Thus, the message in the novel is that it was very important to shake and stir up the slumbering villages and this was only possible through Gandhian strategy, but working for and towards a large social change would necessarily involve technology and modernisation and also for being able to govern India one must have a practical approach and not live in the world of myths. R.K. Narayan's *Waiting for the Mahatma* also ends on a similar note but in retrospect. *Kanthapura*, however, appears to have captured the division in the Indian psyche—the division between Gandhi and Nehru. The ending of the novel is not a defeatist ending for no miraculous or a fairy tale ending was possible in the late 30s. Also a fairy tale ending or a miraculous end of the novel, besides being unrealistic, would have subtracted from the strength of the narrative which is about a process not about a goal: the process of change of transformation, of awareness and of empowerment.

References

Ashcroft, Bill, Gareth Griffiths and Helen Tiffin. *The Empire Writes Back: Theory and Practice in Post-colonial Literatures*. London: Routledge, 1989.

—, eds., *The Post-colonial Studies Reader*. London: Routledge, 1995.

Bose, Subhas Chandra. *The Indian Struggle. 1920-42*. Ed. by Sisir Kumar Bose and Sugata Bose. Delhi: Oxford University Press, 1997.

Dalton, Dennis. *Gandhi's Power: Non Violence in Action*. Delhi: Oxford University Press, 1998.

Fanon, Frantz. *The Wretched of the Earth*. Trans. Constance Farrington. Harmondsworth: Penguin, 1961.

Narayan, R.K. *Waiting for the Mahatma* (1956). Mysore: Indian Thought Publication, 1991.

Rao, Raja. *Kanthapura (1938)*. Delhi: Orient Paperbacks, 1970.

9

Mythologising Indian Freedom Movement in *Kanthapura*

Neelam Raisinghani

Myth is a serious legend, a tale, a story of superhuman will, courage and strength handed down to a people by oral traditions over a long period of time and put into written form by writers to suit their purposes. Myths reflect a society's spiritual foundations and symbolize human experience embodying a strong faith in the cosmic view preserved and worshipped by every culture

T.S. Eliot in *The Waste Land* has made a conscious use of mythical situations or characters in a modern context to bring out the similarities and contrasts between the past and the present. He is conscious of the bewildering variety, complexity and intricacy of modem life. He tries to render in his art this variety and complexity by using myth as a technique.

Other English authors have made an unconscious use of myth. They may not even be aware of using myth, but critics find out those characters and situations in which myths have operated. These authors use archetypal situations unconsciously.

In Indo-Anglian fiction the writers have made a conscious use of not only the literary stories from the *Ramayana* or the *Mahabharata*, but also the folk tales and fertility rituals. They weave various legends, myths and folk-lores into the structures of their novels to heighten the effect of their purposes. They succeed in their purposes because there is the sharing of a common mythology between the narrator and the audience

Raja Rao has used this method deliberately and has depended upon mythological sources in *Kanthapura*. He is an outstanding exponent of using the mythical parallel to extend our understanding of the contemporary historical situation. He weaves in many stories within a story. In his famous foreword, Rao admits:

> There is no village in India, however mean, that has not a rich *sthala-purana*, or legendary history, of its own.... Episode follows episode, and when our thoughts stop our breath stops, and we move on to another thought. This was and still is the ordinary style of our storytelling. I have tried to follow it myself in this story.

Raja Rao has used a mythology which is shared by him and the readers. He has made use of well known epic or purnanic tales which can be easily understood by his Indian readers. He has used the famous myth of Rama and Ravana to describe Gandhi's struggle against the British empire. Raja Rao uses the local myths of South India, which he calls 'sthala-purana'. These regional tales are limited to the legendary history of a place or village. The author has taken pains to describe these folk tales in detail to enhance their appeal. Besides the national and the regional myths, he uses rites and rituals of worshipping with *kumkum* and camphor, fasting, or offering of betel and coconut.

By weaving these epic myths, folk-tales and rituals, Raja Rao tries to raise a socio-political theme to epic dimensions. Political confrontation is the life blood of *Kanthapura*. Gandhi's fight against the central theme of the novel. The story of *Kanthapura* is narrated by an old grandmother, who reminisces about the glorious past of her village long after the actual events had taken place. Like an inveterate myth-maker she links the gods and goddesses with historic figures. Mahatma Gandhi is Rama, while the Englishmen or their brown agents are the soldiers of Ravana's army.

Rao juxtaposes legendary religious heroes of the past with real and fictional figures of the present. Jayaramachar, the Harikathaman, uses the ancient Indian legends to give a sacred background to the rise of Gandhi. Rao dramatizes the whole novel along the same principle of making the past a vital part of the present. Moorthy is a functional device used to apotheosize Gandhi.

Gandhi's spiritual presence dominates *Kanthapura*, though he is an invincible god, whose avatar or physical manifestation is Moorthy. K.R.S. Iyengar points out that "Moorthy (like Gandhi) becomes the epic hero Rama routing the demon Ravana's sinister army of occupation, namely the British intruders" (391).

Raja Rao has tried to rewrite history with a view to unravel the mysterious nature of reality by mythologising it. He has constructed and deconstructed some classical or existing myths and blended them with politics through the Harikathas read by Jayaramachar, Ramakrishnayya and Ratna. These Harikathas have a sprinkling of gods and mythological figures, a junction of the past and the present, a juxtaposition of god figures with mortals, of history and the contemporary background.

Myths convey messages easily. The myth of Brahma and Valmiki, narrated by Jayaramachar to the villagers, performs this role. It exposes the ruthlessness and brutality of the Britishers. Sage Valmiki during one of his sojourns to Brahma implores Brahma!

> Rise up O God of Gods ! I have come to bring you sinister news. Far down on the Earth you chose as your chief daughter Bharatha, the goddess of wisdom and well being... you who sent us the Prince propagators of the Holy Law and Sages that smote the darkness of Ignorance, you have forgotten us so long that men have come from across the seas and the oceans to trample on our wisdom... to bind us and to whip us, to make our women die milkless and our men die ignorant. (11)

Valmiki requests Brahma to send one of his Gods so that he may incarnate on Earth and bring back light and plenty to enslaved India. Brahma assures him to send Siva's incarnation on earth and free India from her enforced slavery. Mahatma Gandhi is the embodiment of Lord Siva to free Bharatha. Like Siva, the Mahatma is also "three eyed", believing in "self purification, Hindu-Moslem unity, and Khaddar" (10). Siva and Mahatma are one.

> For, after all, sister, when one has a light on the forehead, one can march a thousand leagues. Siva is poison-throated and yet he is the three-eyed. May the three-eyed Siva protect us. (113)

Jayaramachar through other myths of Damayanthi, Shakuntala and Yashodha tries to bring his spell-bound audiences to understand something about India and its struggle for swaraj.

The dominant myth is of Rama-Sita and Ravana.

> People are confident of their victory as "the Mahatma will go to the Redman's country and he will bring them Swaraj... and Sita freed, and he will come with Sita on his right in a chariot of the air, and brother Bharatha (Nehru) will go to meet them with the worshipped sandal of the Master on his head. And as they enter Ayodhya there will be a rain of flowers. (189)

When Raja Rao makes a mythic reference to the mystified legends and fictionalized history, the innocent villagers are immediately electrified into the vision of the nature of the conflict in terms of good principle in the Avatara and the evil principle in the adversary. When Mahatma Gandhi and Jawahar Lal Nehru are identified with the *satvic* principle the villagers have no difficulty in identifying the adversary with the Red-men, the British military colonial establishment, in the encroaching Skeffington Estate, a wing of the British industrial empire that is choking Indian industry and commerce, or in the. spiritually dead Indians like Bhatta, Swami, Bade Khan and others or the evil characteristics of Hinduism which internalize power structures in the name of religion. By projecting the ancient myth of Lord Krishna who had to fight-against demons and had killed the serpent Kaliya, Raja Rao refers to the non-violent war Gandhi has waged against tile British empire. More and more men follow Gandhi "as they did Krishna, the flute player" (12). Whenever there are atrocities, darkness of ignorance and corruption such *'Avataras'* appear on the Earth to defend *'Dharma'*. Gandhi is raised to the level of a God. His activities are compared with Lord Krishna's feat.

While Gandhi is called the "Great Mountain" Moorthy is the "Little Mountain." He is the local Gandhi for the villagers. Moorthy tries to eradicate untouchability. He contemplates building "a thousand pillared temple in which we are one and who shall say, he is at the head of the one and another at the foot.... whether brahmin, or bangle seller, pariah or priest, we are all one as the mustard seeds in a sack are equal in shape and hue and all" (123). Moorthy is excommunicated by the Swami, who exploits religion as a cover to conceal his temporal interests. Moorthy kindles Kanthapura with a series of religious activities like the installation and consecration of the Siva Linga to knit the people of Kanthapura into an alliance and work under one banner to repel the common enemy. Moorthy is an idealized character, who like Christ takes all the sins of the people upon himself and undergoes a penance for purification, a young man who conquers physical desire and interest. Like Parvati, he undergoes penances to win Siva: changing he changes not, ash-smeared, he's Parvati's sire, moon on his head, and poison in his throat (113). Moorthy is presented as a super-human figure. He is a dedicated and selfless soul and regarded as a local Mahatma. Range Gowda, the village headman, describes Moorthy as their Gandhi:

> The state of Mysore has a Maharaja but that Maharaja has another Maharaja who is in London, and that one has another one in heaven, and so everybody has his own Mahatma, and this Moorthy who has been caught in our knees playing as a child is now grown up and great, and he has wisdom in him and he will be our Mahatma. (103)

Moorthy is the local god, while Gandhi is the greater god. By deifying Moorthy, Raja Rao has attempted to create a *sthala-purana*, or a local legendary tale.

Raja Rao envisions the *'Matri Shakti'* or mother-principle as the supreme quality in woman and he sees her at the centre of the family. The mother image is seen in woman, in animals, in nature, in goddesses. Raja Rao has applied the ancient Vedic image of 'Gomata', cow-mother to his women characters, goddesses and Mother India. K.R.S. Iyengar comments:

> It is with sure racial insight that Raja Rao has made the cow's mother-gait and silent tears symbolic of India's, the mother's travails and the cow's infinite patience and veiled power as symbolic of the mother's genius for surviving her sorrows and transmuting them into great joy to come. (390)

The idea of the protective mother is uppermost in the minds of the women satyagrahis when police surround them 'If mother-earth had opened and said, come in children' we should have walked down the steps and the great rock would have closed itself upon us" (214). Kenchamma is the mother goddess of Kanthapura. She protects them through famine and disease, death and despair. They pray to her:

> Kenchamma, Kenchamma,
> Goddess benign and bounteous,
> Mother of earth, blood of life,
> Harvest-queen, rain-crowned,
> Kenchamma, Kenchamma,
> Goddess benign and bounteous. (3)

People of Kanthapura have immense faith in the powers of their goddess Kenchamma, whose descent is wrapt in a myth. She had killed a demon long long ago who demanded young men as food and young women as wives. "Kenchamma came from the Heavens... and she waged such a battle and she fought many a night that the blood soaked and soaked into the earth and that is why the Kenchamma Hill is all red" (2). Kenchamma has always protected the people of Kanthapura from disease, death and despair. She is an unfailing source of help to them. They are sure, "she will now free them from the clutches of Red-man. They are sure that the Goddess will free Moorthy from the prison. She will appear before the judges and free him" (96). Kenchamma is the mother protector. The goddess steps down to live among the villagers. The bond between the people and their mother-goddess is very strong. She protects the village Kanthapura as a greater God protects the entire Universe.

Mythical and human figures jostle with each other in *Kanthapura*, "Some of the chief characters are gods and other human beings larger in power than humanity" (Frye 30). Raja Rao has blended the age-old protective mother ideal with the new times. For though the ancient life pattern is changed by the Gandhian struggle, the images are the same and they are fused in the national context, "Mother is in tattered weeds and a poor mother needs clothes to cover her sores" (67). The family is the country, the country men are the children of Mother India. She protects her children, but when she is ill or weak, or in need of help, the children work for her, for it is a reciprocal relation.

Apart from the literary myths of Rama, Krishna, Siva and Brahma; and the regional myths of Moorthy and Goddess Kenchamma, there are references to local rituals of sacrifice done to please the deities. Moorthy's fasting for self purification and the sacrifices made by the women to bring rain are the archetypal situations. The ploughing of the fields in Vaisakh, the coming of the rains, the worshipping of the cows, the yoking of the bulls to the plough under the Rohini star (144) or the description of the Kartik festival of lights, which proclaim the impressed footsteps of gods, "who walk quietly by lighted streets... Kartik is the month of gods....blue gods and quiet gods and bright-eyed gods" (85).

These rituals increase their faith in their greater gods and the local gods. The innocent people of Kanthapura have blind faith in Gandhi's powers to release them out of their slavery.

> There is something that has entered our hearts, an abundance like the Himavathy on Gauri's night, when lights come floating down from Rampur comer, lights come floating down from Rampur and Maddur and Tippur, lights lit on the betel leaves, and with flower and kumkum and song we let them go, and they will go down the Ghats to the morning of the sea, the lights on betel

leaves, and the Mahatma will gather it all, he will gather it by the sea, and he will bless us. (160)

Women satyagrahis, when locked in the temple, light oil lamps, clap their hands and sing bhajans to please the Siva of the Meru Mount. Under the guise of the religious ceremonies like blowing the conch, lighting camphor, breaking coconuts and singing *Satya Narayan Maharaj ki Jai*, they suddenly shout 'Vande Mataram' (172).

These references create an atmosphere for the old narrator, who weaves all facts into a mythical fabric and transcends and assimilates the political, and historical facts into myths and legends. K.R.S. Iyengar has called *Kanthapura*, "a veritable Grammar of the Gandhian myth—the myth that is but a poetic translation of the reality" (396).

But Meenakshi Mukherjee in *The Twice Born Fiction*, after an analysis of the use of myth in Indo-Anglian Fiction contends: "that the use of myth so far has been more successful technically, than thematically, that the myths chosen are often part of an established literary convention and do not show any unusual insight on the part of the author in perceiving links between the present situation and its parallel situation..." (167).

The Harikatha woven by Raja Rao into the matrix of his story "may not be a thematic success on the part of the author", but an essential aspect of Indian cultural experience. A part of our oral tradition has been expressed by Raja Rao in *Kanthapura* to implant the ethical sense and human values in the minds of his readers, justice and benevolent social and political order in the society through myths and mythological characters, gods and heroes. Through these myths he is trying to lay down a code of conduct for human beings. His basic purpose is to expose human weaknesses and to set models of human behaviour for the society.

References

Eliot, T.S. *The Waste Land*. London: Faber and Faber, 1940.
Frye, Northrop. *Fables of Identity: Studies in Poetic Mythology*. New York: 1963.
Iyengar, K.R. Srinivasa. *Indian Writing in English*. London: Asia Publishing House, 1962.
Mukherjee, Meenakshi. *The Twice Born Fiction*. India Heinemann Educational Books, 1971.
Rao, Raja. *Kanthapura*. Bombay : O.U.P., 1974.

10

Rhythms of Language in Raja Rao's *Kanthapura*

Jyoti Bhatia

Written in an enchanting style, Raja Rao's *Kanthapura* is a story of a small south Indian village caught in the whirlpool of the independence movement, under the influence of Gandhian ideas in the 1930s. The impact was so deep that "it created an awareness of the self" (Jain 84) and motivated the simple villagers to actively participate in the freedom struggle. As D.S. Maini says, "*Kanthapura*... is born out of an act of faith. Raja Rao is quite clearly fascinated by the revolution wrought by the Mahatma in Indian consciousness. To bring out the energy and poetry of the revolution, and to dramatise the power of an idea, once it has gripped the imaginations of the people, is the seminal impulse behind the novel" (Maini 3).

Though the novel is set against a backdrop of political awareness and struggle, it incorporates a number of characteristics from traditional Indian life and culture. Raja Rao presents realistic image of life in an Indian village community with its belief in old traditions, customs, rituals, superstitions, caste system; heavy reliance on religion and local deities, manners of speech and address, and with the help of the elderly female narrative voice gives an oral flavour to the tale, in the Puranic style, with "story within story" (Raja Rao, "India's Search for Self-expression", 1962). Commenting on this aspect of the novel, K.R. Srinivasa Iyengar observes:

> ...the tremors of Gandhi's impact on a South Indian village are recorded here in the chatty language of an elderly widow, and we see everything through the film of her memory, sensibility and temperament and the manner of her telling too is characteristically Indian, feminine with a spontaneity that is coupled with swiftness, vivid with a raciness, suffused with native vigour, and exciting with a rich sense of drama shot through and through with humour and lyricism... the heroes and heroines of epics jostle with historic personalities, and time past and time present are both projected into time future.... The political revolution is thus transcended and assimilated into the racial heritage as myth and legend. (305-306)

In short as another critic Suresh Nath has also pointed out, "Her account bristles with the beautiful blending of the factual, the mythical and the poetical" (Nath 56).

The clue to the form of the novel is given by Rao himself in the 'Foreword' to the novel. He says, "The tempo of Indian life must be infused into our English expression... we, in India, think quickly, we talk quickly, and when we move we move quickly... we tell one interminable tale. Episode follows episode, and when our thoughts stop our breath stops and we move on to another thought. This was and still is the ordinary style of our storytelling. I have tried to follow it myself in this story" (*Kanthapura* 5-6). Reed Way Dasenbrock in his essay "The Politics of Stylistic Experimentation: A Commonwealth Perspective", writes in support of Rao's statement:

> *Kanthapura* rushes and tumbles on: Its sentences are not only based on Kannada syntax instead of English, they are also interminable... Moreover, adding to the rush and tumble quality is the fact that *Kanthapura* is a tale told by a storyteller, which gives a

strong oral voiced quality to the complex syntax. As this village storyteller is not from a westernised or even educated background, she tells the story entirely within her Indian cultural references, betraying no awareness at any point that any aspect of her work need be explained... references to current events... combined with the "rush and tumble syntax creates" a novel "of almost impenetrable density". (66)

Charles R. Larson in *The Novel in the Third World* has appreciated the connection between culture and literary form (11). And this applies to *Kanthapura* perhaps more than it would to a work of another kind for in it he creates a work that is "Indian both in its theme and technique" (Belliappa 158). The novel which is termed, 'a classic', has been interpreted and analysed from various angles as a Sthala-Purana; a Gandhi Purana; its mythical structure and narrative methods and its blending of political and religious elements and on the basis of its language.[1] Several critics have commented on Raja Rao's style and use of language in *Kanthapura* but there are many features in the novel that, I think, need to be focused and elaborated upon further in order to understand the contribution of Rao to the postcolonial novel.

M.H. Abrams, has pointed out that style which is the "manner" of linguistic expression in prose or verse, is how a speaker or writer says whatever he says. The characteristic style of a work or a writer may be analysed in terms of its *diction*, or characteristic choice of words; its sentence structure and syntax; the density and types of the figurative language and the patterns of its rhythm, along with a study of its component sounds and its rhetorical aims and devices (165-166). Syed Amanuddin, in his essay, "Style is the Thing" says, "Style... involves the mode of expression, design, construction, and execution. Its stands for distinctness, originality, and excellence". Diction constitutes an important element. Indo-English writers inevitably have to defend their use of English. Almost fifty years after the writing of the novel Rao in an interview with Ranavir Rangra said reinforcing what he had said in his foreword to the novel, "I would have like to express myself in Sanskrit. It is the richest language in the world. It is the most sophisticated language. You can use it, play with it in the way you like. But I am afraid, my Sanskrit is not good enough. Though my mother-tongue was Kannada, I was brought up in Hyderabad. So my Kannada was not good either. I did not think it sufficient for my intellectual perversities. So I needed some language that I knew better than Kannada and that was English. I have tried to reshape the English language for my own needs. I refuse to write English as an English man or an American. Therefore, my English is, as people said, rather unusual. I try to be authentic with regard to what I write...."

English, being a foreign language, was not the language of what Rao calls "our emotional make-up". It had however appropriated intellectual space therefore it was almost inevitable that writing should be done in English, but it was equally necessary that it be written differently and be made to "carry the weight" of languages native to the writers of the colonialised countries.[2]

And Raja Rao, in *Kanthapura*, indeed succeeds in reshaping the English language for his own needs making it distinctive and colourful using "the syntactic resources of an Indian language" (Dasenbrock 56). The grandmotherly Achakka helping Rao to capture every "nuance and detail of real life and real language" (Turner 9). So effective, forceful, evocative and unique is the style and so masterly is the use of words that we are able to visualise the sounds, the colours, the lights and movements of Kanthapura and its inhabitants. A cinematic picture of a South Indian village emerges, which is in a way representative of the common Indian spirit and style. There is a kind of breathlessness in the narration throughout. The choice of the narrator, I think, has facilitated Raja Rao, greatly to express the tempo of Indian life infused in the English expression. It is Achakka, who helps Rao to capture the speed, the vitality, the very life of an Indian village. She also authenticates the presentation because she has been a part of the struggle, has witnessed the ups and downs of the movement and also because she has been there for a long, long time. She gives a true and unbiased account of everything and everybeing—effortlessly linking the past with the present.

The novel begins with a graphic description of the village Kanthapura, situated "in the province of Kara. High on the Ghats..., high up the steep mountains that face the cool Arabian seas, up the Malabar Coast..., up Mangalore and Puttur and many a centre of cardamom and coffee, rice and sugarcane". The description of the geographical location of the village with its "narrow dusty rut covered roads" which *wind through* the forests, *hang over* bellowing gorges and *leap over* elephant haunted valleys, the *groaning* of the carts as they begin to *grind* and to *rumble*, the singing of the cartman and 'ho' and 'he-ho' of Subba Chetty create an atmosphere at the beginning of the novel itself and acquaint the reader with sounds peculiar to the rural environment (7).

In a similar picturesque manner is the rain, day and night described and one striking feature of the language used here is that human and animal movements have been attributed to all these, and the movement is described in a manner that the prose gains momentum, becoming lyrical and poetic. Such foregrounding is a common feature in Rao's language. The monsoon rain:

> It *churns* and *splashes*, beats against the tree-tops, *reckless* and *wilful*, and suddenly *floating* forwards it *bucks back*. and *spits forward* and *pours down* upon the green, weak, coffee leaves, *thumping them down* to the earth, and then *playfully lounging* up, the coffee leaves rising with it, and *whorling and winnowing, spurting and raffling*, it jerks and snorts this side and that,... The rain swishes round and pours, beating against the tree-tops, *grinding by* the tree-trunks and *racing down* the waving paths. It *swings* and *swishes, beats* and *patters*, and then there is but one downpour, one steady, *full, ungrudging pour*. (56-57)

and the Vaishak rains,

> ...come, the fine, first-footing rains that *skip* over the bronze mountains, *tiptoe* the crags, and *leaping into* the valleys, *go splashing* and *wind-swung*, a winnowed pour... to paw upon the tiles, and the cattle come running home, their ears stretched back, and the drover lurches *behind* some bel tree or pipal tree, and the people leave their querns and rush to the courtyard, and turning towards the Kenchamma Temple, send forth a prayer, saying, 'There, there, rains have come, Kenchamma; may our houses be

white as silver' and the lightning flashes and the thunder stirs the tiles, and the children rush to the gutter slabs to sail paper boats down to Kashi. (114)

Raja Rao creates an onomatopoetic effect in these descriptions and one can hear the swishing, beating and pattering of the monsoon rain, the shivering of trees, the creaking of the bamboos and the clash of thunder. The whole scene is so pictorial, so full of visual images that it is possible for the reader to follow the passage of the rain water which goes skipping, tiptoeing, leaping into the valleys.

The description of the rising day is another example of Rao's masterly and unusual use of languages:

The day *dawned over* the Ghats, the day *rose over* the Blue mountain and *churning through* the grey, rapt valleys, *swirled up* and *swam across* the whole air. The day rose into the air and with it rose the dust of the morning, and the carts began to creak round the bulging rocks and the coppery peaks, and the sun *fell into* the river and *pierced* it to the pebbles, while the carts rolled on and on, fair carts of the Kanthapura Fair... with lolling bells and muffled bells, with horn-protectors in copper and back-protectors in lace.... (45)

Notice here, Rao's use of alliteration, verbs and phrasal verbs. The verbs used suggest that Rao personifies the various elements of nature following the Indian tradition and thus ascribes to them a will of their own—the ability to control their movements. This also helps Rao to give more pace to the narrative.

The description of Kartik is one of the most beautiful and evocative passage in the novel. Kartik comes "...with the glow of lights and the unpressed footsteps of the wandering gods" (87). In a most poetic manner Rao describes the movement of 'night' ...and night *curls through* the shadowed streets and *hissing over* bellied boulders and hurrying through dallying drains, night *curls... and flapping through* the mango grove, hangs clawed for one moment to the giant pipal, and then shooting across the broken fields, *dies quietly into* the river—and gods walk by lighted streets, blue gods and quiet gods and bright-eyed gods, and even as they walk in transparent flesh the dust gently sinks back to the earth,... and night *curls again through* the shadows of the streets (87-88). Achakka's tone full of grandeur and awe can be felt by the reader when she asks after describing the whole scene "Oh! have you seen the gods, sister?" (88).

Raja Rao creates a beautiful and mysterious atmosphere through these words, giving life to all the inanimate objects. The abundance of movement and adjectives is a marked feature of Rao's language in *Kanthapura*, making it breathtaking and colourful. The unusual collocation of words catches our attention and makes us look again at the scenes described. The language possesses both grace and beauty suggestive of poetry and simultaneously it is also steeped in the typical local flavour of Kannada. Commenting on this rhythmic style of Rao's prose, Iyengar writes:

> There is a lilt and seductive rhythm, a curious incantatory power, in this kind of speech which coils round one more and more, and involves one inextricably in the experience. Words here are not mere words, they are more than blocks of stone; they are indeed streams of suggestion, dark rooms with central lights to lit them up, waves of sound, making haunting music, and even nucleii charged with tremendous power. (Iyengar 311)

To portray the Indian sensibility Rao has very successfully infused a number of local and Indian myths, Kannada idioms, phrases and proverbs, similes, metaphors, terms of endearment and abuse into the novel making it more rich, vibrant and original.

In the world of Kanthapura or for that matter any Indian village, religion is of central concern. The local gods and goddesses are living presences to the villagers and as P.C. Bhattacharya points out, "To believing Hindus, gods and goddesses are not distant entities living in a far off heaven. They are involved in all earthly activities.... A believing Hindu verily walks through his life in the company of his gods" (243). Kanthapura, too, has its local deity—Kenchamma, their goddess "Great and bounteous. She killed a demon ages, ages ago". Kenchamma came from the Heavens, never has "she failed us in our grief" (8). The Kanthapurians turn to Kenchamma for protection from famine and disease death and despair (9). They sing and dance in her praise and offer her "... flowers and fruit and rice and dal and sugarcandy and perfumed sweetmeats...." (9) and ask her to protect them.

To the simple, god-fearing villagers, all aspects of life are linked to religion. In the novel also at every step, we find, the villagers invoking the gods to protect them. It is again faith in God and religion that gives them an inner strength to brave all the hardships of the independence movement. In fact it is the various jayanthis, mass prayers, bhajans, puja-feasts which bring the whole village together, instil in them a sense of participation and community feeling and inspire them to fight for 'Swaraj'.

Rao recognises this aspect of rural life and presents it convincingly by interweaving religious myths into the structure of the novel. In the 'Foreword' to the novel, Rao, has said, that in *Kanthapura* he has tried to tell a story from the contemporary annals of his village, in the nature of a 'stathlapurana' in which "the past mingles with the present, and the gods mingle with the men" (5). In Kanthapura with the help of mythical tales and associations with historical legends, Moorthy, Jayaramachar the Harikatha man and Rangamma easily reach the hearts of the villagers. They associate the struggle for independence to a pilgrimage, a holy mission and thus touch the emotional chord in their hearts and get them actively involved in the movement. And at one point in the novel, the political and religious slogans occur simultaneously, "Vande Matram", "Mahatma Gandhi ki Jai" echo with "Satyanarayana Maharaj ki Jai" (169). Jayaramachar and later Rangamma in their narrations show how religion which is a potent force can be used to transform the thoughts and attitudes of the people. In Jayaramachar's kathas, as Achakka tells us, there is always "...something about our country and something about Swaraj (16). It is Jayaramachar who acquaints the villagers with Gandhi—the man and his struggle for freedom in the manner of a Harikatha, thus ensuring people's acceptance of Gandhi as a legendary figure, a son of God who would free them from the clutches of slavery by slaying the serpent of foreign rule (48). Jayaramachar and his special Harikathas change the outlook of the Kanthapurians especially the young folk and instil in them a feeling of revolution against the 'Ravana Raj' of the British. Rangamma too uses the stories from Vedas and Puranas to create awareness among the masses especially the women folk. During discussions "... she would always bring the British Government into every page and line." she would say, "Sister, if for the thorny pit the illusioned fall into, you put the foreign Government, and for the soul that searches for liberation, you put our India, everything is clear;'..." (107).

The religious aspect of the Indian psyche has been fully brought out by Rao in the novel for not only the good, honest and pious characters employ religious myths but the corrupt, greedy, selfish and hypocrite characters like Bhatta, Swami and his agent also use the same myths of Ram-Sita-Ravana-Krishna inversely because of their dishonest intentions and thus exploit the credulity of the naive villagers.

In the novel, Rao, presents, an authentic picture of village life in all its complexity and uniqueness. Like all Indian villages, Kanthapura, too, is neatly divided according to caste and occupation of the villagers into a Brahmin quarter, a Potter's quarter, a Weaver's quarter and a Sudra quarter. The socio-economic condition of the people is evident from the houses they live in. Postmaster Suryanarayan has a double storied house; Patwari Nanjudia has a veranda with the rooms built on to the old house with glass panes to the windows---and this finds special mention by granny Achakka; Kannayya House people had a "high veranda with a house generations old, but as fresh and new as though it had been built yesterday"; Pock marked Sidda has a "real thothi house, with a big veranda and a large roof"; and the Patel has a nine beamed, house (9-12).

People know their place on the social ladder and move accordingly until as P.C. Bhattacharya says, "its placid routine is disturbed by irresistible forces" (247).

Raja Rao uses adjectival names to acquaint the reader with the status, occupation, temperament, habits and physical features of the different characters. We have postmaster Suryanarayan, Patwari Nanjudia, Waterfall Venkama, Snuff Sastri, Temple

Lakshamma, Front-House Akamma, Coffee-Planter Ramayya, the temple people, the Fig Tree people, Beadle Timmayya, Pock marked Sidda, Corner—House Moorthy, Old Mota, One-eyed Linga, Jack tree Tippa, Nose Scratching Nanjamma, Advocate Ramaswamy-the three pice advocate, Sankara the Ascetic and walking Advocate, Rice-Pounding Rajamma, Husking Rangi, Gold Bangle Somanna, Mota Madanna, Concubine Chowdy, Khadi Shop Dasappa, Boatman Sidda, Goldsmith Nanjudia Trumpet Lingayya, Pipe Ramayya, Gaptooth Siddayya, Horn Nanjappa, Betel Lakshamma and many others. These adjectival appellations, peculiar to the Kannada culture not only individualise the characters but also show the kind of familiarity that exists in an Indian village where everyone knows everyone else and refers to them in a manner that "immediately establishes their identities" (Bhattacharya 249).

The modes of address further convey the attitudes of the speakers towards the addressee and so Moorthy who is loved by all becomes Moorthappa; Sankara becomes Sankarappa or Sankaru and Bhatta becomes Bhattare when he is requested to come for an obsequial dinner or applied for an appropriate date for some ceremony as he is the first Brahmin of the village. All women in South India especially in villages are called 'amma' and in the novel too are addressed as such. Words like 'sister', 'brother', 'aunt', 'daughter' and 'mother' have been used even when there is no actual relationship in keeping with the Indian forms of address. Relations too are explained very explicitly as 'he is my wife's elder brother's wife's brother-in-law' (34).

Another very interesting feature of the novel is the use of names for places. Again as per the Indian tradition descriptive names are given so that places are identified easily for example 'Haunted-Tamarind Tree field' (27); 'Bear's Hill', 'Bhatta's Devil's Fields', 'Horse-Head Hill' (50), 'Buxom-Pipal bend', 'Devil's Ravine Bridge', 'Parvatiwell Corner' (51). 'Tortoise-rock' (63); 'Black-Serpent's ant-hill' (116); 'Siva's Gorge' (136) and many more.

Exclamations and phatic expressions, 'Ho', 'he-ho' (7); 'He, He, He' (53), 'Thoo! Thoo! Thoo!' (65); 'Ayyo-Ayyoo' (55); 'Hele

Hele' (89) 'Hoyla! Hoyla!'; 'Hoye! Hoye! Hoyee-la!' (117) 'Hoy-hoy' (147); 'Ahe, Ahe' (157) are typical Indian sounds rooted in the rural culture. Further, the language is laced with figures of speech—all conveying the Indian manner of describing people and objects. Rao, successfully translates some of these expressions in the novel.

Moorthy, is like a noble cow, quiet, generous, serene, deferent and brahmanic, a very prince (11), as honest as an elephant (15), straight as an aloe, strong and calm (129); Patel Range Gowda is a veritable tiger (12); Rangamma is as tame as a cow (101); Waterfall Venkamma is like a banana trunk. (43) and as important as a buffalo (84-85); Narsamma grows thin as a bamboo and shriveled like a banana bark (48); Vasudev's mother is an old sour milk (63); Policeman Bade Khan is the bearded goat (66); Dasi is as hale as a first calved cow (108); the Skeffington estate coolies have bamboo legs and are goat eyed (141); The quinine pills are as bitter as neem leaves (58); gold has wiles as a wanton woman (60); Seenu is Anjanyya Moorthy's fire tailed Hanuman (81); when the rainy season approaches, the darkness grows thick as sugar in a cauldron, the drops fall big as the thumb and the thunder goes clashing like a temple cymbal through the heavens and when the days become broad-sky becomes blue as a marriage shawl (56-57).

The ease with which the villagers employ similes and metaphors in their day to day speech, is perfectly captured by Rao in the novel. It also helps Rao to succinctly convey the attitudes of the different characters towards each other. When Moorthy shows surprise that Bhatta had come to see the Patel, Range Gowda—the Patel explains, "Yes, learned Moorthappa. He had, of course, come to see me. He wanted me to be his dog's tail. But I said to him, the Mahatma is a holy man, and I was not with the jackals but with the deer. At which Bhatta grew so furious that he cried out 'this holy man was a tiger in a deer's skin',.... and I said to him, 'So it may be but the Red Man's Government is no swan in a Himalayan lake" (77-75). Whereas to the Patel, the British Government is no swan, for the swami's agent the red man is 'the protector of their Dharma like Krishna and if the white man leaves us.... it will not be Rama-rajya we shall have but the rule of the ten-headed

Ravanna' (94) and 'when the British rule disappears, our eternal Dharma will be squashed like a louse in a child's hair' (95).

When to propagate non-violence Moorthy goes on a fast for three days in the temple, the sceptical and spiteful Venkamma and Bhatta use the metaphor of cat for him. Venkamma says, "Ah, the cat has begun to take to asceticism" (68) and Bhatta swears that he "would beat the drum and denounce this cat's conversion to asceticism" (71).

Range Gowda is so enraged with Bade Khan that when Moorthy mentions him as the representative of the Red Man's Government in Kanthapura, the former boils over and says, "I shall not close my eyes till that dog has eaten filth" but Moorthy wants him to be non violent both in speech and action, to pluck hatred out of his heart and to love even his enemies. He reasons with the Patel thus, "Every enemy you create is like pulling out a lantana bush in your backyard. The more you pull out, the wider you spread the seeds, and the thicker becomes the lantana growth. But every friend you create is like a jasmine hedge. You plant it, and it is there and bears flowers..." (75). To explain the oneness of all, Moorthy uses the metaphor of the mustard seeds, all equal in shape and hue (123).

The farmers and workers in agricultural fields also employ very interesting comparisons and Rao brings out the difference in the speech habits of people belonging to different strata of society in the novel. Notice the crudity and coarseness in the comparisons of the farmers and workers at the Skeffington Estate. To the farmers, the earth after rains is as a soft dame; soft as a pumpkin's kernel; the unfriendly wind is like a prostitute showing her tricks (117); Pariah Siddaya of the Skeffington Coffee Estate gives a vivid account of snakes. The cobra is a "Maharaja—clever, nice, clean, shining with glittering eyes"; the water snakes are "silly like the tongues of village hussies"; the green snake is wicked and when fails to sting he "runs back into a thicket like a barking puppy"; the flying snake is "a sly fellow, monster, fine gentleman who is not like a cobra, frank in his attack, never aggressive" (53-55).

Besides these, at a few places, Rao uses quite long and vivid comparisons to suggest the confusion and chaos, both within and without that the women experience when they are attacked by the policemen. The women "feel like mad elephants.... The whole world" seemed to them "a jungle in battle, trees rumbling, lions roaring, jackals wailing, parrots piping, panthers screeching, monkeys jabbering, jeering, chatter-chattering..." (153-154). When later the policemen open fire "there was a shuddered silence, like the silence of a jungle after the tiger has roared over the evening river, and then like a jungle cry of crickets and frogs and hyenas and bisons and jackals" the women "groaned and shrieked and sobbed" and "rushed this side... and that side... fell and... rose, and... crouched and... ducked..." (172). "The bullets scream through the air, like flying snakes taken fire, they wheeze and hiss and slash against the trees, or fall hissing into the canal..." (174).

The rural tone in all its individuality has been perfectly captured by Rao in these expressions which convey the living vibrancy of Indian provincial speech, the essence of Indian speech habits. Rao, effectively harmonises the Indian idiom with the English language recreating actual characters, "people whose mannerisms and speech issue from the sing-song lilting rhythms of a Dravidian language" (Jussawalla 31).

All the similes and metaphors are earthy, taken from animal and plant life and other common objects and experiences of rural life. And it is interesting to note that to convey the various shades of the personalities of the characters, the associations are usually from the animal and plant world whereas animals and elements of nature are given human attributes. Instead of using the pronoun 'it' for inanimate objects and animals, Raja Rao uses the personal pronouns, 'he' or 'she' to describe the wind, earth, snakes etc. thus ascribing feminine and masculine qualities to them. This again is a common feature of Indian speech. As Cecil Nelson points out, "The English used in *Kanthapura*.... is used in a new cultural and linguistic setting; it has to be especially creative,.. because it has to meet new references and situations (1)". The language has been adapted in appropriate, "linguistically classifiable ways to its new environment"(5). Braj Kachru, also says, "the form of a *speech event* in English and a parallel *social event* is determined by the culture in which English is used. This interaction of an alien language in a non English context results in the newness in the new varieties, styles, and registers of English." (quoted by Nelson 5).

Further Raja Rao's portrayal of the different characters in the novel is full of life. He shows how their manners, behaviour and speech are conditioned by their nature and position in society. Range Gowda is the most powerful man in Kanthapura. Achakka describes him as a fat, sturdy fellow, a veritable tiger amongst them, his words were law in their village, an honest man who has helped many a poor peasant but was a terror to the authorities (12). When Moorthy has to begin the 'Don't touch the Government campaign', he first goes to see Range Gowda, "Nothing can be done without him. When Range Gowda says 'Yes', you will have elephant and howdahs and music processions. If Range Gowda says 'No', you can eat the bitter neem leaves and lie by the city gates, licked by the curs," (74). The blessing the plough' ceremony begins only on his arrival. He comes like a born aristocrat "on his horse, his filigree shawl thrown over his shoulders, his durbar turban on his head and his English reins in his hands, and Mada running behind him,...."

When Policeman Bade Khan comes to Kanthapura, he goes to the Patel and says, "He, Patel, the Government has sent me here and I need a house to live in". But the Patel has none to offer and bluntly refuses to accommodate him. Bade Khan, who is the representative of the British Government knows his importance, cannot take in the Patel's indifference, and threatens the veritable tiger of the village Range Gowda and says, "the first time I corner you, I shall squash you like a bug." But the Patel is a powerful man, not to be coerced by an outsider. He retaliates by saying, "You'd better take care not to warm your hands with other's money. For that would take you straight to the pipal tree...." (20-21). This attitude of the Patel exasperates the policeman greatly and he goes straight to the Skeffington Coffee Estate Sahib and says, "Your Excellency, a house to live in?" (22). The contrast in his tone and mode of address to the Patel and the Sahib is very very obvious. The assertive tone with the Patel and a humble one with the white Sahib. A similar servile attitude is seen in the Skeffington Estate coolies who fall down to kiss the feet of the Sahib-'their Maharaja', and call themselves 'the lickers of his feet' (52).

Range Gowda, in the novel, comes out as a powerful, confident and authoritative person but his comic strain is also quite evident. Whenever mentally tickled his speech and gestures both reflect his amusement. He "chuckles and spits and munches on" (75). For Bade Khan, on the other hand Rao use words like 'spat', 'grumble', 'growl', 'thump', 'kick' etc.

Bhatta, who began life as a pontifical brahmin and was always ready and punctual for obsequious dinners where he ate greedily munching and belching, drinking water and then munching again gradually becomes a rich moneylender and a landowner. He becomes an important man and his voice is no longer a sparrow's voice. He becomes 'a learned Maharaja', 'a great father' to his debtors and also 'a lawyer' to the simple village folk. Under the influence of the Swami, his voice acquires a new authority and he expresses his dislike for Gandhi business and calls it 'Gandhi vagabondage' and says, "What is this Gandhi business? Nothing but weaving coarse hand-made cloth, not fit for a mop, and bellowing out bhajans and bhajans, and mixing with the pariahs" (33). He tries to prejudice Rangamma against Moorthy and his activities by saying, "Rangamma, you are a sister to me, and I am no butcher's son to hurt you. I know you are not a soul to believe in all this pariah business. But I only want to put you on your guard against Moorthy and these city boys" (35) and when he fails to convince Rangamma he threatens to have Moorthy "outcasted."

The Swami too would like to crush the pariah movement in its seed, before its cactus roots have spread far and wide. Their language conveys their fear, hypocrisy and greed. They are afraid that if this Gandhi business continues, caste discrimination will vanish and they will have no power, no hold over the common man, on whose simplicity and faith they prosper.

Waterfall Venkamma is a typical jealous, loudspoken, spiteful woman with a venomous tongue. She cannot bear anybody's happiness and prosperity and takes pleasure in mocking, hurting and insulting others. She says to Narsamma, Moorthy's mother that, "the next time I see him in the Brahmin Street, he will get a jolly fine marriage welcome with my broom-stick" (43). And to the daughters-in-law of the village, in a tone full of mockery, says "what do you know of the outside world, you kitchen queen?... You think the cock crows only because of you, young women." (44). Bhatta exploits her spiteful nature to set fire wherever he wants. The narrator describes her way of speaking with words like 'roared', 'howled', 'clapped her hands', 'mocked' and 'spat' and 'cried out'.

Moorthy, the noble cow, is gentle in his approach and uses religion and soft similes to convince and persuade the villagers to spin, to speak truth, to follow ahimsa and equality. To the women he says, "To wear cloth spun and woven with your own God-given hands is sacred..." (23). He mixes with the pariahs, educates and involves them in the struggle for independence and the pariahs feels so obliged that they call him 'learned one', 'our master', and 'our Gandhi' and feel sanctified by his presence and touch.

Moorthy returns from the prison with his confidence and strength doubly renewed. He prepares the villagers for action and says, "we are out for action. A cock does not make a morning, nor a single man a revolution but we will build a thousand pillared temple... and each one of you be ye pillars in it..." (123). He wants to involve everybody in the struggle for independence and therefore says, "Brothers, we are yoked to the same plough, and we shall have to press firm the plough-head and the earth will open out, and we shall sow the seeds of our hearts, and the crops will rise God-high." He then asks them to await the harvest with hearts "as clean as the threshing floor, strong as the pivot of the pressing mill..." (123-124). And thus he goes on converting villagers into Gandhi's 'soldier saints' (130).

It is Moorthy's second exposure to the prison and the city that changes his outlook and he who had blindly followed Gandhi up to now begins to question his teachings and decides to follow Nehru—the equal distributionist (183). In direct contrast is the experience of Rangamma whose faith in Gandhian ideology is strengthened. She who knew about many things through her newspapers was earlier unable to explain things and satisfy the curiosity of the villagers, is now filled with confidence and strength and effortlessly explains the complex vedantic texts, knitting together past and present legendary figures and the freedom struggle in her narration. She organises the women and forms a 'Sevika Sangha' and prepares the women to be strong physically and mentally. She says, "We shall fight the police for Kenchemma's sake and if the rapture of devotion is in you, the lathi will grow as soft as butter and as supple as a silken thread..." (172). And she becomes mother Rangamma to the villagers. It is to be noted that this is reflected in her use of the soft similes. It is men like the Patel, Bhatta, Bade Khan, the Skeffington Estate Sahib and maistri, who have power, who use coarse language laced with hard similes or words of abuse. Rao translates some of these expressions in English in the novel.

Even women and other villagers, who are with Moorthy, when angered, use abusive language. When Moorthy is stopped at the Skeffington Coffee Estate gates, there takes place a battle of oaths between them and the maistri, the butlers and Bade Khan— 'Son of concubine'—'Son of widow' 'I'll sleep with your wife'— 'you donkeys husband'—'you ass'—'You pig'—'you devil'—'you pariah-log' (65). The prison warders call Seetharamu 'Ass! Pig! Badmash!' (147); and later on when men are arrested the women feel like mad elephants and call the police—'monsters, butchers-dung-eating curs' (152), the villagers call the toddy booth owner Boranna, 'a life-drag and a nail-witch and a scorpion' (142).

Other linguistic features of the novel are a slight change in the syntactic structure with the inversion of the verb and the subject/noun in sentences like, 'Kanthapura... High on the Ghat is it... up the Malabar coast is it,...' (7); 'Kenchamma... Great and bounteous is she... never has she failed us in our grief' (8), 'And he can sing too, can Jayaramachar' (16); 'And there were other stories, he told us, Jayaramachar' (18) 'I tell you, he was not a bad man, was Bhatta' (32) 'Then he goes, Moorthy, to Pandit Venkateshia' (26) 'Him, they put into a morning bus,...' (91).

The use of plural pronouns 'we' and 'our' to depict the collective consciousness of the villagers; The use of personal pronouns for elements of nature like, "there is still many a good heart in this world, else the sun would not rise as he does nor the Himavathy flow by the Kenchamma Hill" (97); the farmers refer to earth after rains thus, 'why, she has gone four fingers deep' (115). The use of direct speech, colloquial words, the connective, the mixing of the tenses as the narrator shifts from one subject to another, the use of songs, bhajans, Harikathas—all help Rao to fuse the rapidity and interminability of the Indian thought and speech into the novel. Rao, also Indianises some words in the novel like 'younglings' (8), 'feedless', 'milkless', 'clothless' (18), 'vengefulness' (76) 'sobless' (91) 'clayey' (92), 'unmuddied' (95) 'seeable' (127), 'tongued' (134). He also uses some very unusual transferred epithets—'gaping sacks' (25), 'sobbing lantern', 'frothing milk-pot' (32), 'pungent tamarind', 'suffocating, chillies', 'lolling bells and muffled bells' (45), 'hanging mountains' (51), 'bellied boulders', 'dallying drains' (87) 'winkless night', 'wakeful night' (125), 'thunderless rain' (143). Raja Rao, also uses the Indian sense of time and says, 'Moorthy would come by the blue bus.... That will be when the sun has passed over the courtyard' (120) and other words, like 'dawn', 'dusk', 'Vaishakh', 'Kartik', 'Sravan', 'Ekadashi', 'Dasara' etc. to refer to time of the day, year and seasons.

Many Indian words are used without translation in the novel like patwari (9), paysana (10), sari (13), vidwan (15), palanuins and howdahs (15) annas, banya (24), charka (25), taluk (27) khir, dal (28) chutney (29), ghee, pheni (32), happalams (42) ragi, kumkum (45), prayaschitta (46); dhoti (56) mandap (67) panchayat (77), laddu (85), vakils (92) maidan bazaar (93) pandal (106) cummerbund (119), copra (135) etc.

Rao, also translates some Indian expressions into English in the novel for e.g. 'I shall squash you like a bug' (21), 'You had better tell those tales to white washed walls. Nobody who has eyes to see and ears to hear will believe in such a crow-and-sparrow story' (22), 'Our granary is empty as a mourning house' (25), 'I swear he would have done had not the stream run the way it did' (27), '... let our family creepers link each other' (29), 'You cannot put wooden tongues to men' (38), 'the youngest is always the holy bull' (39), 'what are you waiting for? Nobody's marriage procession is passing' (53), 'Tell me, does a boar stand before a lion or a jackal before an elephant?' (62), 'Our Moorthy is like Gold—the more you heat it, the purer it comes from the crucible' (99), 'When you strike a cow you will fall into the hell of hells and suffer a million and eight tortures and be born an ass' (99), 'The sinner may go to the ocean but the water will only touch the knees' (100), '... the sword can split asunder the body, but never the soul?' (111), 'Why, my right eye minks, we shall have a grand harvest' (115), 'ten heads make a herd and one head a cow' (126), 'you cannot straighten a man's heart' (140), 'Only a pariah looks at the teeth of dead cows (166), 'Our hearts are squeezed like a wet cloth' (175). Some of these expressions also point at the beliefs held by Indian people.

That the story of *Kanthapura* is narrated by a person who has no experience of the larger world is communicated by the narrator's frequent use of 'they say' and 'so they say', 'she told us' and 'he told us'. The story is being narrated to a live audience is further shown by Achakka's including her listener's into the narrative with 'If not, tell me sister Tell me, how could this happen, if it were not for Kenchamma and her battle?' The novel abounds in such rhetorical questions. And there are no technical words used by Achakka—planets are described as 'a great tube with a chink, to which you put your eyes and see another world with sun and moon and stars, all bright and floating in the diamond dust of God'; Aeroplanes are described as 'air vehicles that move, that veritably move in the air, and how men sit in them and go from town to town'; radio is 'the speech that goes across the air... you could sit here and listen to what they are saying in london and Bombay and Burma (35-36). The narrator's tone full of wonder and disbelief is easily felt in these exclamatory descriptions.

There are many aspects of Raja Rao's style and language that can still be elaborated upon but I will sum up by saying that Raja Rao's use of language in the novel is unique and original which comes by his use of regional expressions. It is clear that he uses English creatively to convey the Indian sensibility and succeeds to adjust it to the Indian emotional make up. It would not be wrong to say that he concretises the experience of an Indian village in the novel. I conclude with M.K. Naik's words, "in Raja Rao's hands the language has shaken off all trace of foreign acquisition and begun, to assert its inalienable rights as an independent idiom and calls *Kanthapura* a fine example of the genuine Indo-Anglian novel with its sensibility, its form and its style—all rooted firmly in the soil and drawing sustenance from it" (quoted by Bhattacharya 279).

Notes

1. K.R. Srinivasa Iyengar, in his book *Indian Writing in English* (1962) succinctly comments on the theme, manner and expression of Rao in *Kanthapura*. In *Indo-English Literature-A Collection of Critical Essays on Indian Creative Writers* in English edited by K.K. Sharma (1977), Harish Raizada assays to evaluate the progress of Rao from *Kanthapura to The Serpent and the Rope* in his essay "Literature as 'Sadhna'" and Atma Ram Sharma comments on the "Peasant Sensibility in *Kanthapura*". Again in *Perspectives on Raja Rao* edited by K.K. Sharma, in the *Indo-English Writers Series*-2, 1980. D.S. Maini writes on "Raja Rao's vision, values and Aesthetic", Suresh Nath on "Gandhi and Raja Rao": J.B. Alphonso-Karkala on "Myth, Matrix and Meaning in Literature and in Raja Rao's Novel, *Kanthapura*"; Ramesh Srivastava on "Structure and Theme in Raja Rao's Fiction"; Harish Raizada on "Point of View, Myth and Symbolism in Raja Rao's Novels"; Atma Ram Sharma on "Raja Rao's Prose-Style"; and N.C. Soni on "The Achievement of Raja Rao". P.C. Bhattacharya in *Indo-Anglian Literature, and the Works of Raja Rao*, 1983, presents an interesting account of *Kanthapura*, touching upon all aspects of the novel. Cecil Nelson in his essay "Syntactic creativity and Intelligibility published in *The Journal of Indian Writing in English*, July 1984, gives a linguistic analysis of *Kanthapura*, focusing on "the interaction of the English mono-lingual reader with a bilingual bicultural text" (v). Prem Prakash in his essay "Stylistics in Raja Rao's *Kanthapura*-An Indian Response" published in *Indian Writings in English* Vol. 1 (1996) edited by Manmohan K. Bhatnagar, uses the literary theories and principles of the Upanishads and the Vedantic system to explain "how the English vocabulary in the novel achieves an Indian ontology enabling Raja Rao to forge an idiom where the transtemporality of works become uniquely

his own" (9), and in a recent publication, *Gandhism and Indian English Fiction*, 1997, Dr. V.T. Patil and Dr. (Smt.) H.V. Patil study how Gandhi provided a frame of reference to novelists like Mulk Raj Anand, Raja Rao and R.K. Narayan for their novels.

2. Achebe also voices similar sentiments on experimentation in the English language when he says, "I feel that the English language will be able to carry the weight of my African experience. But it will have to be a new English, still in full communion with its ancestral home but altered to suit its new African surroundings." (quoted by Dasenbrock 59).

References

Abrams, M.H. *A Glossary of Literary Terms*. 3rd ed. Madras: Macmillan, 1978.

Amanuddin, Syed. "Style is the Thing". *The Journal of Indian Writing in English* 12.2, July 1984: 105.

Belliappa, K.C. "The Question of Form in Raja Rao's *The Serpent and the Rope*." *Journal of Commonwealth Literature* xxvi-1 1991, 158.

Bhattacharya, P.C. *Indo-Anglian Literature and the Works of Raja Rao*. Delhi: Atma Ram & Sons, 1983.

—. "Book Sense" *The Times of India*. 2 Jan. 1999,12.

Dasenbrock, R.W. "The Politics of Stylistic Experimentation—A Commonwealth Perspective." *The Journal of Indian Writing in English* 12-2. July, 1984.

Iyengar, K.R. Srinivasa. *Indian Writing in English*. Bombay: Asia Publishing House, 1962.

Jain, Jasbir. *Problems of Postcolonial Literatures and Other Essays*. Jaipur: Printwell, 1991.

Jussawalla, Feroza. "Beyond Indianness: The Stylistic Concerns of *Midnight's Children*." *The Journal of Indian Writing in English* 12.2. July 1984: 31.

Larson, Charles R. *The Novel in the Third World*. Washington, D.C.: Inscape Publishers, 1976.

Maini, D.S. "Raja Rao's Vision, Values and Aesthetic". *Perspectives on Raja Rao*. Ed. K.K. Sharma. Ghaziabad: Vimal Prakashan, 1980.

Nath, Suresh. "Gandhi and Raja Rao". *Perspectives on Raja Rao*. Ed. K.K. Sharma. Ghaziabad: Vimal Prakashan, 1980.

Nelson, Cecil. "Syntactic Creativity and Intelligibility". *The Journal of Indian Writing in English* 12-2 July 1984.

Rao, Raja. "India's Search for Self Expression", *The Times Literary Supplement*, August 10, 1962.

—. *Kanthapura* (1938). New Delhi: Orient Paperbacks, 1970.

—. "Interview with Ranavir Rangra". *Indian Literature*. New Delhi: Sahitya Akademi, xxxi 4, 1988.

Turner, G.W. *Stylistics*. Harmondsworth: Penguin, 1974.

11

Judith Wright's Treatment of Love

Pradeep Trikha

The poems in *Woman to Man*[1], as is obvious from the title, are about man-woman relationships. They are about Judith Wright's attitude to love. The important thing to pinpoint at the outset is that to the poet love covers 'myriads' of meanings and functions. Her concept of love is not traditional, or to use a hackneyed word Romantic[2], at least in the broad sense. But in her poems, we find, that love is a power which has underlying psychological, physical, psychic, metaphysical and spiritual significance. Not using too much embellishment in her love poems, she employs sexual and natural imagery to give a heightened effect of these various aspects of love imbibed in her poems. Noteworthy is the point that when we talk of different levels of love and their significance in her works, we need not go pin-pointing and jotting down that such and such a poem reveals physical love or spiritual love and so on, but in more than one instance, a single poem is found to embody all the different levels, varieties, and aspects of love.

Consider the poem "Woman to Man" (1). This poem reflects a

dramatised situation. One finds at the surface level love projected in its most primitive form: sex. The primordial image of "the eyeless labourer" who bears responsibility for the "selfless shapeless seed" the beloved holds, is the lover-husband who with his beloved performs the sexual act for the birth of the "third who lay in their embrace", and as for last stanza, it is in itself an illustration of the rhythmic motion of the sexual act:

> This is the maker and the make,
> This is the question and reply
> the blind head butting at the dark,
> the blaze of light along the blade
> Oh hold me, for I'm afraid. (1)

This stanza has been cited at length to illustrate that love in the entire poem at the surface level is seen in its sexual aspect. The "blind head butting at the dark" is symbolic of the phallus. It stands for the child too. The tone of the poet is one of realised appetency in the sexual act, and to put it in bare terms: it calls for both man and woman to be united for the emergence of the child. Judith Wright celebrates fulfilled love. But love to her is not a mere physical compulsion. It has metaphysical overtones. She considers love as a force leading to gestation and thence to resurrection. In the poem, for instance the "selfless, shameless seed" stands for chaos and the child symbolise the primal triumph of creativity over chaos. Every sexual union celebrates such a triumph. Love is raised to a higher pitch, it ensures the continuity of life, though it might be achieved through sex. It counters both time and death beneath whose sickle everything in this world suffers annihilation. But love with its power of creativity overwhelms temporality and speeds continuity.

If we delve a little deeper, then, perhaps, our understanding of her concept of love is enriched. For Judith Wright, love is not merely the physical force behind creation, not only the symbol of creativity and rejuvenation, it is also spiritual, impregnated with a Platonic nuance. The poet feels that the abiding relationship between men and women, amongst mankind in general is achieved through love which cements human beings together. No doubt "pain and darkness must claim" ("Woman's Song"), everybody but the permeation of love sustains mankind. Father, mother and child together constitute the trinity of love; this primal love diffuses itself in great variety fighting decay and speeding rebirth.

The last stanza which says:

> We are the white grave-worms of the grave.
> We are the eyeless beginning of the world.
> Oh, blind kind flesh, we the drinking seed
> that aches and swells towards its flower of love. (33)

illustrates how the lovers through their creative power transmute death into life. Love has to pass through pain to produce that flower—the child which defies time.

The point which absorbs the reader is that 'love' which is seen operating through nature and mankind not only acts as a binding force but transforms and extols the Woman involved in the act of love. Love raises the Woman to the stature of a Creator, the Mother Earth, the Mother who says:

> I am the earth, I am the root
> I am the stem that fed the fruit
> I link that joins you to the night. (2)

Perceptibly enough beneath the creator-figure of the Mother, the abiding relationship between the child and its mother lasts for long; it is she who gives both death and birth to a child. That is she fights death through her love and triumphs with a child. In this light, love is seen as an integrative power linking man to nature, death and rebirth.

The poet's attitude to love is positive and life-affirming. But as Shirley Walker points out, "the poet is equally clear about the misuse of sex" (Walker 38) denial of the creative power. A poem like "The Unborn" sets out to illustrate the adverse effect on the mother, and a sense of loss associated with the child which had been aborted. If love and life are denied, vitality is destroyed and sterility reigns. Perverted love leads nowhere, succumbs to death and time. It fails to conquer time as the life-affirming power as love does. The "Metho-Drinker" is one such instance in which the person has chosen love which is consuming and

> melts away the flesh that hides the bone
> to eat the nerve that tethers in time.

"Typists in a Phoenix Building" carries with it the same theme but more intensified and trenchant. The world she depicts in the absence of love and sexuality is shallow and impotent, regeneration and creativity merely relegated to nihilism. Some critics consider this poem representative of anti-sexuality, defining its meaning in terms of aridity and shallowness. While female frigidity is expressed in the phrase "immaculate and dumb", male sexuality is connoted in the "train". The society portrayed is sexless and has crushed human sexuality and love. The poem undoubtedly has kinship with Eliot's *The Waste Land*. Particularly this passage when compared to some in Eliot's poem which reflect the same idea, is more effective, more impersonal than them.

> The train goes aching on its rails.
> Its rising cry of steel and wheels
> Intolerably comes and fails
> on walls immaculate and dumb.

The failure of male sexuality and the female frigidity are pictured symbolically in these lines.[3]

In Eliot's *The Waste Land* the section, "The Fire Sermon" ferrets out lust and hatred in the affairs of man and woman, as shown through the typist and the clerk. There is a sense of indifference and impassivity. There is neither aversion nor gratification and this absence of emotions is a measure of the infecundity of the age:

> Flushed and decided, he assaults at once
> exploring hands encounter no defence.
> His vanity requires no response
> and makes a welcome of indifference.
>
> ("The Fire Sermon")

The mechanical movements of the typist and the clerk are the measure of the sterility of the age. Davidson feels, "*The Waste Land* strongly reveals the unruly forces of improper desire in its emotional yearning, in its constant return to sexual tragedy, and in its disorienting juxtapositions and displacement" (Davidson 124). Like Eliot, Wright speculates on the sterile existence of humanity in the contemporary mechanised environment. The sexual experience in which the typist is seeking "shelter" proves fruitless and desolate. The poem concludes on a melancholic note describing the Australian landscape, and leaves behind a sense of despondency. The imagery is very suggestive that is to say that life giving forces like fire or water are not able to retrieve. It ends on a note of vacuity:

> no fires
> consume the banked comptometers;
> no flood has lipped the inlaid floors
>
> ("Typists in the Phoenix Building")

Wright's vocabulary in this poem does not allow us to delve deep into the human emotions. The words are borrowed from the machine world and the tall buildings are suggestive of enclosed human sensitivity, resulting in an impotent waste of human seed. Eliot's poem in contrast has some 'unruliness' about its language.

In some of her poems she treats sexual love not merely at physical level but sublimates it to depict it as a force that is a part of reality, which creates as well as destroys. The intimacy of love and creativity to the fertile world is a point which she often emphasises in detail, showing the integration of child to nature, the collation and identification of life and death to the regenerative patterns in nature. Thus love is a force that unifies all beings and underlies the unity of mankind. To discuss this at 'psychic' level love is associated with the psychic imagination—the initial conception of a poem, its flowering out.

A changing attitude to love is discernible in some of her poems. As earlier pointed out she believed love to be a counter force to death and time. Of course, in some of her later poems, she does not refute the transience and ambivalence of love. This ephemerality and ambivalence is clearly indicated in "The Blind Man: II Country Dance".

Faced with this strange disease of modern life, with imminent longevity and enveloping aridity, the only resort is love; the only panacea is love for all pain. "The Cycads" illustrates this observation. Consider "The Company of Lovers" in which love is not a mere Protector, but a moment of unison. The fierce exhilaration that love produces is a counter to the "dark preludes of the drums" and achieves a timelessness that breaks the "cordons that death draws in", with the promise of rebirth. The idea pervasive is that love may be transient but to live life to its full brim and rhythm is an affirmation of love itself.

Judith Wright treats love as a great humanising force "working through the unconscious levels of the psyche to release the individual from the imprisoning demands and inhibitions of the ego and to integrate him into mainstream of humanity and creativity" (Walker 114). Love is moreover seen as an emancipatory power. It allays fear, it fights against the dark forces of the world and releases our unconscious imbued with "ancient terrors". Love gives "the very life by which we live/the power of answer love with love". Love is simple, easy, natural:

> Nothing is so hard as love—
> love for which the wisest weep
> yet the child who never looked
> found it easily as his sleep
> Nothing is as strange as love—
> love is like a foreign land.
> Yet its natives find their way
> Natural as hand-in-hand
>
> ("The Man Beneath the Tree")

Love while banishing fear, triggers off the visionary power of the poet, it informs the psyche. This is illustrated in "The Maker":

> ...love who cancels fear
> with his fixed will,
> burned my vision clear
> and bid my vision still.
>
> (*Collected Poems*: 1942-1970)

An examination of Judith Wright's attitude to love is quite illuminating. For Wright love operates at three different levels: as a physical compulsion instrumental to the propagation of mankind; as a vitalistic force animating the entire natural world; as a spiritual force fighting evil, hatred and fear. In her poems as such, love is primarily a unifying power, reconciling individuals with one another, integrating the individuals into cycles of the natural world and guaranteeing the unity and continuity of all aspects of being, for all the manifestations of the primal creative force of life itself (Walker 32). She surveys love as a great humanising force, concluding that "all men are one man at last" ("Nigger's Leap"). Herein lies the difference between a poet like Sylvia Plath and Judith Wright—the one negating life and love and expressing a sense of self defeat; the other upholding and positively affirming life and love.

Notes

1. Judith Wright, *Woman to Man*, (Sydney: Angus & Robertson, 1949). All verse citations in this paper refer to this edition and the relevant page numbers are given in brackets within the text itself. Verse citation from other collections are separately cited.
2. This is not to deny any influence of Romanticism. In some of her poems the lament of the loss and destruction of Nature and Love is distinctly Romantic.
3. T.S. Eliot's *The Waste Land* has some passages that echo the same idea, but they are usually bare and ironical; Judith Wright's passage is powerfully symbolic and in fewer lines says as much.

References

Davidson, Harriet. "Improper Desire: Reading *The Waste Land*", *The Cambridge Companion to T.S. Eliot*. Ed. David Moddy. Cambridge University Press, 1994.

Walker, Shirley. *The Poetry of Judith Wright*. London: Arnold, 1980.

Wright, Judith. *Collected Poems: 1942-1970*. Sydney: Angus and Robertson, 1971.

—. *Woman to Man*. Sydney: Angus and Robertson, 1949.

12

Race-retrieval in Chinua Achebe's *Things Fall Apart*

Amina Amin

The text of Chinua Achebe's *Things Fall Apart* becomes a site for what Abdul JanMohammed terms "a Manichaean code of binary oppositions" such as white/black, civilisation/savagery, rationality/sensuality, modern/traditional, individual/community (Jan Mohammed 62). What is remarkable is the way Achebe accommodates these binary oppositions and holds them in artistic balance. Achebe does it both thematically and technically.

At the thematic level, Achebe explores meticulously and faithfully the cultural and social patterns of the Igbo society as also its primordial qualities. He devotes more than half the text to portray this society with all its myths, legends, beliefs, customs, superstitions and taboos which are deeply rooted in the consciousness of the people. It is as if he has taken upon himself the moral role of a 'teacher' or an 'interpreter' to retrieve his race, to recover what has been repressed and denigrated by dominant forms of cultural productions and coloured by Eurocentric biases. It is as if he wants to bring back an entire society into the folds of history.

As Wole Soyinka observes, the situation in most African countries needs a double retrieval "first from the colonial deniers of their past but also from the black neo-colonial deniers of their immediate past and present" (Soyinka 1990: 114). In *Things Fall Apart* Achebe is primarily engaged with retrieving the history of his race from the imperial deniers of his past. In this respect, he seems to have conceived his role as one of addressing in his fiction the social, political and religious concerns of Africans. Achebe's muse has been the Igbo of Southeastern Nigeria and his ambition has been the "celebration of our own world . . . the singing of the song of ourselves, in the din of an insistent world and song of others" (*Current Biography Year Book* 1992). As he has himself admitted *Things Fall Apart* was written partly in response to inaccurate depictions of Africa and Africans, particularly by British writers. In his successive works Achebe examines the consequences of the black neo-colonial denial of his country's immediate past and present.

Things Fall Apart, like any other novel of colonial consciousness in its early stages, can be termed a 'resistance' novel. Without being overtly political, it draws attention to the cultural imperialism of the white men and portrays how a community falls apart because of the collision that occurs when Christian English Missionaries arrive among the Igbos of Nigeria. Tribal society though it is, it has been bound by centuries-old laws of right and wrong, good and evil. Therefore it has not been one night of savagery from which the European, acting on God's behalf "delivered his people" (Achebe 1975: 44-45), as it has been made out to be.

Depending for their subsistence on land, the African people have lived closely and in harmony with nature. As Achebe shows, they respect the seasonal changes with an almost religious fervour, preparing themselves for the best and the worst. These seasonal changes and the myths and beliefs associated with them compel them to perform certain rites and rituals which shape their consciousness and their daily lives. Again, they have their own social system and cultural practices which are closely bound by their beliefs and superstitions. They even have their own judicial system; a village council to settle disputes and punish offenders. The daily lives of these people are governed by the belief in gods and goddesses whose "omnipotence" they dare not challenge lest they incur their wrath. Ancestral worship as also respect for old people are as deeply ingrained in their psyche as the need for the worship of the deities. The novel's appeal lies primarily in Achebe's portrayal of the communal life of the Igbos. Where the claims of an individual clash with those of the community, the individual must gladly forfeit his claim. Indeed as Achebe shows very clearly, the individualism of an Okonkwo has no place in the strongly bonded kinship of the Igbos. If the community falls apart with the advent of the European missionaries and bureaucrats, it is also ruined because of the tragic intransigence of the Okonkwos. To be sure Achebe also points out the weaknesses of these people: the ruthless laws of a tribal society, its treatment of women and children and the custom of discarding new-born twins etc. are deftly woven into the fabric of the text to lend them the legitimacy of a tribal way of life. The central character of the novel, Okonkwo, is a kind of an African Everyman, a staunch champion of the Igbo tradition. In his tragic fall we witness the disintegration and fall of an ancient society. Okonkwo is a hero, an exceptionally brave man in every sense. So great is his prowess even as a young man that he has won battles and has had five heads severed. "He was well-known throughout the nine villages and even beyond. As a young man of eighteen he had brought honour to his village by throwing Amalinze, the Cat" (Achebe 1987:3). He is a man of titles, has large acres of land and can afford to have many wives. In short, he has become a living myth. It is through his life from birth to his tragic suicide that Achebe portrays the intricacies of the Igbo culture. However, Achebe refuses to romanticise Okonkwo's achievements, for he shows how strength and bravery of the kind the Okonkwos have, if honoured to the exclusion of open mindedness and flexibility, lead to disaster. It is not merely the tragic flaw in his character but also his obsessive hatred of the white men who he fears will tear his own culture apart, that brings his tragic end.

The texts produced in the colonies during the early years of Imperialism were in the language of the colonisers. These texts were written by people whose identification with the colonisers was near total. Hence such texts could hardly credibly reflect an indigenous culture. Even when they began to be written by the English-educated upper classes like in India, they were written under 'Imperial licence', in the language of the dominant culture. It was only when the restraining influence of the imperial discourse was set aside and new usages were evolved and appropriated that the texts acquired the flavour of the regional culture. Needless to say that postcolonial literatures developed through several stages corresponding with the stages in the development of both the national and regional consciousness of a people as also the abrogation of the imperial canonical centre.

One of the important factors that made imperial domination over the colonies possible was the control over language. It was through the language of the rulers that concepts of 'truth', 'reality', 'universality' etc. were established as the only valid ones. And such concepts dominated the minds of the people even after the political domination of the rulers ended. Where literary activity was concerned, the cultural hegemony of the rulers continued even after the colonies gained independence. It was only after an effective and confident postcolonial voice began to be heard that such domination began to be weakened. It is out of "the political tension between the idea of a normative code and a variety of regional usages that some of the most exciting and innovative literatures of modern times have emerged" (Ashcroft 1989:8). And it is in the way Achebe handles such a tension that the greatness of *Things Fall Apart* lies.

A major feature of the novel is Achebe's concern with the crisis of identity a particular community experiences because its culture is being gradually and systematically denigrated and a "supposedly superior" cultural model imposed. Again, although the community that Achebe portrays has not undergone an actual "geographical displacement" or was not entirely subjugated, it is likely to experience a sense of linguistic alienation, because through its educational system, the Empire has sought to impose on the colonised an alien language which is incapable of bearing the burden of their experiences. Hence the need for writers like Achebe to transform the language of the masters and mould it in such a way that it becomes an apt vehicle for expressing the geographical or physical conditions of their land as also their sociocultural practices.

D.E.S. Maxwell identified two groups of colonies while offering his model of examining literatures of postcolonial societies—"settler" and "invaded". In societies like India and Nigeria which according to him were colonised on their own territories, writers were not compelled to adapt to a different landscape as it happened with "settler" colonies like Australia, New Zealand, Canada and the United States. In case of the "invaded" colonies, people had responded to their landscape since ancient times in their own indigenous languages. They had their own "sophisticated" responses to it which eventually got marginalised because of the imposition of a different world view expressed through an alien language (Maxwell 1965: 82-83). But whether "English" was used to express the experiences of an alien environment or whether it was used to describe a people's social and cultural inheritance, there was an "intolerable wrestle with words and meanings" and the compulsion "to subdue the experience to the language, the exotic life to the imported tongue" (Maxwell 1965: 82-83). Although Maxwell's model is not entirely acceptable to critics of postcolonial literatures, the fact remains that the dominant imperial language and culture were privileged over the people's. Literatures written in "english" (Ashcroft 1989: 8) were considered to be off-shoots of "English" literature and therefore marginalised.

However, it would be interesting to examine how Achebe evolves a counter-discourse through innovation and experimentation, using fictional techniques to portray his culture in the best possible manner. Though story-telling has been part of African culture from times immemorial, Achebe uses an "alien" genre i.e. the "novel" to narrate the story òf Okonkwo's life. Asked whether his work has been translated into Igbo, Achebe said he hoped to translate *Things Fall Apart* into Igbo some day. But being bilingual, the "novel form" seemed to go with the English language. Again, Achebe's use of the English language for his artistic purpose must have been a kind of political engagement which as

JanMohammed says was "co-terminus with formal experimentation". The "political orientation" and "experimental formulations" of *Things Fall Apart* seem to have been deliberately designed to counteract Western/European hegemonic domination. It is as if Achebe is challenging the European master narrative and offering an alternative both in terms of the metaphysical system of his culture as also the narrative strategies he has employed to represent the multicentredness of human life. Helen Tiffin puts it succinctly:

> In *Things Fall Apart* Western historicising is kept at bay while the complexity and communal destiny of culture through proverbs, seasonality, festivals, rituals, multitheism and power-balancing and power-sharing are established. Simultaneously this serves in each of its facets, to comment on a British system of theological exclusivity, ethnocentrism and hierarchical structuration. (Tiffin 62)

Things Fall Apart is a rich source of the Igbo customs, beliefs, myths, legends, rites and proverbs. These elements are used both explicitly and implicitly in the form and structure of the novel to show how they shape the life and consciousness of the people. The novel gets its life and source from the oral tradition of Africa. It is a fine example of the art of story-telling and Achebe proves to be a great folk tale teller. The way he makes use of the native proverbs in English shows how he exploit native elements of speech to give authenticity to the language he employs. The short crisp sentences he uses to narrate amusing stories within stories, typical of his people's cultural consciousness, lend an authenticity to his language and give to the novel a regional flavour. The seemingly loose structure of the novel acquires a tautness because of the precision Achebe brings to his language, a language that easily slips from 'English' to 'english'.

References

Achebe, Chinua. *Things Fall Apart*. New Delhi: Arnold Publishers, 1987.

—. *Morning Yet on Creation Day*. London: Heinemann Education Books, 1975.

Ashcroft, Bill, Gareth Griffiths, and Helen Tiffin. *The Empire Writes Back*. London: Routledge, 1989.

Current Biography Year Book. 1992.

JanMohammed, Abdul. "The Economy of Manichaean Allegory: The Function of Racial Difference in Colonial Literature". *Critical Inquiry* 12, Autumn, 1985.

Maxwell, D.E.S. "Landscape and Theme". *Press*, 1965.

Soyinka, Wole. "Twice Bitten: The Fate of Africa's Culture Procedures". *PMLA*, 105, January, 1990.

Tiffin, Helen. "Post-Colonialism, Post-Modernism and the Rehabilitation of Post-Colonial History". *Journal of Commonwealth Literature*, 22, 1988.

13

Proverbial Resistance to Authority: Chinua Achebe's *Things Fall Apart*

Supriya Agarwal

Language has a dual character, it is both a means of communication and a carrier of culture. For it was speech which came first, with the written form following in due course. For example in Nigeria, the oral culture was predominant and the written was introduced only with the advent of colonialism. Thus, while writing, the African novelist uses language as a technique for cultural inferences which were orally transmitted through generations. Language is used in their writing to create a texture and tone which in itself defines certain themes and meaning. Though much of colonial writing is written in English but what marks the work of Afro-Asian writers, is their conscientious use of the English language in depiction of the society to which they belong. Their fiction is governed by the habits, customs, norms and manner of their own group or community and so their speech is steeped in a perceptible quaintness. Commenting on the use of language as a technique, Mark Schorer in his essay "Technique as Discovery", remarks:

For technique is the means by which the writer's experience, which is his subject matter, compels him to attend to it; technique is the only means he has of discovering, exploring, developing his subjects, to conveying its meaning and, finally, of evaluating it. And surely it follows that certain techniques are sharper tools than others, and will discover more, that the writer capable of the most exacting scrutiny of his subject matter will produce works with the most satisfying content, works with thickness and resonance, works which reverberate, works with maximum meaning.(387)

Achebe in *Things Fall Apart*, appropriates the English language for the purpose of expressing his native culture and for a non-African reader his novel becomes an induction into it. Through conscious manipulation he has successfully conveyed the larger meanings, thus succeeding in universalising the particular. He has focused on those little remnants like myths, rituals and proverbs so as to translate and transfer the cultural perceptions. The novel is set in tribal society and the narrative itself is studded with proverbs and similes which help to evoke the cultural milieu in which the action takes place. Achebe selects the type of imagery appropriate to the time, place and people he is trying to picture and it is his sensitive use of appropriate language that lends an air of historical authenticity to his novel. As when the author talks about the personal god or Chi in the novel, he says "The Ibo people have a proverb that when a man says yes his Chi says yes also. Okonkwo said yes very strongly: so his Chi agreed. And not only his Chi but his clan too"(29). A sentence like this opens a complete world of native beliefs and moral for the reader to understand and appreciate. The novel is a faithful record of the transitional and turbulent period of African history, whose cultural identity with the advent of Christianity and colonialism came under direct attack till things in the culture fall apart. This book thus, has immense sociological and historical importance, for it explores the basic cultural patterns and social past of Nigeria. One notices that the book opens with the Arcadian atmosphere that exhibits the essential qualities of a primitive society which is bound by laws of nature, good and evil, totems and taboos, beliefs and superstitions, myths and legends, rites and religion, customs and observances punctuated by folk speech, proverbs, songs, anecdotes etc. And each of these has a meaningful function in the total structural pattern of the novel because each tends to serve as a technique when examined from the context of the culture. Also collectively they are the metaphors of a culture.

More than folk tales and myths, the central or core part of the oral literature in most African societies is embodied in proverbs which are drawn from experience and from observing the behaviour of human begins: their feelings, emotions, thought process, habits, beliefs, values, the prevalent folk stories and the surrounding world of plants, animals and natural happenings. Their attributive quality is the aptness with which they convey the meaning effectively in a very concise and pointed manner, symbolically bringing home that which has to be said. Thus, the proverb is an important part of the expressive mechanism of the African speech and this has been amply expressed by Achebe in his work. The theme and climatic development of the plot, the portrayal of the central character, especially in close proximity with the stage of the novel's growth are subtly indicated by the proverbs.

In the novel Achebe says "Among the Ibo, the art of conversation is regarded very highly and proverbs are the palm oil with which words are eaten" (6). Each proverb is richly connotative, compressing wealth of associations into a pithy phrase. By the use of proverbs, a speaker is looked upon, as the owner of traditional values and wisdom locked in them. Thus proverbs constitute one of the most potent factors for individual conformity and cultural continuity and in *Things Fall Apart* they succeed in translating Ibo thoughts and words into English, adding an extra dimension to the novel. While reviewing the novel in 1959, for its vernacular expression Ben Obumselu in his review said:

> The African writer is not merely to use but to expand the resources of English and also that the verbal peculiarities of *Things Fall Apart* suggest that Chinua Achebe has reflected much on this problem. His solution is to attempt literal fidelity to translate where ever possible the actual words which might have been used

in his own language and thereby preserve the native flavour of his situations. (43)

An Ibo proverb as Achebe uses it, besides giving a local color lightens up a situation and gives it a significance which otherwise could be missed. As we see in the novel, the proverb "If a child washed his hands he could eat with kings"(7), indicates the character of Okonkwo, whose fame rises to be a man of title and one of the lords of the clan. The phrase gives an insight to the reader, of the native tradition that age was respected among his people but achievement was revered. Not by birth but by merit of one's personal qualities and gains, respect could be earned in society. Thus proverbs are used both to give information and to express the motives and thoughts of characters. When an old man says about Okonkwo "Looking at a King's mouth, one would think he never sucked at his mother's breast" (65), the whole ethnic framework is brought to life. A lot of critics have noticed and commented on the use of proverbs. Bernth Lindfors in his work *Folklore in Nigerian Literature* remarks, "the function of proverbs in Achebe's novels is to reiterate themes, sharpen characterisation, clarify conflict and define values"(6). Palmer refers to them as vivid "illustrate analogies" (62). They are used as imagery is used in the novel and tend to rein force and hold together the various strands of theme handled by the author.

Proverbs are woven into speech and dialogue, which far from detracting the flow of the narrative or making for climaxes in structure, make it integral. Each proverb has a story behind it and this is the triumph of Achebe's art. He knows how to achieve big effects economically by fastening on what is most significant and setting it in a context which gives it a wider application. The proverb, "A toad does not run in the daytime for nothing"(19) and "whenever you see a toad jumping in broad daylight then know that something is after its life" (178), basically express one and the same idea that whenever there is something unusual in the movement or decision of people then, it is enough to suggest that there is some obvious reason. The former is directed at a person called Obiako, a palm wine tapper by profession, who abandons the trade so suddenly that it arouses public speculation and the reason is not far to seek. The man gives up the trade following the prediction of the Oracle, that he will fall off a palm tree and die. The second time the proverb appears at the end of the novel, then it refers to the fall of the traditional culture of Umuofia in face of the advent of the white man's religion and cruel laws. Achebe poignantly expresses the prevailing fear and uncertainty of Umuofia with the help of animal imagery. "Umuofia was like a startled animal with ear's erect, sniffing the silent ominous air and not knowing which way to run"(173). The toad in the proverb is a symbol of the terror-stricken natives of Nigeria and the pursuer is the white colonial aggressor.

Each of these proverbs carry on the theme of the novel and strengthen the structure. The proverbs themselves became a hall mark of *Things Fall Apart*, as the setting, characterisation and the very structure of the novel are coherently cemented within the repository elements of the given culture. Commenting on the technique and usage of proverbs, Donatus Nwoga says:

> The Ibo proverbs can be relevant in two ways, depending on the context—the illuminative and the corrective. In Achebe's novels both types of uses are found. Corrective use refers to that which is not direct, is oblique in its usage, designed to produce an understanding or reaction in the person concerned, without directly involving the speaker. The illuminative use on the other hand, directly reinforces ideas by recalling traditional wisdom to support a given statement and is mainly to be found in formal address, oratory, discussion etc. (*Language and Culture* 198)

The novel depicts various cultural tensions and conflicts arising out of a clash between tradition and modernity, the real and the occult and so on. But it is the conflict between the individual and the society and the way in which it is resolved that seems to lend a typical flavour to the novel. In the end, it is the society, the larger entity which emerges triumphant as against the individual who dissociates or delinks himself from the society to assert his pride and individuality. Here the question is not so much about the right or wrong of the individual's convictions or credentials as about the necessity of the people to adhere to the society with its roots in a traditional faith. This fact is very subtly highlighted through appropriation of language by Achebe, thus opening a subtext for the reader to understand. For example in the Umuofian society laziness and poverty have no place and it is a subject of gossip for the ordinary folk. They heartily laugh when they talk about Obiako's father who died a poor man but demands ritual offers after death, through the Oracle. The son then questions the spirit, if he had left even a fowl or a goat when he died. Okonkwo's self pride is defeated when people crack this joke and he is reminded of his own-weak, idle, poor, contemptible father. And he is apparently reduced to an old woman, as the saying goes, "an old woman is always uneasy when dry bones are mentioned in a proverb" (19). This proverbial expression has a derisive effect on Okonkwo who strives hard to outdo his father, in all respects.

Okonkwo is a self-willed, self-made man with firm determination. This is illustrated thus: "The lizard that jumped from the high iroko tree to the ground said he would praise himself if no one else did" (22). The same proverb is used towards the end of the novel but to get a different effect. When the question of salvaging the Umuofian culture becomes the sole concern of the people, they are to be on the alert like eneke to make the final assault on the white man, his religion and his government. The rural idiom used in *Things Fall Apart* not only conveys a great deal but also evokes authentic tribal culture and sensibility, rural expressions and analogies. Expressions like "I shall give you twice four hundred yarns"(20), "the drought continued for eight market weeks" (22), "from cock-crow till the chickens went back to roost" (81), are some of the expressions which take the non-African reader by surprise and give an understanding of the ways in which time and space were measured in rural society. In the novel, one comes across a number of rural sayings which add to the inexhaustible source of cultural references. Thus the traditional and mythical framework in the lives of the tribal people of Umuofia has successfully moulded the narrative structure of the novel. Making use of the local dialect Achebe has presented not only the tragic irony of the hero, Okonkwo but also the rural world of religiosity, customs, superstitions, faiths, taboos and agrarian life. George Awoonor Williams, a critic, was quite enthusiastic about the use of such phrases by Achebe. He commented:

> I think Achebe's *Things Fall Apart* achieves this overall effect of freshness by the translation of Ibo thoughts and words into English. Proverbs are woven into speech and dialogue. Far from being a desecration of the English language, which seems to have come to stay, this transliteration of thoughts, concepts and images give the language a freshness and a new scope for which I am sure the native speakers of English will thank us. (44)

Achebe is painstakingly accurate and precise in recording the colonial penetration into the bush land. Despite their being absolute fidelity to historical truth, the colonial experience is presented from the perspective of the native residents—Igbos. The conscious and attentive reader is forced to ask the question " Is the use of proverbs in some way a protest against oppression and domination? Are they setting in motion the reactions against the European powers and voicing the native resistance?". This thought can further be substantiated when we reflect on what Chinua Achebe himself had to say on the role of the writer. In November 1969 during his visit to the University of Texas at Austin, Achebe when asked in an interview, "Do you believe literature should carry a social or political message?" His reply was:

> Yes, I believe it's impossible to write anything in Africa without some kind of commitment, some kind of message, some kind of protest. Even these early novels that look like very gentle recreations of the past - what they were saying, in effect, was that we had a past. That was protest, because there were people who thought we didn't have a past. What we were doing was to say politely, that we did - here it is. (Palaver 7)

Thus, the novel takes into account all the rooted nuances of class, custom and culture that differ inherently from the homogenised cosmopolitan defacing and focusing on those little remnants like myths, rituals and proverbs. Achebe has metaphorically made use of them as a resistance to authority.

References

Achebe, Chinua. *Things Fall Apart*. London: Windmill Series, 1989.

Lindfors, Bernth. *Folklore in Nigerian Literature*. New York: African Publishing Company, 1973.

Nwogo, Donatus. "Appraisal of Igbo Proverbs and Idioms". *Language and Culture*. Eds. F.C. Ogbalu and E.N. Emenanjo. London: O.U.P., 1975.

Obumselu, Ben. "*Things Fall Apart*: A Critical Review", *African Culture, African Critics*. Ed. Rand Bishop. New York: Green Wood Press, 1988.

Palaver. *Interviews with Five African Writers in Texas*. The University of Texas, 1972.

Schorer, Mark. "Technique as Discovery", *20th Century Literary Criticism: A Reader*. Ed. David Lodge. London: Longman, 1992.

Williams, George Awoonor. "African Literature, an Evaluation". *African Literature, African Critics*. Ed. Rand Bishop. New York: Greenwood Press, 1988.

14

Deconstruction of the Savage Myth in Chinua Achebe's *Things Fall Apart*

Veena Jain

> But the war goes on; and we will have to bind up for years to come the many, sometimes ineffaceable wounds that the colonist onslaught has inflicted on our people. (Fanon 201)

Fanon's words may seem a bit too harsh to a First World critic but the fact remains that the "wounds" have been inflicted and the postcolonial writer cannot help but write about these wounds. Though the word postcolonial has become controversial of late, the postcolonial writing is the healing process that takes the form of resistance writing: resistance against oppression, onslaught and dehumanisation of man. I use the word "Man" for the civilised West has justified its actions on the grounds of transforming brutes, subhuman creatures, Niggers and Blacks into man. As Fanon points out, " The native is declared insensible to the ethics; he represents not only the absence of values, but also the negation of values. He is let us dare to admit, the enemy of values and he is in this sense absolute evil" (32).

Chinua Achebe in *Things Fall Apart* (1958) deconstructs this very myth by proving that society and culture did exist however primitive, that "Man" did exist, but was converted into a brute by the aggression of the French on the Nigerian soil. The process of humanising the so called "animals" of Africa and bringing enlightenment to the world of Africans through the spread of Christianity, culture and science by the West, was one of violence. Peace was brought about by mass slaughter, splitting up of the native community, uprooting of traditions, religion, language and elimination of tribes in the name of education. Hence Achebe picturises a perfectly cohesive society with its values, traditions, customs and religious leanings; a humane society which exhibits feelings of love, hate, violence, worship, marriage, recreation and earning from the land. It is a society with a past that Nigerians need not be ashamed of and Europeans need to take cognisance of. In an address to the conference on Commonwealth Literature held at Leeds University in 1964, Achebe declared:

> I would be quite satisfied if my novels (especially the ones I set in the past) did no more than teach my readers that their past—with all its imperfections—was not one of a long night of savagery from which the first European acting on God's behalf delivered them. (Quoted by Phelps 331)

The choice of the title taken from Yeats's famous poem *The Second Coming* is not therefore without significance. When Yeats writes: "Things fall apart, the centre cannot hold mere anarchy is loosed upon the world", he foresees the end of Christian civilisation. Achebe predicts the end of the traditional African society. To stretch the parallel a little further, it would mean an affirmation of the African civilisation which resembled the utopian Byzantine world of arts and nature in its proximity to nature and Mother Earth. The Second Coming of Christ as a horror vision of the "rough beast" is ironically akin to the advent of the white missionaries and white administrators. They bring about the catastrophic end and disjunction of Umuofia and consequently of Okonkwo, the hero who stands for Africanness.

Things Fall Apart holds a special significance in colonial history, for it is history: the unravelling of reality seen through the eyes of the colonised and the sufferer. It is a representative novel, as Gilbert Phelps points out in his essay on "Two Nigerian Writers: Chinua Achebe and Wole Soyinka." It was realised, that *"Things Fall Apart* was in effect the archetypal African novel, in that the situation it describes—the falling of a traditional African rural society as a result of the coming of the white man, was a traumatic experience common to all the colonial or former colonial territories" (331).

The opening sentence of the novel plunges the reader straightaway into the heart of Umuofia with the introduction of Okonkwo and his wrestling skill, thereby marking the importance of the socio-cultural value system. His social achievements are summed up in the following words:

> He was a wealthy farmer, and had two barns full of yams, and had just married his third wife. To crown it all he had taken two titles and had shown incredible prowess in two inter-tribal wars. And so although Okonkwo was still young, he was already one of the greatest men of his time. (12)

Regarded as a man of action and highly esteemed for his physical strength and courage, Okonkwo is an antithesis to his father Unoka. Unoka is lazy, is perpetually in debt, loves music and hates the sight of blood. He is a man of gentle emotions and loves the "intricate rhythms of Ekwe and the Udu and Ogene." But the Ibo people have no place for such weaklings and social failures. Hence Okonkwo is afraid to reveal the finer emotions of sensitivity, love and feeling for fear of being considered a coward. His love for his daughter Ezinma and the hostage Ikemefuna is masked by a rough and rugged exterior. He is obsessed with the idea of preserving his manliness in reaction against his father's effeminacy.

Farming is the main occupation. Hence land occupies a central place in their life. Land is solid and it gives them dignity. Okonkwo's social status is determined by the land he owns. Before the harvest, Umuofia has its festive season; a thanksgiving to Ani—the earth goddess. It is the feast of the new yam—a kind of New Year celebration. Huts and walls are scrubbed with red earth, women paint themselves with camwood, draw beautiful patterns with uli on their body, shave their head in designs and wear beads on their waist. Yam foo foo and vegetable soup is in plenty and a wrestling match accompanied with the beating of drums marks the end of the festival. Palm wine and kolanut are offered to the guests as a sign of hospitality and honour. They drink the wine in drinking horns usually kept in goatskin bags. The partaking of wine entails an elaborate ceremony. Achebe, the skilled craftsman, leaves out nothing. He writes:

> The younger of his sons, who was also the youngest man in the group moved to the center, raised the pot on his left knee and began to pour out the wine. The first cup went to Okonkwo, who must taste his wine before anyone else. Then the group drank, beginning with the eldest man. When every one had drunk two or three horns, Nwakibie sent for his wives... Anasi was the first wife... She walked up to her husband and accepted the horn from him. She then went down on one knee, drank a little and handed back the horn. She rose, called him by his name and went back to her hut. The other wives drank in the same way, in their proper order, and went away. (23)

Such ceremonial details and more, and their fondness for proverbs, stories and folk tales add up to the picture of a society with a rich traditional and cultural heritage. Idioms, allusions and folklore point to a live oral tradition. Their socio-moral value system is self-sustaining.

The Oracle of the Hills and Caves is the final authority of justice on all social and political matters of the village. It represents their ancestral gods. Worshippers go to the Oracle with awe and reverence to know all about their future. Personal disputes are settled in public by the nine egwugwu, the judges. "It is communal self-criticism, and relaxed and in the last resort we all want the same things:... at that level we can say the community triumphs, and that it spreads its own light and reason" (Fanon 37).

Punishment follows transgression of laws. Okonkwo is punished though not severely for beating his wife during the week of peace. But he is exiled from his home! and for committing a "female crime" by inadvertently killing a clansman when his gun explodes during the burial rites of Ezeudu.

Umuofia has its strange and irrational ways. Cheilo when possessed with the spirit of Agbala acquires superhuman strength carrying Ekwefi's daughter Ezinma on her back round the nine villages to the Oracle of Hills. With Ezinma on her back she disappears through a hole hardly big enough to pass a hen, chanting-"Agbala do-o-o-o! Agbala ekeneo-o-! Chi negbu madu ubori ndu ya nato ya uto daluo-o-o!..."

Similarly Ikemefuna, the hostage, is killed as ordained by the Oracle, though he is loved by Okonkwo and calls him father. Surprisingly Okonkwo participates in his killing as he is afraid of being considered a weakling though he is filled with guilt and remorse for days after the incident. Okonkwo is incapable of compromise; of blending the "masculine" and the "feminine" within himself.

Again, if a woman gives birth to twins they are abandoned and left in the evil forest to die and so is a man afflicted with stomach ailment, for he is considered to be an abomination on mother earth. Unoka faces such a death. Such events are shocking to the rational mind. But Achebe weaves them so skilfully in the fabric of social framework that the reader accepts them with the same calm that the writer narrates them. Achebe is successful in juxtaposing conflicting values and actions within the accepted beliefs.

Okonkwo's exile is the turning point in the novel. With his downfall begins the disjunction of Umuofia. During his stay in Mbanta his friend Obireka brings news that Abame has been wiped out. He says, "After a few days a few white men came to the market place which was full and began to shoot. Everybody was killed except the old and the sick who were at home.... their clan is now completely empty" (129).

The white missionaries arrive in Mbanta and begin to educate the natives about the falsity of their own gods and religion. Ironically, it is Okonkwo's son Nwoye who is lured by their talk and becomes a convert. Nwoye like his grand-father is the softer sort. Hence the missionaries attract him with their songs and prayers. "The words of the hymn were like the drops of frozen rain melting on the dry palate of the panting earth. Nwoye's callow mind was greatly puzzled" (137).

When Okonkwo returns to Umuofia the church has made its impact and there is a white man's government to judge cases against the natives. Some of the natives are imprisoned and subjected to the indignity of clearing the ground or fetching wood for the White Commissioner. The natives are men of title. They are pained and angered at such treatment. Others are hanged. In despair they sing:

Kotma of the ash buttocks,
He is fit to be a slave
The white man has no sense
He is fit to be a slave. (161)

It is ironical that the white man in the eyes of the native is ignorant, foolish and high handed, hence fit to be a slave. Okonkwo's blood boils to hear incidents of assault on his kinsmen. But as Obierika explains, the white man has acquired power by dividing their clan, by driving them apart with his religion and turning their own kinsmen against one another. The white man has taken away their power to fight back. Obierika tells Okonkwo, "He has put a knife on the things that held us together and we have fallen apart" (162).

When the Christians desecrate the personal gods of the natives, they invite their wrath. Okonkwo and the leaders of Umuofia decide to demolish the church that has parted them. It results in their imprisonment and a fine of two hundred and fifty bags of cowries. Their stay in the prison is one of hunger, humiliations and insults. They are not allowed to go out to urinate, their heads are shaved and then knocked together by the court messengers. Okonkwo is filled with hate and vows to avenge his honour. He has survived personal failures: his exile, his son's treachery or the failure of crops. But when the very existence and dignity of his clan is threatened, he is ready for war. Seething with anger, he kills the court messenger who tries to disrupt their meeting, He seeks the support of his people, but they are divided and Umuofia backs out of war, unable to take action like Okonkwo. Okonkwo is filled with despair. Umuofia has failed him. Rather than accept the white man's slavery, he decides to take away his life. His act is a crime against mother earth. Okonkwo's despair finds release only in death. His friend Obierika says ferociously to the District Commissioner who has come to arrest Okonkwo, "That man was one of the greatest men in Umuofia. You drove him to kill himself; and now he will be buried like a dog..." (191).

Okonkwo's death is recorded in the White Commissioner's book in a paragraph. The name of the book is *The Pacification of the Primitive Tribes of the Lower Niger*. This ironic note by Achebe and his cool objective tone that he uses throughout, heightens the tragedy of Okonkwo. Okonkwo's death is the result of a dilemma that all natives face. "If he shows fight, the soldiers fire and he is a dead man; if he gives in, he degrades himself and he is no longer a man at all; shame and fear will split up his character and make his innermost self fall to pieces." (Sartre's "Preface" to *The Wretched of the Earth* 13).

The end of *Things Fall Apart* is a displacement of Ibo culture, language and traditions by the English language, religion and culture. The process of colonisation has begun with the death of Okonkwo. The novel is a work of epic dimension in its magnitude of subject matter. It unveils the complete life history and tragedy of Okonkwo and consequently of the African tribe. *Things Fall Apart* resembles Patrick White's *The Tree of Man* in its vastness of human life history. Achebe adds life and vitality to the novel by introducing native usage in the English language. He thus pushes the frontiers of English language a little further, thereby adding another feature of postcolonialism to his writing.

One aspect of decolonisation takes into account the acceptance of guilt and self introspection on the white man's part. Writers like Conrad in *Heart of Darkness* and Sartre are relentless in their incisive criticism of imperialism. But the imperialistic stand continues even today seen both in America's dictatorial policies on nuclear disarmaments and the continued oppression and killing of Negroes in America. The latest Cosby murder case as reported in the *Times of India* dated 25th July, 1998 says,

African Americans as well as Americans are brainwashed everyday to respect and revere slave owners and people who clearly waffled about race.

America's Educational Institution's Dictionaries define "black" as "harmful"; "hostile"; "disgrace"; "unpleasant" aspects of life. White is described as "decent", "honourable", "auspicious"; "without malice."

Sartre's scathing denunciation of colonialism should be an eye opener to the West. "First, we must face that unexpected revelation, the striptease of humanism. There you can see it, quite naked, and its not a pretty sight. It was nothing but an ideology of lies, a perfect justification for pillage; its honeyed words, its affection of sensibility were only alibis for our aggressions" (Preface to *The Wretched of the Earth* 21).

Note

1. Viney Kirpal in her introduction to the *Post modern English Novel* has made a comprehensive survey of the Indian postcolonial scene where she discusses the various stands taken by postcolonial theorists. She writes, "Said—like Rushdie privileges the migrant writer and downgrades the idea of national literatures as ideological narrations." Critics who have rejected this claim are Aijaz Ahmad, Timothy Brennan, Revathi Krishanaswamy. Similarly T.N. Dhar in his essay "Historiographic Contest and the Post-Colonial Theory" in *Literature and Ideology* has taken the stand of Rushdie and Said to give the term a wider implication. He writes, "Coercion may not necessarily inhere in the methods of their adversaries, but in the ones which are a part of their cultural traditions and style."

References

Achebe, Chinua. *Things Fall Apart*. New York: Ballantine Books, 1959.

Dhar, T.N. "Historiographic Contest and the Postcolonial Theory". *Literature and Ideology*. Ed. Veena Singh. Jaipur: Rawat Publication, 1998.

Fanon, Frantz. *The Wretched of the Earth*. Preface by Jean Paul Sartre. Harmondsworth: Penguin Books Ltd., 1961.

Kirpal, Viney. ed. *The Postmodern Indian English Novel*. Bombay; Allied Publishers, 1997.

Phelps, Gilbert. "Two Nigerian Writers: Chinua Achebe and Wole Soyinka", *The Present, The New Pelican Guide to English Literature*. Ed. Boris Ford, Vol. 8, Harmondsworth: Penguin, 1983.

15

Too Close and Yet too Far: Naipaul's View of India as a Wounded Civilisation

Purabi Panwar

Sensitive western travellers to India have often been baffled by their Indian experience, overwhelmed by the vast physicality of India and the diversity of the ways of life of the people living here. Their responses range from blatantly colonial ones like those of George Otto Trevelyan who writes, "It is difficult to imagine how any business was done before we came into the country how anyone ever made a road, or a boat, or a journey" (Trevelyan, 258), to more perceptive ones who transcended their itineraries in an attempt to know more about the country and the people, something that can be read in their travel impressions.

Where does one place V.S. Naipaul in this tradition of western travel writing about India? Two basic questions that need to be answered at this point are, (a) Can one refer to him as a 'western' writer, taking into consideration his Indian ancestry? and (b) Do his writings about India fit into the generic framework of travel writing? To answer the second question first since that is simpler. As all of Naipaul's books on India are based on travel impressions, they can be broadly classified as travel writings. The socio-political/ethnographic analyses are based on travel impressions and not research and what appears to be reportage is often laced with fiction. After repeated visits to this country, Naipaul's views on India show a greater understanding of the country and its people, though an Indian would still find it fragmentary.

This brings one to the first question as to whether one can refer to Naipaul as 'western'. Naipaul himself would not consider it debatable, he would take his adopted western identity for granted. One is reminded of the time he was so offended at being categorised as a West Indian writer that he promptly changed his publisher.

His doubly diasporic status (his ancestors migrated to Trinidad from a village near Gorakhpur and he went to England as a student and decided to stay on) and the image of the wanderer that he consciously projects, makes any kind of classification somewhat difficult. However, the fact that he chose to live in England and has been writing mainly with the western reader in mind, establishes him as a western writer who has taken on the added responsibility of interpreting happenings in developing countries, condescendingly referred to as the third world, for the benefit of the western reader. It is quite another thing that the people of these countries might find his interpretations inadequate. Sharp reactions to his latest book *Beyond Belief* from non-Arab Muslims, who according to Naipaul, have been deprived of their socio-cultural heritage by Arab Muslims in the name of Islam, can be cited as an example.

To come back to *India: A Wounded Civilization*, and Naipaul's responses to India recorded in it. He realised after the first visit that India was not and could not be his home. Yet he could not reject it or remain indifferent to it like any other tourist. In his own words, "I cannot travel only for the sights. I am at once too close and too far" (Naipaul, *India: A Wounded Civilization*, hereafter referred to as *IWC* followed by page number in parenthesis, 8-9). In 1971 he came on a visit during the mid-term election called by Indira Gandhi and wrote a long article titled "The Election in Ajmer" (First published in *Sunday Times Magazine*, 15-22 August,

1971. Later included in *The Overcrowded Barracoon and Other Articles*). He came back in August 1975 and stayed on till October 1976. The impressions of this visit, blending his travel impressions with ethnographic—political analyses were put together in *India: A Wounded Civilization*.

The first thing one notices while reading the book is the absence of anxiety which had made him hysteric during his first visit, right from the time he landed in Bombay and was harassed by the customs authorities for possessing bottles of liquor without the right papers at a time when Maharashtra was a dry state. This can be read as symptomatic of a shift from his earlier colonial stance. This can be seen in his impressions of Bombay. To quote:

> The Indian—Victorian—Gothic city with its inherited British public buildings and institutions—the Gymkhana with its wide veranda and spacious cricket ground, the London-style leather-chaired Ripon Club for elderly Parsi gentlemen (a portrait of Queen Victoria as a youngish Widow of Windsor still hanging in the Secretary's office)—the city was not built for the poor, the millions. But a glance at the city map shows that there was a time when they were invited in. (*IWC* 59)

Naipaul spoke of begging as "precious to Hindus as religious theatre, a demonstration of the workings of *karma*, a reminder of one's duty to oneself and one's future lives" (*IWC* 58), an observation which draws on his brahmanic upbringing, an authorial voice that he consciously subverted. It suited him to use Hinduism to disparage begging as a step towards establishing himself as an agnostic for the benefit of his western reader.

His final verdict on the beggars suggests a deep-rooted dislike of poverty and can be traced to the financial insecurity of his early life, in Trinidad where his father did not have a permanent job and made a living of sorts doing odd jobs here and there, while the rest of the family lived with Naipaul's mother's family, the rich and influential Capil Deos of Chaguanas, a district in Trinidad. So he distanced himself from beggars as he had distanced himself from his poor relative Ram Chandra Dubey in *An Area of Darkness* and remarks, almost like a typical western tourist, "the beggars have become a nuisance and a disgrace. By becoming too numerous they have lost their place in the Hindu system and have no claim on anyone" (*IWC* 58).

Another instance of this distancing can be seen in Naipaul's response to the ruins of Vijayanagar which made him wonder about "...the intellectual depletion that must have come to India with the invasions and conquests of the last thousand years" (*IWC* 17). It is possible that Naipaul's inability to establish an Indian identity is responsible for his total rejection of India's history.

In the ruins of Vijayanagar, Naipaul clarifies, Hinduism "had already reached a dead end, and in some ways had decayed, as popular Hinduism so easily decays, into barbarism" (*IWC* 16). This attitude of considering Hinduism decadent, even barbaric, is part of an acquired Prospero Syndrome that made Naipaul side with the coloniser, putting forward the argument that the crisis faced by India was neither political nor economic but that of being fettered to the past which impeded any growth or progress. In his works, "The... crisis is of a wounded civilization that has at last become aware of its inadequacies and is without the intellectual means to move ahead" (*IWC* 18).

Denial or suppression of socio-cultural heritage to a country that was once a colony, closely indicates an affinity with the coloniser for whom it was a tool of cultural imperialism, to ward off feelings of national pride that could at some stage become an assertion of identity and snowball into attempts to overthrow the coloniser. That Naipaul adopts this stance, clearly indicates his ideological preferences and a conscious process of distancing from India.

In the course of his post-1962 visits to India, Naipaul concerned himself with ethnographic analyses of the people here, at the same time keeping a distance from the common man most of the time, talking mainly to those in authority and power, like the IAS officer in Bombay, the commissioner in Rajasthan, among others. With his colonial conditioning, he was unable to meet Indians on an equal footing till recently, always judging them on the basis of standards borrowed from the west. This accounts for his desire to improve the people, in the sense arousing in them a desire to progress materially, something that he attributes to the commissioner in Rajasthan to whom he talked about the "remaking of men" (*IWC* 30) so that they would work and make a success of the projects irrigation and reclamation projects started by the government. As the special commissioner saw it,

> this was not simply making men want, it meant, in the first place, bringing them back from the self-wounding and the special waste that come with an established destitution. (*IWC* 30)

Yet his sensitivity to his environs produced some fine descriptive passages of places visited, passages which suggest a closeness, an ability to relate to the scene described. A passage describing a 'model' village in the Kota-Bundi region of Rajasthan, can be cited as an example. To quote:

> The street was unpaved, and the villagers, welcoming us, had quickly spread cotton rugs on the ground that had been softened by the morning's rain, half hardened by the afternoon's heat, and then trampled and manured by the village cattle returning at dusk. The women had withdrawn—so many of them, below their red or orange Rajasthani veils, only girls, children, but already with children of their own. We were left with the men; and, until the rain came roaring in again, we talked. (*IWC* 29-30)

Evocative passages like this, reveal the literary artist in Naipaul but in the multiplicity of authorial voices, the ethnographer and the political analyst are louder than others as the author assumes the role of an interpreter of India to the west. This task is made possible by his unusual position, in the words of the critic Kerry McSweeney "...precisely because he is so uniquely qualified—by his Indian ancestry, Trinidad childhood, British base, and temperamental inability to stay in one place for long" (McSweeney 154). But to Naipaul, India was not a socio-cultural alternative, nor a home away from home, though the latter would have been closer to the persona of the eternal traveller that Naipaul has always chosen to project. For him at that point of time, India was a third world country, without a sense of history, without a racial memory, and had to break off all ties with its past (which Naipaul considered different to history) in order to get the best out of its present, which, according to Naipaul would be progress as understood in the western context.

In this frame of mind, Naipaul understandably criticises westerners who consider India an alternative or a spiritual haven, as their stance undermined his. To quote:

> Out of security and mental lassitude, an intellectual anorexia, they simply cultivate squalor. And their calm can easily turn to panic. When the price of oil rises and economies tremble at home, they clear up and bolt. (*IWC* 27)

The young foreign academic he met at a dinner party in Delhi, particularly evoked derision because Naipaul found his response to India shallow, though his own initial reaction to India as expressed in *An Area of Darkness*, especially with regard to public defecation, had been somewhat similar. His vehemence for the western academic stemmed from the desire to be regarded as an exclusive interpreter of India to the west. He probably felt that the academic and his wife were encroaching upon his territory in the metaphorical sense.

In his quest for an Indian identity and the anger and anguish that gave an edge to his initial travel impressions as expressed in *An Area of Darkness*, Naipaul had been conspicuously silent on current events in India like the third General Elections and had made only a passing reference to the turbulence in Kashmir.

In *India: A Wounded Civilization* Naipaul attempted to analyse the current political set up in India. He was most impressed by Indira Gandhi, whom he had profiled in an earlier essay, one of the first attempts to look at a political event in India. To quote:

> Indira, Mrs. Gandhi, that formidable lady in New Delhi, who had done a de Gaulle on the Congress and taken over, who had abolished the old consensus politics of the Congress. She had declared war on privilege; her appeal was to the poor, the untouchable, the minorities. She had nationalized the banks; she had 'derecognised'

the princes; and, to deprive the princes of their privy purses, she intended to change the constitution.

(Naipaul, *The Overcrowded Barracoon* 110)

He admitted there were excesses during the Emergency, "The opposition spokesmen in exile speak of the loss of democracy and freedom; and their complaints are just. But the borrowed words conceal archaic Gandhian obsessions as destructive as many of the provisions of the Emergency" (*IWC* 172) but his conclusions exonerated her in a way; something drastic like the Emergency was needed, according to him, to jolt India out of an intellectual vacuum/inertia and get rid of the decadent aspect of its civilisation.

Naipaul's attitude to the Emergency and his admiration for Indira Gandhi, stand in direct contrast to the views of other writers from the Indian diaspora, notably Salman Rushdie. Rushdie denounced the Emergency and along with it Indira Gandhi and her son Sanjay Gandhi, vehemently in *Midnight's Children* (1980). For Rushdie the Emergency heralded "the beginning of a continuous midnight which would not end for two long years" (Rushdie, *Midnight's Children* 499-500). Indira Gandhi and her son are referred to as the widow and her son in the novel. One of the characters in *Midnight's Children* showed a newspaper photograph of Indira Gandhi to Saleem Sinai, the protagonist, "Her hair parted in the centre, was snow-white on one side and black-as-night on the other, so that depending on which profile she presented, she resembled a stoat or ermine" (*Midnight's Children* 477).

However, Naipaul's passive support for the Emergency need not be correlated absolutely with his admiration for Indira Gandhi. It can be related to his concept of India "as a decadent civilization …where the only hope lies in further swift decay" (*IWC* 174) implying that the "swift decay" could be brought about by the Emergency which, therefore became a necessity in a way if India wanted to break with the past and start afresh.

As a postcolonial traveller who was unable to establish an Indian identity, Naipaul's view that India should sever all connections with the past, is understandable. It is in keeping with his self-appointed role of interpreting India to the west in a way that his western readers would appreciate. What he failed to see or refused to see was that a race can be uprooted like the Jews in Hitler's Germany and elsewhere in Europe during the Second World War, and yet manage to salvage their heritage and traditions, incorporating them into their present lives. In this context one can quote from Jawahar Lal Nehru's *The Discovery of India* (1946) for a balanced view:

> India must break with much of her past and not allow it to dominate the present. Our lives are encumbered with the dead wood of the past; all that is dead and has served its purpose has to go. But that does not mean a break with, or a forgetting of, the vital and life-giving in the past. We can never forget the ideals that have moved our race, the desires of the Indian people through the ages, the wisdom of the ancients.... We will never forget them or cease to take pride in that noble heritage of ours. If India forgets them she will no longer remain India and much that made her our joy and pride will cease to be. (*The Discovery of India* 522)

It is not simply the past that one has to break with, but "the excrescences and abortions that have twisted and petrified the spirit" (*The Discovery of India* 522) to borrow Nehru's words. Ethnographically, this seems more viable than the alternative suggested by Naipaul.

Naipaul's new found interest in politics led him to profile political leaders along with the movements they spearheaded, something carried over to his latest book on India, *India: A Million Mutinies Now* 1990) On a larger scale Naipaul's observations on Mahatma Gandhi were not quite objective. His remark, "For a reason which he never makes clear—he was virtually uneducated, had never even read a newspaper—he passionately wanted to go to England" (*IWC* 97) shows a lack of perception, as it calls a person uneducated for not having read a newspaper, without considering the fact that a small town like Porbandar would not have one at that point of time.

A discriminating reader would notice certain parallels between Gandhi's first passage to England, "an internal adventure of anxieties felt and food eaten, with not a word of anything seen or heard that did not directly affect the physical or mental well-being of the writer" (*IWC* 98) and Naipaul's first journey away form home, to England. There were hopes and expectations from the "...large world (which) had always existed outside my little island" (Naipaul *The Enigma of Arrival* 98) but there was also "a feeling of menace" of being threatened:

> As the little plane droned and droned through the night the idea of New York became frightening. Not the city, so much as the moment of arrival: I couldn't visualize that moment. It was the first traveller's panic I had experienced. (*IWC* 99)

Naipaul's inability to go into the depths of Gandhi's experiments, discoveries, vows and the correlation that he (Gandhi) tried to establish between the outer and the inner world, only reveals Naipaul's own limitations. He could appreciate Gandhi only when the latter went on a "sad last pilgrimage" (*IWC* 111) to Noakhali, now in Bangladesh, when people there, embittered by communal tension for which they held politicians responsible, scattered broken glass on the roads he was to walk. Naipaul's observations are sensitive though dramatic. To quote, "At this terrible moment his thoughts are of action, and he is magnificent" (*IWC* 111).

While discussing aspects of the political set up in India, Naipaul showed an awareness of the separatist movements. In Bombay he noticed that the Shiv Sena had evolved "within the past ten years, out of bits and pieces of a past simplified to legend" (*IWC* 61). He found the Shiv Sena "xenophobic" (*IWC* 62) and spoke of the "theatricality of its leader, a failed cartoonist who is said to admire Hitler" (*IWC* 62). In 1977 Naipaul's remarks on the Shiv Sena were more referential than analytical. The Shiv Sena for him, at that point of time, was just another decadent Hindu organisation like the Anand Marg, a militant Hindu organisation, which has since been banned.

His perspective underwent a great change while writing *India: A Million Mutinies Now* and he found organisations like the Shiv Sena inevitable in the present Indian context. For him it became one of the many mutinies referred to in the title, an assertion of identity by the middle class. Later, in a newspaper interview, with L.K. Sharma he said:

> The Shiv Sena is a middle class movement and not that of down trodden people. It is part of a larger self-marking process. This process will take a long time. In India, you will have to live with movements like that for the next 100 years.

Movements like this, of the middle class as well as the underprivileged people, in the aftermath of Muslim and later British rule, have been instrumental in shaping a new India, essentially Hindu and "more complex and more unified than any India in the past" (*Million Mutinies Now* 143). Secularists are sure to disagree with this view. Also, one who has come across Naipaul's general advocacy of a global civilisation, would find him paradoxical. But paradoxically is characteristic of Naipaul's style of thinking and presenting his views.

In some ways *India: A Wounded Civilization* reflects Naipaul's attempts to understand India, not dismiss it as an area of darkness. This change of perspective, to an ambivalent one as indicated in the subtitle of this paper, is confirmed by a reading of the text. With this changed perspective, Naipaul can no longer be dismissed as just another colonial traveller with an islander's outlook, trying to cover up his awe and wonder at the vastness of India with a slightly supercilious, know-all attitude.

India: A Wounded Civilization, classified by its publishers as Travel/Current Events, assembles a postcolonial traveller's impressions of India, arising from his visits to this country and travels within it, but related more to people and issues than places. Destinations were important, not for the natural and man made attractions they offered to the traveller, but the socio-politico-economic movements he saw here. Naipaul was not bound by his itinerary. His quest for understanding what he saw in India, and interest in interpreting it to the west grew with every visit. An Indian reader is not likely to agree with his interpretations, consider them fragmentary perceptions at best. However, one has to concede that Naipaul's understanding of postcolonial India grew with every visit. While a study of his latest book on India corroborates this fact, this critic concludes that a fair beginning has been made in *India: A Wounded Civilization* and Naipaul's stance as indicated in the title of this paper (which borrows a phrase from the book) contributes to it.

References

McSweeney, Kerry. *Four Contemporary Novelists*. London: Scholar Press, 1983.

Naipaul, V.S. *An Area of Darkness*. London: Andre Deutsch, 1964.

—. *Beyond Belief*. New Delhi: Viking, 1998.

—. "History is Not a Matter of Licking Wounds", Interview with L.K. Sharma. *The Sunday Times of India* (New Delhi) 18 July 1993, 13.

—. *India: A Million Mutinies Now*. London: Minerva, 1990.

—. *India: A Wounded Civilization*. New Delhi: Vikas 1977.

—. *The Enigma of Arrival*. London: Penguin, 1987.

—. *The Overcrowded Barracoon and Other Articles*. Harmondsworth: Penguin, 1987.

Nehru, J.L. *Discovery of India*. London: Meridian Books, 1960.

Rushdie, Salman. *Midnight's Children*. New York: Avon, 1982.

Sharma, L.K. "History is not a matter of Licking Wounds". *The Sunday Times of India*, 18 July 1993, 13.

Trevelyan, George Otto. *The Competition Wallah*. London: MacMillan, 1964.

16

A Technique of Stimulation: Naipaul's *India: A Wounded Civilization*

M.R. Khatri

In the present paper emphasis is on the scrutiny of the literary text. To speak on content only, as Mark Schorer points out, is not to speak of art but of experience. Content is only experience whereas achieved content includes technique. The more the author is conscious of his technique, the more satisfying will be the achieved content or art. V.S. Naipaul in *India: A Wounded Civilization* draws upon the reader's response by adopting a technique of stimulation. The power of the narrative lies in the author's capacity to provoke the reader's consciousness by causing emotional distortion through a candid portrayal of the shocking elements of Indian civilisation. Naipaul represents and reinterprets a number of aspects of the historical and cultural heritage of India and awakens the reader against the still prevailing uncertainty and emptiness. The author portrays the son called pitiable and shocking condition of India by using a narrative technique that is sharper than his other tools. It is this narrative technique that helps him a great deal to produce a work reverberates with maximum of effectivity.

In 1976 Naipaul wrote this travel book which observes very closely what is changing in India and what represents the incessant continuance. To him India is a country that is slow to understand "that its independence has meant more than the going away of the British, that the India to which independence came was a land of far older defeat; that the purely Indian past died a long time ago" (*IWC* 8). The main weakness that hurts that very sensitivity of the author is the intellectual depletion of India which remains untouched despite a number of wars, plunders and conquests. Throughout the book this message recurs with a degree of regularity even as the focus shifts. He begins the narrative by citing the example of Vijay Nagar, an old Hindu city founded in the fourteenth century, which now in the light of the backwardness of the region seems without a history. Even after a lot of development has taken place since independence the peasantry of the region cannot comprehend properly the idea of change. This intellectual depletion according to Naipaul occurs because:

> The crisis of India is not only political or economic. The larger crisis is of a wounded old civilization that has at last become aware of its inadequacies and is without the intellectual means to move ahead. (*IWC* 18)

He further points out that intellectually for a thousand years India had always retreated before its conquerors and even during the periods of apparent revival it had been making itself archaic, intellectually smaller and always vulnerable. This point of view is accentuated further by his focus on the carload of problems that engulf India—poverty, slums, lack of facilities, illiteracy, exploitation, bonded labour, overpopulation, corruption, lack of planning, lack of leadership, lack of direction and so on. The crux of all these problems is India's inadequacy in terms of intellectual initiative. He even wonders at the viewpoints of those Indian intellectuals like Narayan who feel that despite all these problems "India will go on". Naipaul negates this by regarding Indian "society without a head" for whom habits of analysis are too far outside its tradition. He says:

> The intellectual confusion is greater now than in the days of the British, when the world seemed to stand still, the issues were simpler, and it was enough for India to assert its Indianness. The poor were background then. Now they press hard, and have to be taken into account. (*IWC* 118)

He indicts the Indians for their habit of contemplating over the past ecstatically. Even Gandhi is many times the object of nostalgic memory. Relating his personal experience he says that the conversation of the Indians is an expression of self-indulgence, they only speak about their grievances and thus wallow in self pity—a sweet surrender to a sense of loss. While depicting all this Naipaul carefully keeps shifting from subject to subject from past to present and from fiction to reality. This technique gives rise to a different kind of relationship between the reader, the author and his material. The book does not offer a plot of suspense or climax yet it is not without these. Bits of incidents are arranged in a special order to define the quality of the experience in question. This technique imposes upon the world of action a different kind of rhythm by means of which Naipaul renews to a greater degree our apprehension of contemporary India and its problems.

The author by this way is able to fillip the reader to actively read, redefine and respond to the questions raised in terms of reason and emotion, society and individual and the historical process and its relationship to the present. He warns the reader against a mythology of the past which often lives on as the culture of the present. In this respect he feels that the Indian past is an institution owned by society. But this does not alleviate the burden of the problems, it rather augments them.

Highlighting the magnitude of the problems that surround India he gives a graphic account which is likely to hurt the average Indian. In the Hindu community where the cow is a holy object of worship, he found them eating human excrement; a quack surgeon who on account of his inexperience caused the loss of the eye-sight of seventy patients; workers in Dhanbad, Bihar terrorised by moneylenders and their gangs. The very concept of *dharma* which is such a cohesive force to the Indians accommodates bonded labour, widow burning and other social atrocities. The law also avoids collision with *dharma*. Thus, Naipaul does not offer a surface view of the nature of problems in India, he searches the very marrow of the bones of Indian civilisation to get an answer for what shocks him. The mysterious nature of Indian civilisation in itself poses a challenge to the author who examines it with sharpened tools of perspicacity. The complacency of the Indians puzzles him to an extent which compels him to seek an answer in those very concepts which he rejects at a rational level. Perhaps the conventional philosophical surrender is itself the answer. But this operates only at a subconscious level. At the conscious level he always has in his mind the European method of inquiry which imported in India cannot assume its dynamism. He asks: "How can that system bequeathed to India by another civilisation with other values, give India equity and perform the law's constant reassessing, reforming role?" (*IWC* 132) To seek an answer he quotes the speech of Mrs. Indira Gandhi, published in *The Times of India*, 5 Oct. 1975, who said that *our* legal system should assist in the liberation of the human spirit and of human institutions from the straitjacket of outdated customs. It is in line with our ancient view that 'society' should uphold *dharma* so that *dharma* sustains society (*IWC* 132).

To Naipaul the *dharma* of which Mrs. Gandhi speaks is a complex word, because *dharma* as expressed in the Indian social system, is "so shot through with injustice and cruelty, based on such a limited view of man" (*IWC* 132). He rather feels that *dharma* is the word law must grapple with if the law is to have a "dynamic role". The complexity of the problem intensifies his embarrassment as the language used further echoes his mental perturbation:

> Indians say that their gift is for synthesis. It might be said, rather, that for too long, as a conquered people, they have been intellectually parasitic on other civilizations. To survive in abjection, they have preserved their sanctuary of the instinctive, uncreative life, converting that into a religious ideal; at a more worldly level, they have depended on others for the ideas and institutions that make a country work. (*IWC* 134)

Thus the fusion of the form and content both give rise to a language that wounds the very consciousness of the reader as well. The point the author communicates comes with a potent force and causes counter reaction in the audience in the form of his critical productive response. To lay before the reader the detailed picture of this reality, Naipaul gives his material a broad scope in time. He talks about a number of Indian political leaders of influence and probes thoroughly into their ideologies and political actions but he finds none of them capable of providing India with an ideology of regeneration. He is critical of the cultural primitivism of the leaders like Gandhi, Bhave, Indira Gandhi, Jai Prakash Narayan, Morarji Desai who have not been effective enough to pull India out of the mire of decayed civilisation. He acknowledges the influence of Gandhi who from 1919 to 1930 "drew all India together in a new kind of politics". But he attributes this success to what was unIndian in Gandhi at that time. It was his racial sense, a quality alien to other Indians. This racial sense extended the religious sense of Gandhi in South Africa "teaching responsibility and compassion, teaching that no man was an island, and that the dignity of the high was bound up with the dignity of the low" (*IWC* 154). It was this quality that helped him to get away from the divisive politics of religion, caste and region. But these efforts ended when his role of Mahatmahood as a holy man emerged. It was his Mahatmahood that in the end worked against his Indian cause. Naipaul observes that in post-independence India religious ecstasy and religious self-display reduces Gandhianism to Mahatmahood. Due to this, racial sense which contains respect for the individual, is as remote from India as ever—Gandhi awakened the holy land, his Mahatmahood returned it to archaism, he made his worshippers vain (*IWC* 159).

Gandhi's successor Vinoba Bhave also created for himself the role of a sage. He was the object of regard in India for his developed inner life. But he failed to perform any role for creative change. Naipaul comments "He is not a particularly intelligent man and, as a perfect disciple of the Mahatma, not original; his political views come close to nonsense" (*IWC* 107).

He was important in India just because for thirty years he has been the "authorized version of Gandhi". His preaching also stress upon the rightfulness of the old ways. Talking about the inefficiency of his endeavors Naipaul says: "Bihar, where Bhave did much of his walking, remains—in matters of land and untouchability—among the most backward and crushed of the Indian states" (*IWC* 165). Similarly Naipaul regards Mr. Desai as exhibitionist and hollow. His ways also reflected the "old Indian attitudes of defeat, the idea of withdrawal, a turning away from the world, a sinking back into the past" (*IWC* 141). Thus Naipaul chiefly hits out at the Indian leaders for their fantasies of spirituality. Their ideologies proved as destructive as were the borrowed systems about which Naipaul says:

> India is old, and India continues. But all the disciplines and skills that India now seeks to exercise are borrowed. Even the ideas Indians have of the achievement of their civilization are essentially the ideas given to them by European scholars in the nineteenth century. India by itself could not have rediscovered or assessed its past. Its past was too much with it, was still being lived out in the ritual, the laws, the magic—the complex instinctive life that muffles response and buries even the idea of inquiry. (*IWC* 129)

In the concluding part of the novel, Naipaul talks about his perception of *dharma*, the key concept of Hindu religion, which is in line with what the Aryan Gita says. Nevertheless, he feels that in India ready-made satisfaction pushes people away from individuality and the possibility of excellence. *Dharma* is both, he says creative and crippling, according to what is expected of man, "It cannot be otherwise. The quality of a faith is not constant; it depends on the quality of the men who profess it" (*IWC* 170). Naipaul points out that a true understanding of *dharma* must lead first to oneself as is being practiced by authors like Balzac and Proust for whom action is its own reward—a power "that keeps them in a state of marriage with the Muse, and her creative forces" (*IWC* 169).

Similar use of technique operates at multiple levels in *India: A Million Mutinies Now (1990)*. The very title of this book is marked by the technique of stimulation. It appeared when the country was witnessing problems resulting from the Rath Yatra, anti-Mandal agitations, and the militants in Kashmir, Punjab, Bihar and the North east states. The serious nature of these problems is emphasised through a title that alarms the reader at first glance. Almost every page of the book arrests attention for Naipaul's "close observation, the accurate description and the colourful vocabulary" (Kaul 7). When he depicts the Bombay crowd his use of language brings one the realisation of the forces of dehumanisation generated by overpopulation: "People swept across the road, in such a bouncing froth of light-coloured lightweight clothes, it seemed that some kind of invisible sluice-gate had been opened" (*IMMN* 1).

All along the reader shifts perspectives along with the writer, moving from one frame to another and learning to separate himself from the subject of the work. As an Indian, one undergoes a sense of alienation, even while realising that Naipaul is exaggerating, over-generalising, employing binary structures, painting stark colours and obliterating differences. He is conscious of a strategy which forms part of his need for separating himself from his Indian inheritance. Where do we place him? Is he a conscious artist, deliberately using language and strategy to provoke the reader? Do we thereby assure that his targeted reader is India? Is he using his exaggerations judiciously mixed with facts to present India to the rest of the world—an India which has inherited a great tradition but lacks vitality? Or is it a self indulgence for exorcising his own ghosts? There is perhaps a segment of each of these strands present in his work. But *India: A Wounded Civilization* makes us conscious of our vulnerability, of our strength as well as our failures, proving once again the point that civilisations in order to survive must seek their own vitality.

References

Kaul, R.K. "Naipaul the Renegade". *Jodhpur Studies in English* Vol. 6, 1995.

Naipaul, V.S. *India: A Wounded Civilization*. Penguin, 1977.

—. *India: A Million Mutinies Now*. London: Minerva, 1990.

17

Thematic Perspectives of Culture in Wole Soyinka's *Death and the King's Horseman*

Meenu Bhambhani

In analysing Soyinka's *Death and the King's Horseman* one has to invariably consider the author's warning, which he gives in the prefatory note, of not discounting the play as projecting cultural confrontation between the coloniser and the colonised. A surface reading of the play, in fact, suggests that the thematic thrust is on the conflict between the so called progressive, civilised white imperialist British culture and the black, 'barbaric' Nigerian culture. But if one does indulge in this kind of simplification it will be difficult to highlight the complex issue of values one attaches to the culture. Indeed *Death and the King's Horseman* is a play about cultural resistance in the colonial backdrop in which the African characters, whether having gone through British education in London like Elesin's son Olunde or the natives belonging to the Yoruba tribe, strive for the identity of their selves and culture by adhering to its customs and traditions, thus holding it in dignity.

Although Soyinka cautions that "the Colonial Factor is an incident, a catalytic incident merely" (*Death and the King's Horseman*, 145) yet as the play proceeds he goes on hinting or dropping cues about how colonialism came to Africa under the garb of Christian missionaries and gradually by imposing their religion, education and through the use of military power they tried to sever the umbilical links of the natives from their roots. We do not see in the play one to one fight or violent clashes between the two cultures but there is the intrusion of alien culture which has not only prevented the natives from pursuing their traditions—an encroachment on their freedom and space—but also tried to estrange and alienate them. Soyinka has exposed the hypocrisy of western culture at the same time showing its shallowness. This shallowness is exemplified in the behaviour of the prince who was on a pleasure trip to the city when the entire world including Britain was "in the midst of a devastating war" (194). It is evident even in the behaviour of Simon Pilkings who does not hesitate to call the holy water 'nonsense' before his steward boy Joseph, a tribal converted to Roman Catholic by the missionaries (170). In his last work in English, Ngugi Wa Thiong'o has observed that undervaluing the native religion over Christianity was the first step towards cultural colonialism. He says:

> Colonialism's... most important area of domination was the mental universe of the colonised, the control through culture, of how people perceived themselves and their relationship to the world.... To control a people's culture is to control their tools of self-definition in relationship to others.
>
> For colonialism this involved two aspects of the same process: the destruction or the deliberate undervaluing of a people's culture, their art, dances, religions, history, geography, education, orature and literature, and the conscious elevation of the language of the coloniser.
>
> (*Decolonising the Mind* 16)

This undervaluing is done by imposing the coloniser's system of education. Education is not only a vehicle and carrier of the colonial culture but is also one of the most important means of disassociating and alienating the natives from their immediate environment and roots. Wole Soyinka has shown the failure of imperialist efforts to uproot the natives from their environment which lies in their customs and traditions regarded and condemned by it as barbaric and uncivilised He, indeed, has been fanatically obsessed with the idea of preserving one's culture as he saw it as a potent means of projecting the future and "renewal of society." (David 75). To prevent the society and nation from degenerating, he pleads for respecting one's tradition not only in *Death and the King's Horseman* but also in his political plays like *Madmen and Specialists* and *Opera Wonyosi*. In these latter plays there is no imperial power imposing its culture but the power hungry native rulers who ape the alien cultures consolidating their position and dictatorially alienating the natives from their own traditions. Soyinka sees the native culture as saviour of democracy and man's freedom which was under threat in the African continent by tyrannical autocrats like Idi Amin of Uganda and Macias Nguema of Equatorial Guinea in early and mid 70S. In *Madmen and Specialists* (1971) he pleads to preserve the culture and says:

> It was our duty and a historical necessity. It is our duty and a historical beauty. It shall always be. What we have, we hold. What though the wind of change is blowing over this entire continent, our principles and traditions—yes, must be maintained. For we are threatened, yes, we are indeed threatened, yes, we are indeed threatened.
>
> (*Madmen and Specialists* 285-86)

In *Death and the King's Horseman* the threat comes from imperial masters who are adamant at transforming the natives into their definition of civilised human beings and thus dissociating them. While discussing the problems of postcolonial literatures in the book and essay of the same title Jasbir Jain has said:

> The colonial period not only created a sense of alienation from the native cultural tradition, but also ingrained an attitude of subjection. There is a division at several different levels: a division between the world of ideas and one of reality and a division in the self. By placing the norm, the measuring stick outside the native

society, it has taken away its centre from it, a kind of hatred for the self has been allowed to grow.

(Jain 3)

In the play Simon Pilkings, who represents the colonial power, by preventing Elesin from committing self-sacrifice takes away the centre from him. We find that there is hatred for self in the mind of the horseman but it does not indicate any feeling of inferiority for the native culture. In fact the hatred for self is because of Elesin's failure to bring honour to his self and to his tribe which resulted because of alien culture's intrusion and exercise of sophisticated power over the inhibited natives. This imperialist culture held the native African traditions in disrespect and contempt which is camouflaged by their so called educational and religious reforms whose purpose is not to educate and civilise but which are meant to alienate the natives and thus subjugate and exploit them.

Soyinka has here reversed the scene as none of the characters seem to be influenced or over-awed either by the claims of British cultural, social superiority or their progress in the field of medicine, economy and military power. They do not look for an anchorage in the west. This is evident in the character of Olunde who is sent to London by Pilkings to study medicine. He is sent without the approval of his father Elesin. Study of medicine is significant here as metaphorically it is suggestive of rationality and logic over adherence to emotions and values attached to meaningless and illogical customs and traditions. Although he finds the English "people quite admirable in many ways" yet fails to appreciate their rationality and thus exposes the myth of white superiority. He feels that they "have no respect for what" they find incomprehensible (*DKH* 192); and "saw nothing, finally, that gave you the right to pass judgement on other peoples and their ways. Nothing at all" (196).

Indeed he is the only truly right thinking character in the play who objectively analyses the two contrasting worlds of the coloniser and the colonised and appeals for freedom of the native culture. We find his character transforming and growing and yet retaining the individual quality of loyalty to his roots and people. He is sent to England where he lives for four years and learns that his own civilisation is not so primitive "the like of which has so far only existed in" the imagination of white races. He admires their courage and realises that their "greatest art is the art of survival" (195). The transformation there takes place at two levels; physical as well as mental. It is important here to note how the author has introduced him:

> A figure emerges from the shadows, a young black MAN dressed in a sober western suit. He peeps into the hall, trying to make out the figures of the dancers. (191)

The use of capitals in the word man is significant as it symbolises that he is a human being "Grand but solemn" compared to the masked white figures (191). on the mental level we find that the study of medicine and English people has made him more analytical and sharpened his perceptivity. He has learned to argue and as Mrs. Pilkings says "returned with a chip" on his shoulder (192). This transformation has however not estranged Olunde from his roots and he holds in high esteem not only the big issues involving the matters of maintaining the freedom to observe ones traditions and customs which are part of his native Yoruba culture he belonged to, but even the native ethnic ancestral dress "egungun" which he feels is being desecrated by Mrs. Pilkings. The respect for ancient traditions and ancestral dresses is evident even in minor characters of Amusa and Joseph who serve their white masters. Their religious identities are merged with their cultural identities.

Towards the end of the play there is a re-transformation of Olunde's character which signifies that he has retraced his steps to his roots and not deserted it. That he would not sever his links is implied and hinted in the very first scene itself. The links or roots lie in traditions and nothing and nobody could ever alienate anybody from his roots. Elesin says: A hive

> Is never known to wander. An anthill
> Does not desert its roots....
>   Coiled
> To the navel of the world is that
> Endless cord that links us all

> To the great origin. If I lose my way
> The trailing cord will bring me to the roots.
>
> (157)

Olunde had returned to participate in the burial ceremony of his father who was to perform the ritual of self-sacrifice which would win him veneration of his tribe. He is disturbed by the intrusion of the whites on their cultural territory and pleads for non-interference. His requests go unheeded which force him to change his decision of returning to England and instead sacrifices his own life to save the honour of his tribe. Thus, by upholding the ancestral tradition he re-establishes his severed links with his roots. This ritual self-sacrifice is then symbolic of man's quest for an identity of self which he tries to trace in his culture. It also signifies the struggle of natives against the authoritarian control of colonialists "who play with stranger's lives, who even usurp the vestments of the dead" (219). Apart from this there are other reasons too that cause or stimulate men to revert to their own traditions. It would be apt here to quote Jasbir Jain's words who has rightly observed the motives behind men's search for self in culture in the context of newly independent colonies. She says:

> Motivated variously, perhaps by a need to trace one's origins, as a protest against inequality, a need to free oneself from cultural domination, to prove one's credentials and in order to seek self assurance, the newly independent countries turned to their own traditions.
>
> (Jain 156)

Olunde's fulfilling of the task left unfulfilled by his father symbolises that by saving the honour of his family and tribe and thus upholding the native culture he has proved his credentials and asserted his self. Culture is then not just a matter of individual belief in its various aspects but is a mode of self-expression. It gives identity to a nation thus building an image for it and granting a standing to it as a separate entity in the world.

References

David, Mary T. "Wole Soyinka: Individualism vs. Social Commitment". 71-79 *Littcrit: A Literary Half Yearly*: Volume 18, Number 1 & 2 June, December, 1992.

Jain, Jasbir. *Problems of Postcolonial Literatures and Other Essays.* Jaipur: Printwell, 1991.

Soyinka, Wole. *Six Plays.* London: Methuen, 1984.

Thiong'o, Ngugi Wa. *Decolonising the Mind: The Politics of Language in African Literature.* Oxford: James Currey Ltd., 1986.

18

The Unfolding of a Text: Soyinka's *Death and the King's Horseman*

Jasbir Jain

What kind of a play is Soyinka's *Death and the King's Horseman*? The obvious answers—that it is a play about the colonial situation, or about cultural clash—are not only discounted by the author,[1] but do not in any way offer an understanding of the play. It happens to be different from Soyinka's most characteristic plays, for neither the satiric nor the comic purpose dominates.[2] The dominant strategy of the play is irony, and the reversal at the end happens to be a tragic reversal.[3] It is here that a distinction has to be made between the narrative and the dramatic levels of the play. At the narrative level, following closely the sequence of events in the play, Elesin Oba is distracted from his purpose of "committing" death, first by his own desires and later by external interference, and the burden of fulfilling his task falls on his eldest son, Olunde. But in dramatic terms these issues acquire a metaphysical dimension,[4] while the colonial issue and the historicity of the main event are treated as of incidental significance.

Death and the King's Horseman is suffused by the purely dramatic: ritual, song, storytelling, masque, mimicry, and dance. It does not seek to be a representation of life in realistic terms; in fact, there is a conscious awareness of the theatrical, of the nature of spectacle, also of color, pageantry, and ceremony. As Soyinka writes in "Drama and the African World View":

> ritual theatre establishes the spatial medium not merely as physical area for simulated events but as a manageable contraction of the cosmic envelope within which man—no matter how deeply buried such a consciousness has latterly become— fearfully exists.[5]

A similar point is stressed by Johan Huizanga in his article "Nature and Significance of Play as a Cultural Phenomenon," which points out that the act of performing a ritual is "methectic rather than mimetic."[6] The enactment of ritual, despite its similarity to and affinity with "play," is different in the demands it makes on its audience and in the nature and quality of "theatrical illusion" it seeks to produce. While sharing with "play" the seclusion of space, and its separation from ordinary life, it requires a greater participation from the audience; and as for the degree of illusion, a ritual when performed "ritually" is undertaken with the belief that it is real and not playacting.[7]

Seen from this point of view, the first act is wholly ritualistic. The ritual of the horseman's death comes to embed within it the ritual of a union with a new bride, a rite not consummated or dramatically highlighted until the third act. The second act shows us Pilkings and his wife engaged in preparations for the evening's ball dressed in the ancestral dress of the *egungun*,[8] a ritual heightened by the reaction of Amusa and the other natives. The third, which has three separate subsections, once again places the characters in situations which are of conscious playacting or ritual. The first when the women surround Amusa and his men and through mimicry and ridicule subvert his authority (34-39), the second when the marriage rite, "the union of life and the seeds of passage," contemplated in the first act is consummated but not yet completed (4041). Elesin tells his bride: "Our marriage is not yet wholly fulfilled. When earth and passage wed, the consummation is complete only when there are grains of earth on the eyelids of the passage. Stay by me till then" (40). The third section (41-44) of the third act seeks to complete the enactment of the main ritual initiated in the first act, of Elesin willing himself to death. Slowly the rhythm induces a semblance of distance and gradually the man enters into a trance. It is a shamanistic act and symbolises total withdrawal at a moment of total involvement. This, at one level, is the true ending in which the initial ritual designed to emphasise both will and order is being enacted.

Leaving the audience to cope with the aftereffects of act 3, the author now moves, in act 4, to the colonial setting where a ball is being held to welcome the royal visitor from England. But while the native world holds its own against intervention (as seen in the scene where the women send back Amusa and his men), the white world has to move out of its orbit in its attempt to close the gap between two diverse and parallel ways of life. Pilkings is called out from the party as Elesin is to be called back from the land of death. Finally, toward the end of the fifth act the initial rite is partially reenacted but under remarkably changed conditions: the prison cell has replaced the marketplace; shame has replaced honour; and Elesin finds himself no longer as one whose name would be an honoured memory but an "eater of leftovers" (61, 68).

Thus while the dramatic structure moves from ritual to masque and from mimicry to ironic repetition, it also helps elicit the metaphysical meaning through this structure. For instance the first act opens in the marketplace which at once becomes a metaphor for both life and afterlife.[9] The activity and hubbub of the marketplace are in tune with Elesin's own vivacity, and the packing away of the goods reminds one of the folding away of his life. It is like a homecoming for him, "the beloved market" of his youth (18), the "long-suffering home" of his spirit (9). Elesin tells the praise singer: "This market is my roost. When I came among the women I am a chicken with a hundred mothers. I become a monarch whose palace is built with tenderness and beauty" (10). This act of bidding farewell to life is symbolic of the transfer to another world and of the beginning of a journey. There is no sense of any termination or disruption. Death and life have established a cyclical unity, and the physical union with the new bride is only a prelude to the union of life with death which is referred to as the brand new bride (9). The purely temporal is transferred into the religious. And women have a special role to play in this transference. On this last evening, Elesin desires to be with them: "This night I'll lay my head upon their lap and go to sleep. This night I'll touch feet with their feet" (10). Mircea Eliade in *The Sacred and the Profane* refers to the paradigmatic nature of the cosmic creation, of the sacred union between the sky god and Mother Earth, and comments upon its being a model for human behavior: "This is why human marriage is regarded as an imitation of the cosmic hierogamy." Citing examples from various cultures, Eliade points out:

> For non-religious man of the modern societies, this simultaneously *cosmic* and *sacred* dimension of conjugal union is difficult to grasp. But as we have had occasion to say more than once, it must not be forgotten that religious man of the archaic societies sees the world as fraught with messages.[10]

The dramatic function of the first act is primarily to set Elesin apart from other men—as a man who has been chosen to fulfil a privileged role and who can, by the force of his role, command compliance as he does when he asks for the young girl in marriage (22). Elesin's question-answer sessions, first with the praise singer and later with the women, besides being in the folk tradition,[11] also serve another purpose. They exorcise, at a psychological level, first the love of life and then the fear of death (10-15). Elesin is fully in control of his world and of his own will; the unconscious is discounted by being brought to the surface. While others have been afraid of death, he is not:

> My rein is loosened.
> I am master of my Fate. When the honour comes
> Watch me dance along the narrowing path
> Glazed by the soles of my great precursors
> My soul is eager. I shall not turn aside.
> (14)

The picture that emerges at the end of the first act is not one of fear, but one of strength and harmony, one of a world in which there is order and the human will is in control of the situation. The presence of the external threat is recognised, but there is confidence that it will not have any impact on this world. The dramatic tension shifts from the question answer session between Elesin and the praise singer to the one between Elesin and Iyaloja, the latter suggesting the polarity of the two: life and death and the possible disjunction between them.

During this shift from one to the other, the nature of time—its continuity from the past to the future, from the ancestors to the unborn, and the nature of death as but "another modality of human experience,"[12] is elicited and the nature of the journey about to be undertaken is stressed. And it is on these—time, death, and the journey—that irony, the dominant dramatic strategy, turns upon in the play. Robert Scholes, while commenting upon the nature of irony, writes:

> While metaphor and metonymy are expressed and understood primarily at the semantic level of discourse, irony depends to an extraordinary degree on the pragmatics of the situation. In speech, irony will often be signalled by the nonverbal parts of utterances (intonation and gesture), while metaphor and metonymy are virtually independent of these features.[13]

It is in this connection that the dramatic medium is important in *Death and the King's Horseman*, and the threnodic elements not only provide commentary but, at times, commentary which is ambiguous and confusing.

Irony works at several levels in the play, and true to its nature, it takes us into "codes, contexts and situations."[14] It brings about a reversal of situation. The near fulfilment on Elesin's part in the third act is disrupted, and he finds himself in chains and under strict surveillance, with celebration having turned into mourning and praise into contempt. There is also an ironical reversal of roles which is first highlighted not through a native consciousness but through a remark of Jane's when Elesin is brought as a prisoner:

Olunde (quietly): That was my father's voice.
Jane: Oh you poor orphan, what have you come home to?[15]

Olunde is left with hardly any option but to fall into his father's unfulfilled role, but this is not apparent to the audience at this juncture for several reasons. As for the reversal, it also takes place at the level of language. David Richards has commented upon the change of style in fair amount of detail,[16] but what is more striking than the subdued tone of Elesin's replies is the constant reference, both by Iyaloja and the praise singer to the warnings they had given Elesin in the first act. At that time Elesin had felt confident of overriding all weaknesses and hurdles, but now he has no face to defend what has happened. These accusations which echo the question-answer sessions of the first act (68-76) constitute a kind of confrontation for Elesin with his own past, and while psychologically they help to stir Elesin out of his sense of helplessness, dramatically the spectator begins to view Elesin's failure to die as a tragic happening. The bride so urgently desired in the first act is now confined to a totally asexual role: first she is viewed as a mother, then as a daughter:

> My young bride, did you hear the ghostly one? ...oh little mother... I needed you as the abyss across which my body must be drawn... For I confess to you, daughter, my weakness... was also a weight of longing on my earth-held limbs. (65)

Death, when it finally comes to the king's horseman, does not come with honour and glory but limping and bereft of honour and late, for the "moment" is already past (62). Elesin watches the moon, for it is to its movement that life and death are connected. Mircea Eliade comments upon lunar symbolism and its meaning for religious man. It not only brings together "such heterogeneous things as: birth, becoming, death, and resurrection; the waters, plants, woman, fecundity and immortality"; but also reveals to man the link between life and death and "above all, *that death is not final, that it is always followed by a new birth.*"[17]

Thus the reversal is at many levels, including the reversal in the attitude to time: it has to stop for Elesin because for all practical purposes he is no longer alive. He is a man who ought to have been dead by now but is not. The concept of "honour" in the sense Elesin uses is quite familiar to all cultures. Arthur Miller's protagonists one after the other are willing to die for it.[18] In the first act Elesin had said, "Life is honour. It ends when honour ends" (15). Now Olunde because "he could not bear to let honour fly out of doors" has stopped it with his life (75).

Death, as it appears in the play, has many faces, faces difficult to identify and pin down under any one name. Is death, as it is prepared for and welcomed in the first act, suicide or sacrifice or martyrdom? Pilkings is unable to understand Amusa's description of it and wonders whether it is murder or suicide (26-27). Death is discussed very dispassionately by Olunde (57) as an acceptance of the physical termination of life. There is another face of death in the story of the captain who blows himself up with the ship (51), a story which also offers a parallel to Elesin's proposed death. Death strikes one as a necessity when Olunde offers himself (75) in his father's place and as a superfluity when Pilkings threatens to use violence. (Iyaloja comments on this: "To prevent one death you will actually make other deaths?" [73]). When death comes finally to Elesin, it is a violent death; it is now purely identifiable as suicide bereft of the original significance of the rite and is outside it. But again it is only a completion of something which had already taken place when Pilkings had stopped him from dying. The indignity he has suffered can only be wiped out through death.

It is difficult to see death categorically as barbaric or civilised, for the initial ritual has several overtones. It has to be viewed in its proper context, which is not that archaic cultures are more "communal" and contemporary cultures more "individual," but how does a culture view lineage, time, death, and religion.[19] Seen from the structural point of view, the play has two endings: one in the third act and one in the fifth. They are the two deaths which Elesin faces, and they constitute a contrast to each other. The second and the final death is a weak duplicate of the first. Death and life are seen as parallels in the first act, and even when they meet, they meet in harmony—not so in the final act. Here they become an encounter, and death, instead of being a continuation of life becomes an escape from it. The transformation which takes place, takes place in Elesin's reason for willing death. The final act is also full of dramatic deception; both Pilkings and Iyaloja are hiding the truth from Elesin, though for entirely different reasons: one, to calm him and reconcile him to his fate; the other, in order to excite him and push him over the edge. The truth, when it comes, does free Elesin's will and enables him to complete the task he had begun and to fulfil his pledge.

Is the play, then, a tragedy in the Aristotelian sense? Is the ending Elesin's failure or Pilkings's? Partly, I think, it is both. Pilkings has failed in what he set out to do, but his failure is not the source of tragedy; on the other hand, his action is. The tragedy lies in Elesin's "laggard" will, in the displacement of his world and the reversal of his role; even Olunde's death is not a tragic event in itself but becomes tragic in its effect on Elesin, as an event in the whole sequence. What arouses pity and fear is the contrast between the manner of death Elesin had been preparing for all his adult life and the actual manner of his death, in the necessity of his death even when it has lost its initial purpose. There can be and need be no rational explanation for this need: it is a matter of faith and understanding. There is thus no approval or disapproval in Soyinka's stance[20] but a mere unfolding of the cultural sensibility, of the meaning so firmly and irrefutably embedded within its own world. Compared to its logic, the actions of the white world suddenly acquire a semblance of interference, of disruption or violence, and of an implied logical and cultural superiority somehow determined to displace this world. This, like the whole colonial incident, is also only an incidental by-product of the main event which primarily is concerned with the meaning of Elesin's life and finally his death and which gradually moves out from a religious context into a tragic one.

Notes

1. Soyinka, in his note prefacing the text of *Death and the King's*

Horseman, disapproves of the "facile tag" of "clash of cultures" as a method of interpreting such situations and, regarding the colonial factor, points out that it is "a catalytic incident merely" (London: Eyre Methuen, 1975) 6-7. All references to the play are to this edition, henceforth referred to as *DKH*.

2. I do not mean to suggest that Soyinka is not a serious dramatist; but while the comic and the satirical dominate several of his plays—like *The Lion and the Jewel* (1963), *The Trials of Brother Jero* (1964), *Kongi's Harvest* (1967), and *The Road* (1965) to mention only a few—in *Death and the King's Horseman*, the metaphysical aspect is uppermost. Eldred Jones in a perceptive article on Soyinka discusses the serious element in his work at great length ("Wole Soyinka: Critical Approaches," *The Critical Evaluation of African Literature*, ed. Edgar Wright [London: Heinemann, 1973] 64-65), but Jones's article precedes the writing of *DKH*.

3. There is a great deal of affinity between the plays of John Millington Synge and those of Wole Soyinka. Their plays, no matter whether they are comic or tragic, use irony as a dominant strategy. I would also like to point out that in most of Soyinka's plays the reversal is not tragic. For instance, see *The Lion and the Jewel*, also *A Dance of the Forests* (where it does not turn out to be tragic for the dead ancestors); *The Swamp Dwellers* is in every way a serious play yet not a tragic one, for there is hope at the end.

4. See Author's Note, *DKH* 7.

5. Wole Soyinka, "Drama and the African World View," *Exile and Tradition*, ed. Rowland Smith (London: Longman, 1976) 176.

6. Johan Huizanga, *Ritual, Play, and Performance*, ed. Richard Schechner and Mady Schuman (New York: Seabury Press, 1976) 57.

7. Ibid. 60. Also see Schechner's own article, "From Ritual to Theatre and Back," in the same collection, 207.

8. For detailed background, see Oludare Olajubu, "Iwi Egungun Chants—an Introduction," *Critical Perspectives on Nigerian Literatures*, ed. Bernth Lindfors (London: Heinemann, 1979) 3. The ancestral dress of bright-colored material covering the head and the body is part of ancestor worship based on the "firm belief that the spirit of man never dies, but that after death, his spirit continues to influence the life of the community from another sphere."

9. "We shall all meet at the great market" (17).
10. Mircea Eliade, *The Sacred and the Profane*, trans. Willard R. Trask (New York: Harper & Row, 1961) 146. David Richards, however, does not see this. union in this light. In a recently published article, "Owe l'esin oro: Proverbs like Horses: Wole Soyinka's *Death and the King's Horseman*" (*Journal of Commonwealth Literature* 19.1 [1984]: 86-94), he is of the view that Elesin, on the eve of his ritual suicide, "artificially embroils sexual passion in the wider metaphysical process of the transition from the world of the living to the world of the ancestors" and looks upon the child of this union as an abiku (a half-child), referring among other things to *A Dance of the Forests*. There is, however, no parallel in the two situations. In *A Dance of the Forests*, the woman dies while pregnant, and the unborn child, who by rights belongs to the land of the living, remains unborn. The woman's restlessness and consequent return to the earth is because of the child:

> It is a hard thing to carry this child for a hundred generations. And I thought... when I was asked, I thought... here was a chance to return the living to living that I may sleep lighter (London: O.U.P., 1979) 5.

However, all references in *DKH* to the child of Elesin's union with the new bride are referred to as rare and fortunate. See pp. 20-22, esp. 22, when Iyaloja says, "It is good that your loins be drained into the earth we know, that your last strength be ploughed back into the womb that gave you being." Also see p. 40, where Elesin refers to it as the "promise of future life." Richards's interpretation has no justification in the text.
11. See Oyekan Owomoyela, "Folklore and Yoruba Theatre," *Critical Perspectives on Nigerian Literatures*, 34.
12. Eliade 148-49.
13. Robert Scholes, *Semiotics and Interpretation* (New Haven: Yale University Press, 1982) 76.
14. Ibid. 76-77.
15. *DKH* 60.
16. Richards 90-94.
17. Eliade 156.
18. Arthur Miller's protagonists, one after the other, die or collapse or become victims because of the loss of this honour. Proctor in

The Crucible (1953) chooses death to loss of honour. He asks, "How may I live without my name? I have given my soul; leave me my name!" There is however no such dichotomy between name and soul for Elesin.

19. Besides Soyinka's own rejection of this approach, there are other critics who see beyond this limited approach. See J.Z. Kronenfeld's, "The 'Communalistic' African and the 'Individualistic' Westerner: Some Comments on Misleading Generalizations in Western Criticism of Soyinka and Achebe," *Critical Perspectives on Nigerian Literatures* 237-39.

20. See Richards 90.

References

Eliade, Mircea. *The Sacred and the Profane.* Trans. Willard R. Trask. New York: Harper and Row, 1961.

Jones, Eldred. "Wole Soyinka: Critical Approaches". *The Critical Evaluation of African Literature.* Ed. Edgar Wright. London: Heinemann, 1973.

Huizanga, Johan. "Nature and Significance of Play as a Cultural Phenomenon". *Ritual, Play and Performance.* Ed. Richard Schechner and Mady Schuman. New York: Seabury Press, 1976.

Kronenfeld, J.Z. "The 'Communalistic' African and the 'Individualistic' Westerner: Some Comments on Misleading Generalisations in Western Criticism of Soyinka and Achebe". *Critical Perspectives on Nigerian Literatures.* Ed. Bernth Lindfors.

Olajubu, Oludara. "Iuri Egungun Chants—an Introduction". *Critical Perspectives in Nigerian Literatures.* Ed. Bernth Lindfors. London: Heinemann, 1979.

Owomoyela, Oyekan. "Folklore and Yoruba Theatre". *Critical Perspectives on Nigerian Literatures.* Ed. Bernth Lindfors.

Richards, David. "Owe I'esin oro: Proverbs like Horses: Wole Soyinka *Death and the King's Horseman*". *Journal of Commonwealth Literature*, 19. 1, 1984.

Schechner, Richard. "From Ritual to Theatre and Back". *Ritual, Play and Performance.*

Scholes, Robert. *Semiotics and Interpretation.* New Haven: Yale University Press, 1982.

Soyinka, Wole. *Death and the King's Horseman.* London: Eyre Methuen, 1975.

Soyinka, Wole. *The Plays of Wole Soyinka* (2 vols). Delhi: Oxford University Press, 1979.

Soyinka, Wole. "Drama and the African World View". *Exile and Tradition.* Ed. Rowland Smith. London: Longman, 1976.

19

Arun Kolatkar's "Jejuri": A Spiritual Quest?

Tanuja Mathur

The scrutiny of self and society has taken various forms in modern Indian English Poetry. Poets like A.K. Ramanujan, R. Parthasarthy and Arun Kolatkar are pre-occupied with the problem of roots. Their examination of their Hindu ethos has been in several directions. Ramanujan seems to be perpetually busy in probing the areas of strength and deficiency of his Hindu heritage. R. Parthasarthy is obsessed with his native heritage. His ambitious 'Rough Passage' is an attempt to deal with the theme of identity exposed to two cultures—the Indian and the Western.

Arun Kolatkar, a bilingual poet, who wrote in Marathi, his mother tongue as well as in English, wrote "Jejuri" in 1976, for which he was awarded the Commonwealth Poetry Prize in 1977. This long poem, with several sections, may be understood as a presentation of modern urban scepticism impinging upon ancient religious tradition. This is one of the themes of the poem. Is the religious quest the chief motive behind the protagonist's journey to Jejuri? This motive seems to be evident in the poems describing the poet's visit to the town of Jejuri and the hill-temple of Khandoba, an incarnation of Lord Shiva who is also known as Malhari Martand. This town is fifty kilometers south-east of Pune and is the most prominent temple in Western Maharashtra. The God Khandoba is worshipped by all castes and communities and has Muslim devotees as well.

The visit to Jejuri is completed in half a day, starting early in the morning and ending in the late evening. It seems that the visitor is non-involved, without a sense of devotion. Thousands visit Jejuri with a spirit of worship which this modern visitor lacks. It is noteworthy that the experience is so familiar and yet so foreign to the protagonist who is an Indian.

We become aware of this non-involvement at the very beginning of the poem "The Bus", where the protagonist travels with an old man in the bus going to Jejuri. The poet, while depicting the old man as seated beside the protagonist in the bus, (who may be understood as young) is trying to bring forth a conflict between the traditional Hindu religious faith and the modern value system. The old man's destination is well-defined by the "caste-mark between his eyebrows" (49). The protagonist cannot step beyond the caste mark (49), because he has not such well-defined spiritual destination but has some few questions oppressing him. Shirish Chindhade questions, "Is it the tarpaulin flap that precludes a penetration beyond the symbolic caste-mark? In traditional Hinduism metaphysical ignorance is said to pose a curtain between the devotee and the deity, the same way as the tarpaulin flap prevents glimpses of landscape outside the bus" (93).

The journey to the religious town is made by the state transport bus which is comparatively a comfortable mode of conveyance, in view of the fact that most devotees choose to walk miles together to Jejuri. Later in the poem, the protagonist seems to be rendered incapable of stepping "inside the old man's head" (49) with the caste-mark which symbolises deep devotion. It is at this point that a question can be raised. How far does "Jejuri" appeal as an analysis of the Hindu religious and spiritual sensibility for which India is traditionally known? The experience of the protagonist here is very different from the kind of sensibility defined by other writers where it "exalts minds and makes all the burden light". The impersonal approach in the poem is further enhanced by the use of a persona referred to in phrases like "you look down" "you search for", "your own divided face" (48) "you seem to move" (49). This works as an effective device to detach the modern pilgrim from the state of a heightened religious sensibility defined in Nissim Ezekiel's "Enterprise". The modern sensibility of the protagonist is blunted by forces of rationalism and scepticism with the result that there is an incapacity to see the roots of traditional culture.

The poem "An Old Woman" speaks for the Jejuri ethos and culture. In "The Bus" the poet depicts an old man. Here it is an old woman. With the repetitive use of the word "old", it seems that the poet wishes to emphasise the contrast between the old and the new. The old stands for the cultural or the traditional whereas the new or the modern is symbolic of the rational or the intellectual in order to be religious.

The old women in Kolatkar's poem has no official status but is a self-appointed guide whose only excuse is to pester pilgrims. The poet says:

>   She wants a fifty paise coin.
>   She says she will take you
>   to the horseshoe shrine. (49)

which the protagonist has already visited. The above lines bring forth the socio-economic status of India, where even a fifty paise coin is very meaningful to the old woman. The poet also expresses the fact that the age-old materialistic outlook attached to the religious places does not convince the modern pilgrim at all. The old woman is sticky like a "burr" and the question she asks later in the poem is disturbing:

>   what else can an old woman do
>   on hills as wretched as these? (50)

She may be a one time murli or devadasi, now old, therefore without any commercial prospects. Kolatkar here describes the decay and the ruin of the old religious order. He says,

> the cracks that begin around her eyes
> spread beyond her skin. (50)

It is towards the end of the poem that the poet voices his experience at the temple of Khandoba,

> ...you are reduced
> to so much small change
> in her hand. (50)

In "Makarand", which is a small poem in the Jejuri collection, there is a contrast which is built up by Kolatkar between spiritual faith depicted by the "you" and her atheistic companion—she supplies what he lacks, namely an experiential response. In the absence of such a response, the protagonist's exasperation is noticeable:

> Take my shirt off
> and go in there to do pooja?
> No thanks.
>
> Not me
> But you go right ahead
> if that is what you want to do.
>
> Give me the matchbox
> before you go,
> Will you?
>
> I will be out in the courtyard
> where no one will mind it
> if I smoke. (51)

who is this 'I'—the protagonist or the poet? Who is preparing for a pooja? The question raised by the protagonist in the beginning of the poem and the use of the negatives intensify the fact that the visitor or the modern pilgrim is detached from the scene to the extent that he regards smoking as more rewarding than perhaps performing pooja. There is an assertive and direct finality about the preferences of the protagonist. The burning of incense and the lighting of cigarette by the same matchbox have to be studied in sharp contrast, one illuminates through faith whereas the other simply burns itself to further decay. They throw light on the poet's intention of pointing out the larger contrast at Jejuri—mainly, the slowly wearing off of ancient faith vis-à-vis an impatient modern sensibility. The metropolitan intellectual sensibility is brought in a close encounter with orthodox culture and therefore, fails to register appropriate response. This further suggests the total collapse of modern religious sensibility.

The "Chaitanya" section which takes us back to the 15th century, reveals how the return to the past makes no difference to the protagonist's scepticism. Chaitanya Mahaprabhu, the noted Bengali Vaishnava saint, whom some worship as an incarnation of Krishna, is said to have visited Jejuri around 1510 and exhorted the murlis to mend their ways, as a result of which a murli named Indira, is supposed to have reformed herself. In the first of these two sections, Chaitanya's attitude to the stones of Jejuri is described. He found these stones god-like even without the red paint and "sweet as grapes" (50). But the last section of "Chaitanya" makes it clear that the visit of the saint has made no difference to the place. The ignorant ones, like the protagonist, experience a discomfort:

> he popped a stone
> in his mouth
> and spat out gods. (50)

What then is "Jejuri" about? Is it about an emotional, aesthetic, cultural or a spiritual quest? Is it about a need for faith? S.K Desai says, "the protagonist goes to Jejuri not as a seeker... not as a pilgrim.... He is a kind of a traveller... a tourist" (48-49).

When asked by an interviewer whether he believed in God, Kolatkar answered, "I leave the question alone. I don't think I have to take a position about God, one way or the other". "Jejuri" may be understood as a confrontation of the ancient religious tradition and the modern industrial civilisation—the latter overpowering the old religious order. Arun Kolatkar, as a twentieth century poet, ends on the note of doubt and scepticism which does not convey sense of closure or finality but leaves the issue open-ended. Herein lies the richness of meaning which is attached to "Jejuri". R. Parthasarthy's observation regarding the poem is quite succinct and precise. He says, "Apparently it is about the poet's irreverent odyssey to the temple of Khandoba at Jejuri.... In reality, however the poem oscillates between faith and scepticism in a tradition that has run its course" (40).

References

Chindhade, Shirish. *Five Indian English Poets*. Delhi: Atlantic Publishers and Distributors, 1996.

Desai, S.K. "Arun Kolatkar's Jejuri: A House of God". *The Literary Criterion* XV, 1, 1980.

Parthasarthy, R. *Ten Twentieth Century Indian Poets*. Delhi: Oxford Press, 1993.

20

Homecoming of an "Exile" after "Whoring after English Gods"?

Krishna Sharma

In this paper my endeavor is to trace the homecoming of R. Parthasarthy, the exile, after his disenchantment with the English Gods. For instance one would like to ask the question why does he return? Is this homecoming a quest for identity? If yes, whether this quest is personal or cultural? Does he find his "Self"? His native roots? His Indian Gods?

The answers to these questions lie scattered in his poem *Rough Passage* and in his own statements given time and again. The very word "colonial" rings like a bell that tolls an Indian to the nations subjection under the British Raj. The term "colonial" broadly signifies a political subjection but it may also be extended to include ingrained cultural and literal marginalisation/subjection, thus making colonials a rootless throng in their own homes. The end of British rule may have ended in 1947, but the impact of colonial imperialism still appears to persist; they still "rule us" and our normative patterns are derived from them, our intellectual tradition influenced by them. By influencing us deeply at a psychological level, they have converted us into "fractured selves" which Nayantara Sahgal referred to as the "schizophrenic self"[1], Bharati Mukherjee as "hyphenated self"[2] while Jasbir Jain calls the "bicultural self"[3]. Call it what one may, but how long are we going to obfuscate the issues of our rootlessness? These jargons, it is evident, will not help us to find our roots. The very use of words like "colonial", "post-colonial" underlines the irony when we are 50 years old as a "nation", and are on the verge of entering the 21st century. Our writers and critics will have to decolonise themselves, rethink their norms and respond to various political, cultural and philosophical crises specific to our own societies, evolve our own concepts and theories rooted in our social milieu and our literary practice. Let us honestly accept that we have not yet been able to coin our terms; shape our cultural forms and sharpen our own measures in criticism and literature though I admit that the process has begun but it is still very slow.

Edward Said in *Orientalism* has underlined the limitations which a colonial consciousness imposes on a nation. One looks at one's self through the eyes of others and judges oneself by their yardsticks, adopts what is given out. Said says:

> The most important thing about the theory during the first decade of the twentieth century was that it worked, and worked staggeringly well. The argument, when reduced to its simplest form, was clear, it was precise, it was easy to grasp. There are Westerners, and there are Orientals. The former dominate; the latter must be dominated, which usually means having their land occupied, their internal affairs rigidly controlled, their blood and treasure put at the disposal of one or another Western power. (36)

Colonial consciousness may have two facets; first, its acceptance of an imperial model and the other, its rejection. We will have to come out of this colonial cocoon and take a critical look at our own cultural roots, with which we can identify ourselves, in our mirrors with our own eyes as we are—good or bad; measure ourselves not by imported yardsticks or theories/ideologies, but by our own indigenous norms. Ashis Nandy in *The Intimate Enemy: Loss and Recovery of Self under Colonialism* points out colonialism is an attitude of mind and does not necessarily coincide with political control (Preface xvi).

Born in Tiruchirapalli in 1934, educated at Don Bosco High School and Siddartha College, Parthasarthy was a lecturer in Bombay for ten years, before he joined the O.U.P. in 1971 as Regional Editor in Madras. During 1963-64 he was a British Council Scholar at Leeds University where he read Linguistics. In 1978 he moved to New Delhi as Editor O.U.P. During 1978-79 he was a member of IOWA's International Program.

His works include *Poetry from Leeds* (1968) edited with J.J. Healy; *Ten Twentieth Century Indian Poets* (1976) and *Rough Passage* (1977) which published at the age of forty three was a runner-up for Commonwealth Poetry Prize in 1971. *Rough Passage* is a unique book of verse of three tier structure: "Exile" written between 1963-67; "Trial" the second part written between 1961-74; and "Homecoming" the final part written between 1971-78.

Parthasarthy's concern for poetry and literature shows a consciousness, a need for holding to roots in myth and tradition; a cautious and creative return indeed to native modes of perception and articulation. Like A.K. Ramanujan, Parthasarthy's quest for identity is ingrained in his sense of exile. Like Kamala Das's autobiography *My Story*, Parthasarthy's essay "Whoring after English Gods" has many confessional statements about his sense of alienation. He seems to suffer from a feeling of rootlessness, disconnection and disorientation. In a way this essay could be taken as a background to understand "Rough Passage", which takes stock of his history of growing up ("As a man approaches thirty he may/take stock of himself"). It provides not only the background, the historical and personal circumstances in response to which the poem eventually came to be written, but also the terms of reference. At school and in college he was intensely attracted to English ideas and attitudes (while highly critical of everything Indian) so much so that he decided that "England would be my future home" (66). The result was a sense of alienation from his native culture and a distancing from Indian life and its values. But as he matured and took stock of himself he saw the other aspect of English life. He was highly disillusioned and disenchanted like E.R. Braithwaite in his novel *To Sir, with Love* who also felt betrayed by the British ideals of equality, freedom and fraternity. Parthasarthy could feel the attacks on social ethos; the racial discrimination; the fast food values where the soul gets eaten up like a hamburger. He confesses that he found himself an alien in the England he experienced. "...I found myself crushed under two hundred years of British rule in India. My disenchantment was total, I felt betrayed" (66). Along with this came a sense of nostalgia for home, a sense of crisis and an overall failure of nerve; a need for self definition/identity.

"Exile" is, as Parthasarthy says, about the consequences of British rule, "one of the consequences it explores is the loss of identity" and a sense of estrangement from one's own culture and therefore "the need for roots". The failure to associate himself with the alien culture on the one hand, despair to identify himself with his native culture on the other hand converted him into a bundle of nerves. He decided to return home, "to the Indian soil under the hot Indian sky. . .I felt strangely at home. England had been a trial by fire. . . and the ashes are the few poems I have written in English" (70).[4]

In "Homecoming" he describes some events of family re-union since his grandfather's death in 1959. He recalls recognising his cousin, Sundari, the social meetings "on the steps of the choultry" (inn) and gives a vivid image of "...the familiar coconuts out of the fire of rice-and-pickle afternoons" (141) in a spicy language. The memories of the Vikai river, the sea, the streets, the overcrowded buses, the sky at home all seem to bend "in adoration/under a diminished sun" (142). About his intercourse with poetry he says, "Only poetry offered a kind of knowledge I despaired of finding anywhere else: Knowledge of oneself" (70) which he seems to have found in Indian and Tamil heritage.

The chief motif of Parthasarthy's poetry is the very sense of exile which reinforced the need for native roots and quest for self. "Exile" explores the poets search for identity and the self at one level, while at an extended level it also explores his relationship with colonial culture where the reflection of the self's past brings forth sentiments of betrayal and remorse. Love and words are "hunchbacked" and the poetic self searches creative fulfillment in admiring native gods and language.[5] The little of Parthasarthy's essay "Whoring after English Gods" is also very suggestive. By using a religious metaphor he suggests that English gods i.e. English culture, English ideals, English way of life, English language etc. could not give him ease, security and satisfaction which he could have got by marrying his native gods.

A surface reading of the poem reveals the poet's desire to concretise various experiences and his responses to various problems/phases of life. It is a type of loud thinking, taking stock of the poet persona's own life and his inner self. The tests and tribulations, the dichotomy of existence and language generically are different from the dilemma of love of culture and identity. The tensions here are the tensions of a poet's experience and expression i.e. the poet's endeavour to unfold his experiences through a creative medium (language); the tension between his English and Tamil sensibilities. At another level, however, an extended meaning elevates the aesthetic sensibilities and perceptions which D.W. Harding feels may rightly be "telescoped back into the poem and be present to us when we read it again—present to us with immediacy, not through a secondary process of reflection or decoding". The opening lines of "Exile." "As a man approaches thirty he may/Take stock of himself/Not that anything important/At thirty the mud will have settled./You see yourself in a mirror,/Perhaps, refuse the image as yours," (137) at one level indicate that the poet's aim is to take stock of his self which suggests that the persona in 'Exile' is a man in a mood of introspection and has reached an age of maturity. His reflections upon the past experiences of life and the mistakes he had committed, seem prophetic "You stir, and the mirror dissolves/Experience doesn't always make for knowledge/You make the same mistakes" (137).

He refuses to recognise his self and therefore decides to give quality to the other half of his life. Read in this light the poem highlights the personal, not the cultural perspective, while at the same time the focus might be changed and the poem may be used as resisting the culture of Europe and examining the consequences of British rule on an Indian which results in loss of identity of his cultural self. So the "passage" though "rough" proved fruitful in as much as he comes face to face with the falsity of his personal and cultural myths. The conflicting values of idealism and compelling exigencies of reality are portrayed through various images. The poet persona remembers "the woman (which could also be English language) you may have loved/you never married", although "...these many years years/you warmed yourself at her hands./All right your hand has/rested on her left breast" (137). This image suggests his intimate relationship with English literature and culture which proves to be a futile association, the "maya-like veil" is soon lifted. He confesses the futility of this relationship which was barren and one-sided when he says. "He went for the wrong gods from the start./And marriage made it worse./He hadn't read his Greek poets well:/better to bury a woman than marry her" (143). He comes face to face with a crucial reality when he writes,

> There is something to be said for an exile
> You learn roots are deep
> The language is a tree, loses colour
> Under another sky
> The bark disappears with the snow and branches become hoarse.
> (138)

This realisation is neither shocking nor disgusting, it is an unimpassioned realisation that following the wrong gods will never yield a harvest of creative satisfaction. Only one's own place and language are fertile and authentic. Thus running after false gods ultimately exhausts and drains one's faculties. So much so, that a person may never be the same again.

The dichotomy of Parthasarthy's fascination with two cultures, diametrically opposite, can be seen throughout the poem. Ultimately he discovers that the alien imperial culture will not accept him, " 'coloureds' is what they call us/over there" (138). Similarly, the disillusionment about the "jewel city" is also vocalized ". . . the city is no jewel, either" (138). It is again like any other city. The poet voyages from city to city in search of anchors only to encounter the impact and imprints of the West, which he wanted to escape from. Thus, he faces an emotional trauma and finds himself levelling off rather fast. Frustration then sets in. He (the exile) starts donning his Indian clothes and flaunt his Indianness. When he returns, whether for a short stint, or for good, he faces disillusionment. The country and the people he had left have changed (he was not aware of these changes while in the foreign country); the past he wished to return is not there, it also keeps changing. The exile then feels that his genetic make-up, his environment, his experiences, his responses could neither be understood at home (by the Indians) nor abroad (by the English)[6]. The search, however, continues and this modern Ulysses reaches his ancestral home in Madras, where a disillusioned self cries,

> What have I come
> here for a thousand miles.
> The sky is no different
> Beggars are the same everywhere
> The Clubs are there, complete with bar and gold links.

The streets of Madras are disfigured by high breasted cardboard-and-paper goddesses, people are unable to communicate, and worst of all, "The sun has done its worst/skimmed a language/Worn it to a shadow." His urge to share his inner experiences and his craving for fulfillment remains unfulfilled. He regrets that the last thirty years "Have given me (him) little wisdom/and I've dislodged myself to find it."

The city is the same everywhere be it London, Madras, Bombay or Calcutta. If in Madras he finds materialistic western concerns prevalent after uprooting the spiritual essence of the Dravidian values and replacing "The hour glass of Tamil mind/by exact chronometer/of Europe," in Calcutta the sky oppresses him. His old love (his language, people and culture) smells of gin and cigarette ash and "Your (her) breasts/Sharp with desire, hurt my (poets) fingers" (76).

The dislocated, fractured self becomes an alien unable to hold a union or communion with everything around him in this wide world. Yet in the end he learns a lesson that despite the mistakes of the past ("You make the same mistakes") he cannot disown anything and accepts life as it is, with a mixture of good and bad, happiness and sorrow, "Nothing can really/be dispensed with. The heart needs all."

Thus the poet helplessly swings between two extremes from "Whoring after English Gods" to distancing from Indian gods, shall we call it? Is it the inevitable destiny of a cultural schizophrenic or the helpless resignation of an exhausted self? The fact that there has been no poetry forthcoming since the publication of *Rough Passage* tells its own tale.

Notes

1. Sahgal used this title for a talk in the symposium *Asian Voices in English* held in Hong Kong, March-April, 1990. The word according to *Little Oxford Dictionary of Current English* means:mental disorder marked by disconnection between thoughts feelings and actions. Sahgal seems to refer to the disorientation of exile's external and internal, native and alien worlds.
2. in *Jasmine* Mukherjee makes a distinction between the hyphenated self and the transferred one. By "hyphenated" she suggests that the exile adopts the culture and ways of life of imperial/alien country because he is attracted towards it. I recall some lines of K.N. Daruwalla published in *Indian Literature*, Sahitya Akademi Journal No. 188 Nov-Dec. 1998, which expresses the condition of a hyphenated self:

Living on Hyphens

a man needs to anchor himself

Between dream and landscape

and between dream and the dark blood

Congealing on the cobblestones;

between hierarchy and disorder;

between the slow rhythms of the reasons

and the frenetic pace of blood;

a man must arrive

at some sort of understanding.

3. Jasbir Jain uses the term to indicate a person who absorbs/adopts two cultures, but is unable to associate or identify his self with any of them. This hybridity causes frustration and the exile keeps swinging between these cultures.
4. This homecoming reminds one of the sense of ease and satisfaction one feels when one reaches home after a long absence. One also recalls the homecoming of Ram to Ayodhya after fourteen years; of Ulysses returning to his home-kingdom after his long, adventurous voyage.
5. Parthasarthy expresses his feelings in 'Homecoming' thus:

My tongue in English chains
I return after a generation, to you.
I am at the end

of my dravidic tether,
hunger for you unassuaged.
I falter, stumble

Speak a tired language..."(141)

This sense of ambiguity is pathetically verbalised by Mabel IMD Khude in the following lines:

Here we stand
Infants overblown
Poised between two civilizations
Finding the balance irksome...
...
I am tired, O my God, I am tired
I am tired of hanging in the middle may. (67)

('Fingerprints: On Creativity and Responsibility' by Indira Parthasarthy. *Indian Literature* 150 July-Aug 1992.)

References

Jain, Jasbir. *Problems of Post Colonial Literature and Other Essays.* Jaipur: Printwell, 1991.

Mukherjee, Bharati. *Jasmine.* Viking, 1990.

Nandy, Ashis. *The Intimate Enemy: Loss and Recovery of Self Under Colonialism.* Delhi: Oxford University Press (1983), 1989. Preface XVI.

Paniker, K. Ayyappa. ed. *Modern Indian Poetry in English.* New Delhi: Sahitya Akademi, 1991.

Parthasarthy, R. "Whoring after English Gods", *Writers in East-West Encounters: New Cultural Bearings.* Ed. Guy Amrithanayagam. London: Macmillan, 1982.

—. *Rough Passage.* Delhi: Oxford, University Press, 1977.

—. ed. *Ten Twentieth Century Indian Poets.* Delhi: Oxford University Press (1976), 1993.

Said, Edward. *Orientalism.* Penguin Books (1978), 1991.

21
The Divided Self in Parthasarthy's *Rough Passage*

Veena Jain

> There is something to be said for exile: you learn roots are deep.
> (Parthasarthy, *Rough Passage* 17)

Parthasarthy's paradoxical stand forms the very basis of postcolonial writing. The term postcolonial encompasses a wide range of experiences; the basic and foremost being one of uprootedness or marginalisation: be it the migrant, the indigenous, the refugee, the minority or the female writer. Expatriate writing is one of the most important offshoots of postcolonial experience and with it is attached a feeling of exile. Jasbir Jain feels, "the word 'exile' evokes multiple meanings which cover a variety of relationships with the mother country alienation, forced exile, self imposed exile, political exile and so on" (*Writers of the Indian Diaspora* 12). Exile brings displacement and displacement leads to alienation which in turn gives rise to nostalgia. Hence "exile" is invariably linked to "roots" and to the concept of home. The exiled writer looks back from his adopted homeland to his mother country.

The expatriate writer thus reflects the consciousness of someone being trapped between two cultures. Though initially the writer becomes an immigrant when he begins to spread out and seek new sources of sustenance in other cultures, he soon turns back to assert his nativist/ethnic identity. In the case of Indian expatriate writers, along with their feeling of liberation and process of growth (which some times takes the form of rebellion from traditional religious practices) is the awareness of having lost their touch with India. Hence it is nostalgia accompanied by a sense of loss. As Bruce King remarks, "The ability to tolerate, accommodate other cultures without losing the consciousness of being Indian, marks the expatriate poets" (209). The dilemma of the Indian expatriate writer is thus to remain "Indian" while turning "international".

Postcolonial criticism has divided itself on the issue of nationalistic culture versus multiculturalism or hybridity as parameters for genuine postcolonial experience. Hybridity, in the case of the third world migrant writer, would mean his mixing and borrowing freely from other culture/cultures that exist in his adopted homeland. It is the immigrant borrowing from the European and not vice-versa especially in a country like England. In this sense, as an immigrant, the word hybrid becomes synonymous with multiculturalism. Hybridity is privileged over the nationalistic stance of the migrant writer by some of the academicians and theorists as Homi Bhabha[1] and Gayatri Spivak. With the growing popularity of Salman Rushdie's works, his utterances[2] have become pronouncements for theorists like Bhabha. On the other hand we have Aijaz Ahmad[3] favouring cultural nationalism. Ahmad is critical of Bhabha when he writes, "The affinities of class and location then lead Bhabha, logically, to an exorbitant celebration of Salman Rushdie" *(In Theory* 69). Similarly Viney Kirpal in her introduction to *The Postmodern Indian English Novel* argues against a postmodernist reading of all postcolonial works. She writes, "... the idea of a hybrid, multicultural identity, the feeling of belonging to a larger universe has been with our writers almost since the inception of the Indian English novel and not since the 1980s as is being made out because of recent commodification of the metro-based migrant writer as a more authentic representer of India"(9).

So if the criteria for privileging a migrant writer is multiculturalism or multiple identities, it becomes a weak stand and if he is favoured for facing a bicultural conflict, a similar conflictual truth is experienced by the native writer as well in the onslaught of cultural appropriation by the Empire.

Moreover, another important question arises when we talk of the Indian expatriate writer representing India. How much Indian is the Indian writer's experience who is writing in another country? His vision may be fractured like that of Naipaul who eyes India with a sardonic humour or romanticisation of the past may lead to present disappointment and hence may give rise to a satiric vein as in the case of most Indian English expatriate poets.

Rajagopal Parthasarthy's *Rough Passage* claims a special place in the canon of Indian English writing as his poetry assembles in itself the migrant's feeling of exile and the nationalist's strong desire to establish a vital link with his culture. In this long autobiographical poem written over a period of fifteen years, the years between 1971 and 1975 belong to a period of return to India after his brief stay in England. Hence the poem voices the conflicts of biculturalism both in and out of his country. It is, in fact, a projection of the tortured Indian mind, the divided self that remains lonely even after his return to India. The division of *Rough Passage* into "Exile", "Trial" and "Homecoming" is the division of the migrant's experience into three different phases of life where exile leads to trial and then to homecoming.

As a postcolonial piece *Rough Passage is* blatantly critical of the consequences of colonial rule and language is the strongest factor that has contributed towards it. Language is not just a medium for self expression: it affirms one's identity, it relates to one's culture, it is an agency of growth. Hence with the appropriation of language, a man's self is distanced from his native traditions, culture and thought processes.

When in England, the poet (Parthasarthy) finds himself alienated through language, culture and societal change. It is from a feeling of alienation and rejection, of disappointment and a sense of loss of one's identity that he returns to his homeland. He is unable to sustain his selfhood by "accommodating other cultures" within himself and hence returns to India to deepen his links with Tamil culture. The first part of the poem "Exile" depicts the disillusioned poet in England, with his ideal of Englishness being shattered. He experiences it in the racial prejudice of the whites against Indians and in the cultural shock he receives on visiting England. He writes in "Exile 2":

> its suburban pockets
> bursting with immigrants
> 'coloureds' is what they call us
> over there—the city is no jewels, either;
>
> (*Rough Passage* 17)

Parthasarthy feels it is his English language education that has distanced him from his native tradition of Tamil culture. The language itself as a medium poses less of a problem. But it keeps the writer "aware of his Indianness" most of the time in a self-conscious manner. Then there is the quality of experience, the cultural lag that haunts the writer. The poet feels, "at the bottom of it all, one suspects a crisis of identity" (*Ten Twentieth Century Indian Poets* 4). The foreignness of the English tongue does not echo for Parthasarthy his traditional associations with the past. "One of the basic problems for the poets has been to find an adequate and above all a personal language. A few have been successful. But by and large they have not been able to Indianize it" (*Ten Twentieth Century Poets* 7).

The English language has "chained him" as he says in the third section "Homecoming" which consists of poems written since 1971. For him, language divides his very personality he writes,

> My tongue in English chains/
> I return, after a generation to you
> ... I falter, stumble.
> Speak a tired language (49).

It is not just a distancing from his native culture and tradition but ultimate dependence on the foreign tongue that has made him impotent to write in his own language, as well. Parthasarthy voices the dilemma of all third world writers who have to depend on a foreign language for recognition. So the guilt probes deeper into his consciousness when he goes "whoring after English gods" and herein lies the "crisis of identity" that he talks of. An extreme sense of alienation accompanies his sense of failure as a poet. He is filled with disgust when he says, "The son of a bitch fattens himself on the flesh of dead poets". This sense of personal failure in life is linked to his feeling of alienation with his culture.

He attempts to re-root himself with Tamil. But Tamil has lost it's former grandeur. It is "a tired language", it has been "hooked on celluloid, you reel down plush corridors " *(49).* The poet desperately tries to reclaim his Tamil past which he does in "The Trial" section (where he celebrates love as a sustaining relationships) and then in "Homecoming".

Family relationship and his Tamil background are evoked to give him a sense of purpose and security in life. Small touches like "sitting crosslegged on the steps of choultry," rice and pickle afternoons", Sundari his childhood playmate "squirrelling up and down Tamarind trees" build up an association with this past. A family gathering is an occasion for renewing relationships. It is with such small touches of ordinary life that the poet concretises his experience to gain selfhood.

He clings to marriage as he does to his past traditions. Responsibility for personal events gives him strength. Homecoming ends with a sense of disillusionment where he stumbles and trips over the mat outside his door. The poet's concern is also with the choice of his career as a poet. He uses the self-deprecating tone to come to terms with the reality of the present. "I have exchanged the world for a table and a chair. I shouldn't complain" (58). He feels loss of speech towards the end of life, "The balloon of poetry has grown red in the face with repeated blowing". Tamil tradition and language no more provide food for his poetic urges. Hence, the poet decides to remain content with the "small change of uncertainties".

The ironic tone and distancing form a part of Parthasarthy's poems. When he claims to be an expert in farewells, life bids farewell to his father and then he realises the crash----"I crashed, a glass house hit by the stone of father's death". Soon life would toll the death knell for him and after him for his "unborn son". He ruminates on life and its continuity and in the same strain turns towards the Vikai river. The river has now lost its sacredness like Tamil. Its "stale flowers" and "sewer" conjure up an image of decayed tradition and the effect of urbanisation and industrialisation.

Nostalgia is a feature common to all Indian English poets. Some like Ezekiel try to come to terms with the Indian situation through the use of irony and humour as in "Good Bye Party for Miss Pushpa T.S." Keki Daruwalla writes in a satiric vein and so does Kolatkar. Ramanujan feels, it is his preoccupation with Tamil, Kannada, Classics and Symbols that give him his "inner forms, images and symbols" *(Ten Twentieth Century Poets 95)*. Ramanujan becomes an example of combining his earlier Tamil experience with the present in a foreign land to ascertain and resolve the bicultural conflict where he assimilates Kannada and Tamil tradition into English. Complementing Ramanujan, Parthasarthy writes, "Ramanujan's deepest roots are in the Kannada and Tamil past and he has repossessed that past, in fact made it available in the English language. Ramanujan successfully conveyed in English what, at its subtlest and most incantational, is locked up in another linguistic tradition" (quoted by Bijay Kumar Das 128).

A feeling of restlessness governs Parthasarthy's poem. It is perhaps common to all expatriate poets. Parthasarthy's return does not guarantee solidity. The very fact that Parthasarthy is now again in America heightens his sense of shiftlessness. This shiftlessness has been beautifully captured by the images in his poetry. Adil Jussawala has commented on Parthasarthy's use of images. He says, "The strength of his poetry lies almost entirely in its visual positions and the startling image. His lines do not sing. He cultivates the deliberately prosaic style, an undertone of rhythm itself. So at their best, his poems become memorable individual images themselves" (quoted by Bijay Kumar Das 123).

The images are starkly visual. The city becomes a place of non relationship and of solitariness with its "bars, clubs and golf links". The city of London with the river Thames and Westminster Bridge instils a sense of exile and Queen Victoria is an "old hag".

So do the cities of Bombay, Calcutta and Madras disillusion him. He asks, "What have I come here for from a thousand miles? The sky is no different". He uses the tree image for language "Whose branches become hoarse under another sky." The Tamil mind is compared to the hour glass and is replaced by the "chronometer" of Europe. The English are "gods" The unbridgeable cultural gap is depicted by the "holes in a wall" or "lamp burning in the fog". The whole poem is replete with images of urbanisation as smoke, litter, sewer, suburban pockets, noises, early trains etc. "Exile 5" talks about the city itself with its "rickety legs /reeling under the heavy load of smoke."

He writes:

I am through with the city.
No better then ghettos, the suburbs
There, language is a noise,
and streets unwind like cobras
from a basket.

(Rough Passage 22)

Arvind K. Mehrotra in his essay "The Emperor has no Clothes" (*Chandrabhaga* 3, 1980 and 7, 1982) criticizes Parthasarthy for his use of generalized unreverberant language and imagery of *Rough Passage*. He is also critical of Parthasarthy's concern for Tamil tradition and language. Mehrotra wants "a language of particulars, a poetry which embodies experience rather than distances it; by embodying its locale or context within it, such poetry avoids self-conscious generalising about experience" (quoted by King 237). Mehrotra does not realise the urgency with which Parthasarthy started writing at the time of national independence when he was about fourteen. A deep urge to free himself from the shackles of colonial rule was strong in him which Mehrotra did not share for he was born in 1947 and by the time he started writing, a significant body of Indian English poetry was already being written.

Hence, asserting cultural nationalism Parthasarthy's poetry does not cater to Homi Bhabha's position of hybrid location of cultural value (Bhabha 72). He makes a strong plea to return to the native culture. Culture is a survival strategy from the nationalist stand. His poem is thus "a declaration of independence from British Literature and the idealized colonial vision of England" (King 237).

Notes

1. Homi Bhabha in *The Location of Culture* talks of culture as a strategy of survival which is both "transnational" and "translational". He writes, "it is transnational because contemporary postcolonial discourses are rooted in specific histories of cultural displacement...culture is translational because such spatial histories of displacement now accompanied by the territorial ambition of 'global' media technologies -make the question of how culture signifies, or what is signified by culture, a rather complex issue" (172). Gayatri Spivak in *Outside in the Teaching Machine* expresses a similar stand when she asks the "indigenous elite" or the "metropolitan marginal" not to produce a merely "antiquarian history which seeks the continuities of soil, language and urban life in which our present is rooted... "(64).
2. Salman Rushdie in his essay "A Dangerous Art Form" favours the migrant writer when he writes, "The ability to see at once from inside and out is a great thing, a piece of good fortune which the indigenous writer cannot enjoy" (quoted by Viney Kirpal 2).
3. Taking the opposite stand Aijaz Ahmad favours cultural nationalism. He writes, "Inevitably, then, cultural nationalism of one kind or another continues to be the constitutive ideology of the theoretical position from which these issues are raised" (69).

References

Ahmad, Aijaz. *In Theory*. Bombay: Oxford University Press, 1992.

Bhabha, Homi K. *The Location of Culture*. London, New York: Routledge, 1994.

Das, Bijay Kumar. *Modern Indo-English Poetry*. Bareilly: Prakash Book Depot, 1982.

Jain, Jasbir, ed. *Writers of the Indian Diaspora*. Jaipur: Rawat Publications, 1998.

King, Bruce. *Modern Indian Poetry in English*. Delhi: O.U.P., 1987.

Kirpal, Viney, ed. *The Postmodern Indian English Novel*. Bombay: Allied Publishers, 1966.

Parthasarthy, Rajagopal. *Rough Passage*. Delhi: O.U.P., 1977.

—, ed. *Ten Twentieth Century Indian Poets*. Delhi: O.U.P., 1976.

Prasad, Madhusudan. *Living Indian English Poets: An Anthology of Critical Essays*. New Delhi: Sterling Publishers, 1987.

Spivak, Gayatri Chakravorty. *Outside in the Teaching Machine*. London: Routledge, 1996.

22

Midnight's Children: A Fantasy

Urmil Talwar

Fantasy, as a literary device, has often been dismissed by literary critics on grounds that it is opposed to humane and more civilised practices of realistic literature. It has thus occupied the edges, margins or the peripheral regions of literary culture. The last two decades of twentieth century have seen the marginals or the peripheral regions/cultures occupy the centre. By decentering the dominant practices marginality provides a highly interrogative space to explore hybrid or contaminated relationships. One finds that fantasy too has moved from the marginal spaces to receive the attention of literary critics and authors and it has become a major device in voicing the 'Other'.

During the nineteenth century and early twentieth century the novelists for example, Sade, Mary Shelley, Wilde, M.G. Lewis, James Hogg, R.L. Stevenson and the like who had employed the fantastic mode had been relatively neglected[1]. It was only during the sixties and seventies that some French theorists[2] have drawn attention to these texts by formulating and raising some critical problems in a few articles.

The fantastic as a mode has become more popular in the post sixties and has challenged the rationalistic view of realism. It has developed as a reaction to the modernist novel, as a postmodern phenomenon where anti-mimetic is equivalent to non-real and is equated to fantasy. Todorov has defined 'the fantastic' in his book *Introduction a la Literature Fantastique* (1970; trans as *The Fantastic* 1973). He argues that the fantastic narratives involve an unresolved hesitation between the supernatural explanation available in marvellous tales and the natural or psychological explanation offered by the tales of the uncanny. Todorov has given a structural analysis of fantastic literature and has analysed different texts for common structural features that provide a more concrete definition of the fantastic. Rosemary Jackson states that Todorov had little time for metaphysics and he did not take into account the impressionistic attempts to define fantasy nor was he interested in the semantic approach like other critics who look for cluster of subjects and for the meaning of the fantastic in these subjects (Jackson 5). She undertook the writing of *Fantasy: The Literature of Subversion* towards fulfilling these omissions. In the theoretical section of her book she introduces critical material on literary fantasy both from a structuralist position and from a psychoanalytical perspective. She looks at the narrative qualities of the mode and the narrative effects of basic psychic impulses (Jackson 8). The narrative qualities of the mode could be listed as follows:

(a) Fantasy is anti-thetical or in obdurate opposition to the real and is free from the restrains of realistic texts.

(b) It refuses to observe the classical unities of space, time and character and threatens these with dissolution. It does not have a coherent plot; chronological time is exploded with time past, present and future. It loses the historical sequence and tends towards a suspension, an eternal present; characters are inconsistent and incongruent counterparts coexist where transformation can be effected.

(c) Subjective dislocation is achieved when subjects are unable to separate ideas from perception. Ideas become visible and palpable so that mind and body, mind and matter seem to merge together. This could also be achieved through metamorphosis of one shape into the other in a state of permanent flux and instability, through symbiosis of the self with other, or through ambiguous plurality. The subject is multiple and metamorphic and nothing seems stable or unitary.

(d) Other persons and other objects in a fantasy are no longer distinctly other, the limit between the subject and object is effaced and they slide into one another in a metonymical action of replacement.

(e) Uncertainty and impossibility in a fantasy are inscribed on structural level through hesitation and equivocation and on thematic level through images of formlessness, emptiness and invisibility.

(f) The basic linguistic trope of fantasy is oxymoron, that holds contradictions and sustains them in impossible unity without progressing towards synthesis.

(g) The fantastic exists as the inside or underside of the real, opposing the novel's closed monological forms with open dialogical structures, interrogating single or unitary ways of seeing and giving utterance to those elements which are known only through their absence within a dominant "realistic" order. Through these absences fantasy has a tendency towards non-signification. As there is no adequate linguistic representation of this "other" it gives rise to disjunction between signifier and signified and at times the sign becomes vulnerable to multiple and contradictory interpretations and this also gives rise to lack of meaningful signification which is at the centre of the fantastic.

(h) The fantastic thus operates in the paraxis region where the imaginary world is neither entirely real (object) nor entirely unreal (image) and is located somewhere indeterminately in the interstitial space between the two (Jackson 19).

Most fantasies depend on mirrors, glasses, reflections, doors, apertures for transmuting into the world of fancy. Alice moves through "the looking glass" in Wonderland, painted pictures of the self reflect the unconscious other in *The Picture of Dorian Gray*.

Metamorphosis into all kinds of different species is a strategy used by many authors. Mirror is another major motif in literary texts, death also dissolves the limits between this world and the underworld felicitating metamorphosis.

Dostoevsky finds in the fantastic literature an appropriate medium to express a sense of estrangement, of alienation from 'natural origins':

> if there is no soil and if there is no action possible, the striving spirit will precisely express itself in abnormal and irregular manifestations. (Dostoevsky, qt. Jackson 17)

Dostoevsky was imprisoned and exiled in Siberia whereas Rushdie, born in India, bred in Muslim culture, blossoming on English soil is migrant and a traveller across borders who has suffered a 'triple disruption' (*IH* 277). He has entered into an alien land of different cultural pattern and social norms and behaviour; he has lost his roots i.e. the sense of home as a safe place and has entered into an alien language. Rushdie writes, "denied all three, (he) is obliged to find new ways of describing himself, new ways of being human" (*IH* 278). Rushdie uses the fantastic as a mode in most of his novels like *Grimus, Midnight's Children, Shame, The Satanic Verses*. He does not employ the customary bourgeois-rationalistic-humanistic tradition[3] of story telling but he has hybridised the Oriental mode of story telling evident in *Arabian Nights* with the Western form and also the English language with Oriental languages and interspersed it with Oriental myth. But here I would trace the influence of western tradition.

Saleem's story is about the interrelatedness of the personal and the public, of his own life with the history of modern India. Rushdie can be said to have portrayed the history of India with elements of marvellous and the supernatural as this helps to resolve the immigrants' dilemma. In his essay on Gunter Grass, Rushdie writes:

> I grew up on Warden Road, Bombay; now it's Bhulabhai Desai Road. Of course, the new decolonized names tell of a confident, assertive spirit in the independent State; but the loss of past at-

tachments remains a loss. What to do? Shrug. And pickle the past in books. (*IH* 277)

And that is what Rushdie does. Rising form his pages "comes the unmistakable whiff of chutney" (37). Like flavours many—lives, events, miracles, places, rumours—leak into each other in a dense "commingling of the improbable and the mundane" (9). When an emigrant writer wishes to reclaim the past it gives rise to profound uncertainties and indeterminacy due to the disjunctive temporalities that the writer, "create(s) fictions, not actual cities or villages, but invisible ones, imaginary homelands, Indias of the mind" (*IH* 10).

In another essay "Errata; or Unreliable Narration in *Midnight's Children*" Rushdie elaborates on the discrepancies in portraying real India. He denounces Saleem Sinai as an unreliable narrator and that his novel is "far from being an authoritative guide to the history of post-independence India" (*IH* 22-23). Rushdie portrays not the real India but his version of India—one of the many possible versions, and confesses that he wished to attempt a Proustian novel, "to unlock the gates of lost time so that the past reappeared... unaffected by the distortions of memory" (*IH* 10) and that he was writing a novel "of memory and about memory" (*IH* 10). Like other migrants of his age Rushdie was carrying his India down the memory lane.

In his essay on his iconoclastic ancestor, Gunter Grass, he explicitly confesses that he was influenced by *The Tin Drum* and like Grass's Danzig, Kundera's Prague, Joyce's Dublin, Marquez's Macondo, Rushdie packed and transported along in an old tin box his Bombay, Delhi and Aligarh. Other works that influenced him were *The Film Sense* by Sergei Eisenstein, the *Crow* poems of Ted Hughes, Borges's *Fictions*, Sterne's *Tristram Shandy* (*IH* 276). M.K. Ragvendra in his review of *Midnight's Children* points out many similarities in the characters and the portrayal of history in *Midnight's Children*, *The Tin Drum* and *One Hundred Years of Solitude*. He places it between the two giants Grass and Marquez, and writes that the voices of his precursors are heard too loudly as Rushdie employed the same mode of magic realism to describe 60 years of Indian history with landmark events of the sub-continent: Jallianwalla Bagh massacre, partition and its aftermath, upto the declaration of Emergency in 1997. "Magic realism is a development out of Surrealism", writes Rushdie in his essay on Marquez and point out that it expresses:

> a genuinely 'Third World' Consciousness. It deals with what Naipaul has called 'half-made' societies, in which the impossibly old struggles against the appallingly new, in which public corruptions and private anguishes are somehow more garnish and extreme. (*IH* 301)

And this is what Rushdie achieves in *Midnight's Children*. This is a strategy used by the postcolonial migrant writer to recreate history. Rushdie uses levitation, flights, telepathy, dreams, memories, magic potions, invisibility, transformation of matter into mind to depict the phantasmagoric realities of post-independent India. Hallucination, insanity, extraordinary situations become the norm of the novel.

Rushdie's text confounds elements of both the magical and the real[4], the mimetic and the marvellous. His narrator, Saleem asserts in a manner that whatever he is saying seems real and then he introduces within that framework what is unreal or at times vice-versa. The very first sentence of the novel begins with a faery tale narration "I was born in the city of Bombay... once upon a time" and then meticulously introduces data and time and place to authenticate his record, that he was born "in Doctor Narlikar's Nursing Home on August 15th, 1947... On the stroke of midnight" (9). It seems that Rushdie wishes to establish it as a true account of the nation's history and one feels that the author has placed chunks of historical facts from the text book before us. At the same time the text abounds in phrases like "I am flying across the city... I am winging towards the Old Fort" (103), "inside the basket of invisibility, I Saleem Sinai... Vanished... Disappeared. Dematerialised. Like a djinn" (381), "I am the bomb in Bombay, watch me explode" (463), which establish it as a fantasy. Saleem overtly adds that he has been "mysteriously handcuffed to history" and his destiny "indissolubly chained to that of my country" (9). Even the PM of the nation wrote in a letter, "We shall be watching over your life with the closest attention; it will be, in a sense, the mirror of our own" (122).

Rushdie thus intermingles the recognisably realistic with the unexpected and the inexplicable, and the elements of dream or faery tale with the everyday life events and maintains the reliable tone of the objective realistic report while making space for the fantastic events. Saleem states:

> I have become... the apex of an isosceles triangle, supported equally by twin deities, the wild god of memory and the lotus goddess of the present.... (150)

Although the narrator frequently speaks of an urgent need to tell things as they really are, he is unable to do so for instance he wishes to describe "as nearly as possible in spite of this flimsy curtain of ambiguities, what actually happened" (87), he does not want to "obfuscate... further" (37), he argues "like a wild fellow" who does not even agree with himself, his "memory plunging into chasms and being swallowed by the dark, only fragments remain, none of it makes sense any more" (422). The narrator is uncertain whether it was a dream, a nightmare or "Facts as remembered. To the best of one's ability" (422). A little later the narrator wishes to immortalize/preserve these words/pickles, "although distortions are inevitable in both methods" (459). Almost near the end of the novel Saleem says:

> One day, perhaps, the world may taste the pickles of history. They may be too strong for some palates, ... I hope nevertheless that it will be possible to say of them that they possess the authentic taste of truth. (461)

His narration possesses the authentic taste of truth shrouded in curtain of ambiguities as the unreliable narrator Saleem has fallible memory and he reserves his right to be unreliable, "if you are a little uncertain of my reliability, well, a little uncertainty is no bad thing" (212). Saleem is not even sure of his parents, whether he is the son of Amina and Ahmed or of Vanita and Wee Willie Winkie? The question remains unanswered. Mary Pereira changed name-tags and Saleem "became the chosen child of midnight, whose parents were not his parents, whose son would not be his own" (117).

This "ambiguity" or "equivocation" whether to reveal or not, whether to believe or not, is the "hesitation" in the protagonist and the reader. This is incorporated at the level of narrative structure. The narrator in *Midnight's Children* deflects the reader's disbelief by confessing his own and hesitation at the level of narrative structure hinders understanding of the tale in rational terms.

The "ambiguity" or "hesitation" in the narration is due to the geographical distancing, time lag, and physical alienation of the author from the country about which he is writing. Rushdie is a migrant who suffers triple disruption, he is a hybrid of three cultures who has an access to a second tradition. This "double inscription of culture" leads to a double perspective, a second vision and he is simultaneously an "insider" and "outsider" in the society he writes about. Saleem Sinai gives a stereoscopic or a fragmentary vision from the "broken mirrors, some of whose fragments have been irretrievably lost" (*IH* 11).

Looking at India through these fragmented mirrors a multiple self is developed. Saleem says, "Consumed multitudes are jostling and shoving inside me" and to know them one has to "swallow the lot as well" (9). While sitting up one night in a pickle factory Saleem narrates the multitudinous lives in about 450 pages, the experience of three generations of Sinai family intertwined with the nation's history, to Padma his mistress in the Indian tradition of relating a story. Padma, who listens to Saleem's endless verbiage is described as the "Mother of Time" (195). She jolts the protagonist out of his dreams or hallucinations and the two are in "dialogical", interrogating relationship. Padma repeatedly questions the narrator about his birth, his parents and the truth of his life. Saleem cannot "do without her paradoxical earthiness of spirit, which keeps—kept?—my feet on the ground?" (150). Indispensable Padma, who listens patiently to Saleem's "cryptic stories" in fact questions the single or "unitary ways of seeing". Saleem reflects, "it's impossible to stop her being a critic" (32). Padma dislikes the narrator's remarks about her name 'Dung Goddess" and wishes that he should insert "a brief paean to Dung" which the narrator does in an ensuing paragraph. Analogous to the narrator's capacities in the Indian mythologies, Rushdie's narrator persona is gifted with supernatural vision, an all knowing memory, the power to enter into other people's dreams and to gallop through time and be present anywhere he wishes. Saleem not only describes his own life but extends backwards in time and his story begins at a point 32 years before his birth when his grandfather returns after having a medical degree from Heidelberg.

Rushdie dismantles the concept of character and portrays Saleem Sinai as a wildly eccentric narrator-protagonist who behaves accordingly in an hyperbolic fashion, metamorphosing from one to another in a permanent state of flux and instability. While narrating incidents related to other characters his identity slides into the other in a "metonymical" action of replacement. The other person no longer remains distinctly the other and there is an "effacing of the limits between the subject and the object". The 1001 children born with supernatural gifts on August 15, 1947 are all fragmented mirror images of the narrator who had the greatest talent of all—the ability to look into hearts and minds of men. Saleem is also endowed with the ability to become invisible and enter into other's dreams—dreams of his father, his mother, Mary and others. Reverend Mother too eavesdrops and enters her daughter's dream (55). Some other characters too gifted with similar powers are a pair of twin sisters in Orissa who possessed the ability of making every man who saw them fall hopelessly and suicidally in love with them, a Bengali boy who announced himself the reincarnation of Rabindra Nath Tagore, a Delhi beggar girl Sundari, Parvati—the Witch, a Kerala boy who had the ability of stepping into mirrors and emerging through any reflective surface in land (199-200).

Invisibility or vanishing seems to be a characteristic feature that recurs throughout *Midnight's Children*—Nadir Khan vanishes from the underworld leaving behind a note; Adam Aziz disappears and so does Mary Pereira. Saleem says, "I in a basket, disappeared, but Laylah or Parvati went without the assistance of spells" (381). Saleem has the power of a genii. Among the children born at midnight some had the "powers of transmutation, flight, prophecy and wizardry..." (200) but metamorphosis of natural form does not take place although the characters within the novel constantly seem to split into doubles and multiples. Saleem, the narrator, tends to see himself schizophrenically both in the first and third person. Shiva is the alter ego of Saleem as is Parvati of Jamila.

The split is also visible in the fragmented narration as linear time sequence is exploded and time past and time future are suspended into an eternal time present. The writer affected by Disjunctive "Temporalities" makes the narrator look at events piecemeal. Saleem declares that this fragmented vision is a legacy from his grandfather. The first chapter "The Perforated Sheet" sets the tone. Guided by the memory of a sheet with a hole cut in the centre, the narrator reconstructs life as released from a strainer; this vision from the perforated sheet. . . becomes his "talisman", his "open sesame". His grandfather, a doctor, was allowed to inspect the body of his young girl patient through the hole. Over the period he knew different areas of her body but could not imagine how would they look fitted together. Saleem claims that he was "condemned by a perforated sheet to a life of fragments" but he is not a victim like his grandfather, "I have become its master" (121), announces Saleem.

The "hole" recurs throughout the novel. Saleem's mother too was afflicted, she could not love her husband in toto as she had learnt to love parts of him, in segments, separately. She notices a hole in the centre of her father's body (13). Saleem even feels a hole at the centre of himself (193). Crowds of people line up to see his sister Jamila Singer through a hole in the sheet (313). Saleem dreams that his grandmother looks down at him through a hole in "a perforated cloud" (461). Through the peepholes of a private "Dilli dekho" machine Saleem tours the whole of India. And with a master stroke he reveals the history of a nation intertwined with his personal life piecemeal through the perforated sheet. Saleem saw his own life—"its meaning, its structures—in fragments. . ." (170). The hole in the sheet becomes codified into a symbol which is surreal and supernatural. Here the grandfather is trying to join the segments whereas Saleem's mother is breaking the whole into segments. The grandfather is a victim whereas Saleem its master; the sister is being looked at whereas the grandmother is looking through the hole and Rushdie opens up the gap between the signifier and signified and the relation of sign to meaning is hollowed out and Rushdie's fiction becomes "one of semantic excess and semantic vacuity" (Sartre, quoted in Jackson 19).

Similarly, there is a recurrence of the symbols of knees and noses and the pointing finger. The first chapter of the Book II is titled "The fisherman's pointing finger" and Rushdie writes of it in the first chapter of Book 1 "old fisherman... pointed out to sea as he told his fishy tales" (15) and Saleem's grandfather fell in love with the boatman Tai because of his "endless verbiage" that he cherished as "magical talk" (15), Saleem Sinai follows that pointing finger "eyes straining at horizon, beyond which lay my future, perhaps; my special doom, of which I was aware from the beginning" (122) and Saleem narrates his fishy tales with pointed finger which may symbolise the quest, the desire to look into seeds of time, seeking some elusive goal, pointing towards histrionic historiography of the nation. These and many more symbols recur throughout the novel but these signs are vulnerable to multiple and contradictory interpretations and this "lack of meaningful signification is of equal importance to structural equivocation suggesting the same trouble in representing or reaching a 'real', absolute signified" (Bellenium Noel qt. Jackson 38).

For Rushdie the "real" is not the absolute signified; the hermeneutics of "reality" is built on "prejudices, misconceptions and ignorance as well as on our perceptiveness and knowledge" (*IH* 25). The author-narrator persona elucidates with an analogy of sitting in a large cinema hall—

> at first in the back row, and gradually moving up, row by row, until your nose is almost pressed against the screen. Gradually, the stars' faces dissolve into dancing grain; tiny details assume grotesque proportions; the illusion dissolves or rather, it becomes clear that the illusion itself is reality. (165-6)

Rushdie wishes to emphasis the indeterminancy of reality as

the spectral region in this novel is located at the paraxis. Reality depends on the individual perception. As one moves away from the past into the present, the concrete and the plausible become more incredible. Rushdie also believes that no individual can perceive the whole truth as "we are not gods but wounded creatures, cracked lenses, capable only of fractured perceptions" (*IH* 12) and also that this is a result of cultural displacement. Through "cracked lenses" or "guilt-tinted spectacles" (*IH* 15) the individual enters reality from many angles.

> Reality can have metaphorical content; that does not make it less real. A 1001 children were born; there were a 1001 possibilities which had never been present in one place at one time before; and there were 1001 dead ends. Midnight's children can be made to represent many things, according to *your* point of view (200).

So there can be multiple points of view and reality can be multifaceted. Rushdie presents his point of view and invites the reader to have his/her point of view. These multiple and contradictory interpretations revolt against the universal monodic meaning of the text.

At the beginning of the novel the narrator hopes "to end up meaning—yes, meaning something" and then admits, "above all things, I fear absurdity" (9). Throughout the novel there is a constant shift between meaning and absurdity. At times his narrative resembles a dream and at others a nightmare. The dream forest of Sunderbans delta is an "absurd fantasy", Saleem's dream of Midnight's Children Club and his capacity to enter into other peoples dream lead to absurd situations. His freewheeling fancy takes him beyond the temporal and spatial barriers.

Metafiction, the conflation of the narrator and the author, narrator and the protagonist, licences Rushdie to be present throughout the novel and Saleem Sinai explains at length the form of his story and he knows exactly what he is doing" having (for the moment) exhausted this strain of old time fabulism, I am coming to the fantastic heart of my own story" (195). He also admits that endowed with hindsight he is "destroying the unities and conventions of fine writing" (236). Using fantasy as a device Rushdie has liberated his protagonist from the shackles of time. Slowly he erases clock time. In fact time ebbs and flows with incidents narrated. Rushdie's novel *Midnight's Children* thus fits squarely into the model of postmodernist fantasy.

Raised on the literary tradition of the West, Rushdie wrote the fabulist historiography of post-independent India in *Midnight's Children* through fabulist techniques and he follows the great tradition of Sterne, Gogol, Gunter Grass, Marquez and Joyce. Using his special blend: fantasy, the chutnification of history is achieved. It may be too strong for some palates, to others its smell may be overpowering. . . but the author has immortalized it through the process of pickling.

Rushdie's *Midnight's Children* reveals that marginality of the migrant with a double inscription, cross-pollination and hybridisation the gives a second vision and opens up a highly interrogative interstitial space with the use of fantastic and this can lead to the exploration of contaminated impure relationships.

Notes

1. The works of the novelists who employed fantasy as a mode for example, Sade's *120 Days of Sodom* (1785) *Justine, or the Misfortunes of Virtue* (1791) Mary Shelley's *Frankenstein* (1818) *The Last Man* (1836) James Hogg's *Private Memories and Confessions of a Justified Sinner* (1824) R.L. Stevenson's *The Strange Case of Jekyll and Hyde* (1896) Oscar Wilde's *The Picture of Dorian Gray* (1891), had been relatively neglected.
2. Some French critics as P.G. Castex, Marcel Schneider Louis Vax, Roger Caillois had attempted to define fantasy by cataloguing the recurrent themes and motifs in randomly selected literary works.
3. The bourgeois-rationalistic-humanistic-tradition is grounded on the assumption of a sharp differentiation between subject and object, mind and body, fantasy and objective reality, high culture

and popular culture. For discussion see Gerald Graff "The Myth of the Postmodern Breakthrough" in Malcolm Bradbury (ed.) *The Novel Today*. Fontana (1977), p. 237.

References

Baldick, Chris. *Concise Dictionary of Literary Terms*. Oxford: Oxford University Press, 1990.

Bradbury, Malcolm, ed. *The Novel Today*. London: Fontana, 1977.

Jackson, Rosemary. *Fantasy: The Literature of Subversion* (1981). London: Methuen, 1986.

Rushdie, Salman. *Midnight's Children* (1981). Vintage, 1995.

—. *Imaginary Homelands: Essays and Criticism 1981-1991*. London: Granta Books, 1991.

23

Overlapping Territories, Intertwined Histories: *A Passage to India*

Vijaya Singh

> That films are only representations does not prevent them from having real life effects in the world.... Thus although there is no absolute truth, no truth apart from representation and dissemination, there are still contingent, qualified, perspectival truths in which communities are invested. (Shohat and Stam 187-189)

In Forster's own life time, *A Passage to India* (APTI), was his most popular work of fiction. Even today it holds a special position in the canon of Anglo-Indian fiction. Not surprisingly, Forster received offers from the leading filmmakers of his time to film his novel. Foremost amongst these was Satyajit Ray. Forster admired Ray's films but he refused the permission as, "he just did not think his novel should be filmed"[1]. It was only after his death in 1970, as Chidananda Dasgupta points out, that King's College Cambridge, the executors of his estate, merged the film and play-rights[2] and sold the copyrights for the novel to David Lean. The British film director, known for his adaptations of Charles Dickens's *Great Ex-*

pectations (1946), *Oliver Twist* (1948) and for films like *Brief Encounter* (1945), *Bridge on the River Kwai* (1957), *Summertime* (1955), *Lawrence of Arabia* (1962) and many others.

The filming rights of the novel provided Lean the opportunity to make a comeback film, after his fourteen-year absence from cinema ever since the failure of his last film, *Ryan's Daughter* in 1970. Significantly, *APTI* proved to be a strategic choice for him. The timing of the making and release of the film coincided with the politico-cultural realities of 1980s in Britain. In Britain this was a period of intense interest in India and the British Raj. There was, as it were, a ready market for books, films and television serials on subjects, themes related to India and the British Raj. Ruth Jhabvala and Salman Rushdie had only recently (1975 and 1982) won the Booker for their *Heat and Dust* and *Midnight's Children* respectively. Meanwhile, *Heat and Dust* had already been turned into an award winning film by the team of Ismail Merchant and James Ivory in 1982. Television serials based on Paul Scott's *Jewel in the Crown* (1984) and M.M. Kaye's *The Far Pavilions* (1984) were already immensely popular in Britain. *APTI* was therefore, in a sense, just waiting to happen. It was only a matter of time when the novel would be turned into a film.

Now, twenty years later, the debate on the film's representation of India is still a keen one and raises important questions regarding the role of media vis-à-vis third-world histories and cultures. The need to examine Lean's *APTI* for its representation of India, Indians, and its adaptation of the novel is, still, just as acute as when the film was first released. It needs to be interrogated for its rhetoric because it is a pointer to how cinema itself is a site where ideological battles of representation may be fought. This paper proposes to examine the film for its engagement with the issues of colonialism, Eurocentrism, racism and the ways in which it constructs meaning in and around India.

But, before going on to discuss the film, it would be relevant to review the source—the novel—of the film itself to arrive at an understanding of the text in the light of the present day postcolonial debate. This is important not only because the critique of *APTI* (the film) must get beyond the errors and distortions that its source has been subjected to, but also for examining the politics of representation in Forster's novel itself. There is also the need to point out that in case of films like *APTI* the idea is not how true to the source the film is, but to reexamine the source itself for its narrative complicity with the prevalent ideology of its own times. This is significant not only in lieu of the unconscious agenda that the text carries but also because cinema's antecedents itself are located in the tradition of the nineteenth century realist novel.

Cinema's inter-text as Shohat and Stam tell us in *Unthinking Eurocentrism: Multiculturalism and the Media*, is rooted in the colonialist discourse of such "divergent fields as philosophy, literature and history"(8). The very fact that the emergence of cinema as an institution coincided with the "giddy heights of imperialism" (Shohat and Stam 8) is a pointer to its role in disseminating the colonial discourse of Racism, Orientalism and Eurocentrism. It is, as Robert Stam and Louise Spence point out in their essay "Colonialism, Racism, And Representation: An Introduction", "Colonialist representation did not begin with the cinema: it is rooted in a vast colonial inter text, a widely disseminated set of discursive practices" (238).

APTI (the film), thus needs to be viewed as a part of the larger western "ideological substratum" engendering and normalizing the "hierarchical power relations generated by colonialism and imperialism" (Shohat and Stam 2). The novel too as a consequence needs to be examined for its representation of India and the question asked, if all its categories of truth: social, cultural, political and metaphysical, about India, its peoples and its rulers do not come together to form a discourse conterminous with the official discourse of imperialism. It needs to be critiqued along with its film for being a party to the broader discursive network of Eurocentric consciousness. Interestingly then Lean's film provides the occasion for a reappraisal of Forster's novel and for pointing out that in a largely postcolonial world all readings of a text like *APTI* are necessarily political.

The Politics of Forster's Passage

Published in 1924, *APTI* has for long been celebrated as a text which calls for multiple interpretations: as a modernist allegory of human predicament in a hostile universe; as a limit text of liberal humanism; as a metaphysical drama about the categories of truth and untruth; as a political fiction seeking to represent the truth of British rule in India and as an anti-imperialist text disputing the categories of race, culture and class.

Until the early 1980s criticism on the novel was located around the above themes and was mostly of a strong liberal humanist kind. There were mainly two streams of criticism at work here: the liberal humanist and the modernist. Where one concentrated on the inherent humanism and mysticism of *APTI* the other focused on the text's modernist element in terms of its use of language, symbols and rhythm. Not surprisingly, Judith Scherer Herz went so far as to say that "language is at once the subject of *APTI*, its intractable medium, its clarifying agency, and its astounding, if finally hapless accomplishment"(59).

The colonialist critique of the novel was largely limited to re-echoing the rhetoric of liberal humanism. That Imperialism was based on wrong conjectures, hence wrong, was the quintessential criticism to come from this generation of critics. There was no engagement on the level of the novel's ideology or a questioning of its structure and narrative. The political criticism of the novel was more often than not pushed to the background in the face of its aesthetic and modernist elements

Even Wilfred Stone, in his excellent book on Forster, *The Cave and the Mountain*, lavishes praise on the novel for its symbolism, aesthetic wholeness, mythical, mystical and psychological aspects, but simply refuses to admit that the political aspect of the novel brooks any serious attention. He reiterates Forster's opinion regarding political views in *APTI* and agrees that they "...are of a secondary or tertiary importance" (315). Such an attitude was characteristic of critics who viewed *APTI* more as a modernist dilemma about the fate of humankind in an incomprehensible universe rather than an inadequate critique of British imperialism. The colonial critique of the novel was more often than not pushed aside as insignificant and less important than the other more urgent thematic concerns of modernism.

Overlapping Territories, Intertwined Histories: *A Passage to India* • 265

In India too for a long time opinion on the novel was of a gratuitous kind. Opinion on it was often mingled with an appreciation of Forster as a friend of India. It is best expressed in the words of K. Natwar Singh, an ardent admirer of Forster, who said "he came as a blessed relief after Kipling" (38). Forster, for a long time evoked that kind of an emotional response from Indian writers—Raja Rao[3], Mulk Raj Anand, R.K. Narayan—Indian critics—Bhupal Singh[4], G.K. Das[5], V.A. Shahane—and Indian readers in general. In recent times, however, critics like Edward Said, Sara Suleri, Jenny Sharpe, Jeremy Tambling, Harish Trivedi, and many others—some of them drawing on Foucault's critical methods—have shown how the novel itself may be an accomplice in the politics of imperialism: in the tropes, clichés and stereotypes it employs to represent India and Indians; it has been accused of an Orientalist and Eurocentric discourse.

The present reading of *APTI*, the novel, thus stems from a need to understanding the ambivalence of its discourse, which allows for a revisionist interpretation by different readers. That is, to ask, can it be argued that the novel contains within itself elements, gaps, silences, which lend themselves to a colonialist/ racist interpretation? What are the tropes through which it describes India? Does the novel contain an agenda outside the intention of its author? On the level of the plot the questions that need to be answered are: what are the difficulties of Aziz and Fielding's friendship? What really happened in the Marabar caves? What is the final message of the novel?

The plot in the novel revolves around the question of friendship between the colonizer and the colonized in British India. The novel ends on the impossibility of friendship between the English and Indians as long as the British rule India, and defers it to an idealized future when India would be free. Forster constructs Aziz and Fielding's friendship as the site for exploring the social and cultural intercourse between the ruler and the ruled. The difficulties of Aziz and Fielding's friendship arise not only from the fact that Aziz is the ruled and Fielding a member of the ruling race but also from the fact that the two belong to different cultures.

There is, Forster tells us, something uncongenial in the Indian soil—ruled by the British—which is hostile to friendship between the two races. As Hamidullah says in the beginning of the novel, "I only contend that it is possible in England...it is impossible here" (33-34). Nature in India becomes an extension of colonialism. So that during the tea party at Fielding's residence "It was as if irritation exuded from the very soil. Could one have been so petty on a Scotch moor or an Italian alp" (*APTI* 94)? For Nicholas B. Dirks, *APTI's* malevolent geography is a "poetic conceit", a metaphor for the way in which in a colonial state landscape itself becomes a fact of culture. Commenting on this aspect of the novel he says, "...culture in places such as India became, through colonial lenses, assimilated to the landscape itself, fixed in nature, and freed from history...for colonial rulers, the culture and nature of the colonized were erased"(3).

Sara Suleri too in her essay "Forster's Imperial Erotic" is of the view that "Forster turns visualizing landscape as though to an act of cultural description that is relentlessly anti-exotic in its intent...in such a revision, geography assumes the characteristics of a hollow symbolic space upon which the limits of imperial intimacy can both be identified and articulated"(163-164). The Marabar caves, which lie at the center of the novel, and engender the central event in the novel are themselves represented as empty; devoid of any meaning; they represent a "renunciation more complete" than Buddha's; "Nothing, nothing attaches to them" Suleri reads in the nullity of these caves, a denial of "both connection and chronology", in that it forces cultural description into a recognition of its own vacuity. Similarly, Homi K. Bhabha too sees in the negation and echo of the caves a "conspiracy of silence", "it is a silence that turns imperial triumphalism into the testimony of colonial confusion and those who hear its echo lose their historic memories" (123).

In a yet another interesting reading of the geography of *APTI*, Penelope Pether in her essay "*A Passage to India*: A Passage to the Patria" suggests that the "emphasis on the Caves as 'void' springs from an anxiety about the nature of 'Englishness', as against colonial 'Anglo-Indianness'. 'Englishness' in India marks a subject position threatened by the experience of its imagined other" (196).

But what conspires in the caves and the silence around it cannot merely be interpreted as aesthetic devices labouring to emphasize the "inscription of colonialism on India's landscape" (Dirks 2). The implications of Adela's allegation of attempted rape; later her withdrawal of the charge; and Forster's refusal to explain what happened in the caves cannot just be explained away apolitically. There is a psycho-historical materiality behind the allegation of rape by Adela. Neither is it enough to merely draw attention to an actual event that occurred in Amritsar where an English girl called F. Marcella Sherwood was brutally assaulted by a group of Indians, as G.K. Das alludes to in his essay, "A Socio-historical Study"(4-7). At the back of Adela's allegation of "attempted rape" lies the racial and sexual mistrust of the Indian by the British in the backdrop of 1857's "Indian Mutiny", when Indian men supposedly raped British women.

Jenny Sharpe in her *Allegories of the Empire: The Figure of Woman in the Colonial Text* presents a brilliant analysis of "rape as an event that emerges in and is constituted by its enunciation" (4) and shows how Forster uses the "category of rape within a system of colonial relations" to create a site of victimization whose meaning is highly contested. So that an opposition is set between "gender and race", "The ambiguity surrounding the alleged rape thus forces the critic to defend either the native man or the white woman against his/her opponent"(119). She suggests that the discourse of rape and the racial memory of 1857 served dual functions; one, it lent credence to the British on moral grounds to continue ruling a barbaric country, second it justified the racial segregation of the British and the Indian. The novel, she says, restages ironically the drama of Aziz's arrest and Adela's accusation of attempted rape, but it does not however, "overturn the mutiny narratives but merely questions their premises" (124).

But what did actually happen in the caves? Forster's own explanation is not much help, He says:

> In the cave it is either a man or the supernatural, or an illusion. If I say, it becomes whatever the answer a different book. And even if I know! My writing mind therefore is a blur here- i.e. I will it to remain a blur, and to be uncertain, as I am of many facts in daily

life. This isn't a philosophy of aesthetics. It's a particular trick I felt justified in trying because my theme was India. It sprang straight from my subject matter. I wouldn't have attempted it in any other countries.... I call it 'trick': but 'voluntary surrender to infection' better expresses my state. (*APTI* 26)

"Infection" is how Forster describes the state of mind of Adela, who has let her mind be infected by India. India, he seems to be saying, infects the sensibilities of those who "voluntarily surrender" to it. The explanation is an example of a typical orientalist justification for what Forster calls his "particular trick". As Trivedi points out, "His logic here seems to be: India is mysterious; so be my novel." And all the better if such mystification served to distance, obscure and transcend the unpleasant and intractable politics of an alleged inter-racial rape..." (181).

Sharpe too feels that:

Forster does not replace the certainty of an attack with its negation; rather, he replaces it with a narrative suspension that opens up the space for a "mystery" in a colonial discourse of power. "Mystery" not only names the place where the logic of colonialism breaks down but also resolves a contradiction by making a question serve as its answer. (125)

Later during the trial, by making Adela recant her charges against Aziz, Forster defuses the politically charged situation. So that the onus of proving Aziz's innocence circumvented successfully The ahistoricizing of the events in the novel is a general strategy of the novel; it is itself situated outside of history. Though, Forster exposes the racist paranoia inherent in the Raj, the inequities it was based upon and the complete humiliation of the Indian people he does not however situate the event historically and is content only to draw attention to the psyche of the British in India.

Indeed, for Forster, the greatest evil of the Raj lay in its attitude and not in its exploitative machinery. "One touch of regret not the canny substitute" (*APTI* 70), is all he asks of the Empire to redeem itself. Indeed, for Forster the problem is not British Imperialism in "political terms but as a problem in individual human relations"(Gorra 641). His account of British India is a limited one that makes "British colonialism a crisis more for the British than for the Indians" (Gorra 641). His novel "is at its most acute in its analysis of what colonialism does to the colonizer... No novel of the period did more to show just how ghastly the empire-born mask of Britishness could be" (Gorra 643).

So, if for Kipling to know India is to rule India, then for Forster, the British mind's inability to "take hold of such a country"; to indeed acknowledge its "otherness" is a reason for estrangement from it is to invert the absolutism of Kipling's "knowable India" and turn it into yet another abstraction.[6] Forster's India so conspicuous in its difference from the romantic imagination of the 18th century western representation is nevertheless a land outside of history where forces of nature keep "men in compartments"; where, metaphysical truths pounce upon unsuspecting westerners; where well meaning English women undergo hallucinations of sexual assaults in caves. Between these extremes the narrative creates an obscure land where the "secular is scanted, and in which India's traditions of mathematics, science and technology, history, linguistics, and jurisprudence have no place" (Parry 175). Forster turns away from an effective critique of the Raj to the mysterious and metaphysical forces of India. The episode in the caves and the constant refrain of "muddle/mystery" however are not the only example of an orientalist disposition in the novel, there are other instances too where Forster indulges in essentializing the difference of the two races. Aziz's character itself is invested with a decadent sexuality. He visits prostitutes and offers to arrange a woman with "breasts like Bombay mangoes" for Fielding. If Aziz is stereotyped as a licentious Muslim, Godbole, the Brahmin college teacher, is no less stereotyped as an "inscrutable oriental" who, is both unable to keep his appointments and prefers to mystify the happening in the Marabar caves.

Similarly, in the Temple section of the novel the depiction of Gokul Ashtami festival, which is supposed to bring harmony and reunite the estranged friends is so chaotic, solipsistic, and comic in its representation of Hinduism that it is difficult to believe that it can provide any viable substitute to the evils of colonialism. Indian nationalism, which makes its presence in Aziz's declaration, "I am an Indian at last" is not developed as an alternative resistance to the Raj. Indeed Forster could not envision the dissolution of the empire in the next "fifty or five hundred years" (*APTI* 316). Thus, "to the end of his life he (Aziz) remained under observation, thanks to Miss Quested's mistake" (*APTI* 290). Not only is the Raj portrayed as permanent, Indian nationalism itself is not taken seriously even though by the 1920s it was a force to reckon with. Aziz's exhortation "Clear out, all you Turtons and Burtons" is met with Fielding's "India a nation?". Said in his *Culture and Imperialism* is of the opinion, that "one cannot help feeling that in view of the political realities of the 1910s and 1920s even such a remarkable novel as *A Passage to India* nevertheless founders on the undodgeable facts of Indian nationalism" (245-246).

In recent times the underlying homosexual or as Suleri memorably calls it "the hidden tradition of imperial looking" (155) in the novel has received a lot of critical attention and brooks attention here too. Even as the theme of friendship is explored in a colonial set up the narrative engages in the "embodiment of the situation of alternative desire in the construction of colonial encounters." (Suleri 155). India thus becomes a "potential site for an eroticized and Orientalised all male utopia" (Freedgood 123). The desire to form an "alternative colonial intimacy" premised on interracial erotic intermingling begins to take shape in the friendship between Fielding and Aziz, but eventually fails due to the divisiveness inherent in the colonial discourses of the empire. Freedgood however feels that the "epistemology of the closet" is finally unable to overrun the "epistemology of the colony" because *APTI* works to "preserve India as a place where Britons might find sexual liberation without giving up their power and privilege. Accordingly, Forster directs his criticisms away from the empire" (124). Homosexuality, for Freedgood, is therefore not a liberatory discourse in the novel as it too works to "recuperate rather than criticize imperialism" (128). Forster's misogyny too is read as a means of directing his critique of the empire on to the insularity of British women where the Indians are concerned. So the hysteria generated during Adela's allegation of rape is read by Freedgood as Forster's critique of heterosexuality as a politically unstable form against homosexuality, which is "rational and manly" instead of "emotional and feminine". He goes on to say that "Rather than question masculinity" as an oppressive social construction, Forster attempts instead to feminize heterosexuality and appropriate true manliness for an all-male community. The failure of the British to form viable relationships is displaced on to the British women who "make everything more difficult out here" (Freedgood 129).

Forster's representation of India is ambiguous, it neither fully repudiates the categories of British Raj nor does it deny them altogether. His consciousness is deeply rooted in the Mediterranean norms, and in the western structures of form and beauty. It would be interesting to see how the film of David Lean deals with these issues and what reading it provides of Forster's monumental work.

Passage to More than India: The Film

The plot of Lean's film is more or less the same as that of Forster's novel with all the major characters in it except for one or two minor characters, who have been dropped. Lean retains most of the dialogue and imagery of the novel too, though he alters the dialogues and some events during certain crucial scenes. The film begins on a wet rainy day in London where Adela[7] is seen enquiring about her and Mrs. Moore's tickets to India.

The misc-en-scene of the first shot includes in the background a huge globe. It stands as a symbol of Britain's domination of world's major geographical locations in the first quarter of the last century. Not surprisingly then the immediate shot in the film is that of the pageantry at the Gateway of India. The Viceroy and the Vicereine in their colonial splendour are seen disembarking the liner and are literally given the red carpet welcome. In immediate succession are seen the half naked porters, women in burqa, snake charmers, the overcrowded streets; in short, the chaos and disorderliness of India. In stark contrast to them are the glamour, pomp and orderliness of British India. The Viceroy, framed in the centre, surrounded by the poverty stricken multitudes of India gives the impression of being godlike, controlling the lives of millions of uncivilized, illiterate, poverty ridden Indians. This sense of British domination is further emphasized by the use of a low camera angle while focusing on the Anglo-Indians perched on top of the deck of the ship cheering the full dress procession for the Viceroy. But while focusing on the crowd of porters the camera looks down upon them as they clamour to carry the luggage of the disembarking passengers.

From the first scene onwards, Lean establishes the binary of chaos and order in constructing the images of Indians and the British and reinforces these images throughout the film. Not only is glamour there in this story there is also the exoticization of the "other". The journey from Britain to India provides a contrast between the London, of "dull blacks, muted charcoals, and watery gray" (Donaldson 90), and the India of bright colors and brighter sunlight. The camera tracks through the streets of Bombay to Victoria Railway station to focus its attention on the flower vendors, burqa clad Muslim women and Hindu women in colorful saris. It is both a picture of the poverty stricken multitude and exotic natives. The same scene is repeated again as Ronny leads the two ladies- Adela and Mrs. Moore- on his tonga through the streets of Chandrapore, where in addition to the flower vendors, and burqa clad women, there are men in colourful headgear and shops selling Holi colours, spices and exotic fruits, Laura Donaldson in her book *Decolonizing Feminisms: Race, Gender and Empire Building* suggests that such a visually exaggerated opposition between England and India ... [works to produce]... "India as an object of intense desire both for Adela and, vicariously, for the cinematic spectator" (91).

Likewise, the same scene of the reception of the Viceroy is repeated on the arrival of the Turtons at the Chandrapore railway station. So as to emphasize the power structure in the sovereign hierarchy of the Raj, where, even the collector of a small district was no less important than the viceroy for its inhabitants. This works to accentuate the romantic, imperial conceptions of the British Raj. Lean in an interview given to Stills admits that he was "prepared to refashion the 'real' India" to meet these requirements. Hence "carefully framed shots of the Gateway are edited together with footage shot elsewhere (New Delhi, the Malabar coast) to create the effect which the real location, surrounded by a harbour, failed to provide" (As quoted in Hill 100).

Similarly, later in the film, the journey to the Marabar caves results in a grand spectacle. A beautifully painted elephant is seen moving leisurely against the visually splendid backdrop of "Bangalore mountains" towards the Marabar caves. There are many such instances of sumptuous visual display and enticing glimpses of extraordinary landscapes in the film. One such sequence is shot towards the end of the film when Fielding comes to meet Aziz in the Himalayan state of Kashmir. It shows Stella and Fielding surveying the natural beauty of the majestic Himalayas in a moment full of possessive emotionalism. The whole Kashmir episode - the lakes, the houseboats, the festival of lights, earthen lamps floating in the lakes offer a visual treat against the drab contrast to England where the film ends soon after.

The film invests India with a picturesqueness and glamour that the novel took pains to shun. In the opening chapter of the novel, Forster describes the geographical setting of Chandrapore as "nothing extraordinary", its inhabitants are described as "mud moving". As Suleri notes, "in place of the exotic, the ordinary is privileged, so that the narrative need express no desire for either overt possession or a concomitant repulsion" (164). But in the film there is an overt interest in the sumptuous visual display of a lost paradise and an emotional self-indulgence in the romantic images of British India. India becomes a place where the British carry the burden of bringing justice to its benighted natives. There is, it seems, an attempt in the film to re-colonize India culturally through the "cultural production of meaning and perceptions which have justified and supported the relations of domination characteristic of imperial enterprise" (Said: *Culture* 8).

To return to the plot however, once Adela and Mrs. Moore have been introduced to the audience, the film creates the train journey/ the passage from Bombay to Chandrapore. The train motif like the gateway motif is invoked again and again in the film to emphasize the journey /the passage theme of the film All the motifs of rivers, ponds, lakes, gateways, arches, trains, sun, crowd, monkeys are brought into focus again and again to give to the film a sense of unity and also to invoke an India timeless, ancient, seductive and mysterious. Stephen Heath points out, that the ideological force of such scenic space exists in the image that carries over into a suggestion of the whole world as a kind of,

> ...spectacle to be recorded in its essence in an instantaneous objectification for the eye...a world, that is, conceived outside of process and practice, empirical scene of the confirmed and central master-spectator, serenely 'present' in tranquil rectilinearity. (Quoted in Donaldson 94)

The train journey is important not only because it serves to bring homepassage theme of the film but also because it functions to introduce the Turtons and establish them as the insular people who along with the Callendars and Mcbrydes represent the reason of failure for the Raj in forming lasting relationship with the Indians.

In the meantime, Adela, Mrs. Moore and Ronny are seen arriving at their bungalow in a tonga. On Adela's arrival at Ronny's bungalow, the Marabar Hills are stressed again as Adela asks Ronny about the Marabar caves. In the following scene Adela is seen waiting in her room for Ronny's goodnight kiss and seems disappointed when he wishes her goodnight from outside her room. She looks at her reflection in the mirror in a moment of sexual self-reflexivity, while at one level the film is about representing a particular period of British Raj in India, there is at the same time a parallel text of the emergence of Adela's sexuality. Right from the start Lean builds the story of the development of her sexuality so that her desire for an exciting life with Ronnie in an exotic backdrop is beginning to look disappointing on account of Ronny's transmutation into a proper Sahib. Gradually she begins to displace her desire from Ronny on to India and Indians. Donaldson too makes a similar point in her essay "Colonialism and Filmic Representation" that from the start of the train journey, the film begins building the theme of awakening Adela's sexuality. She translates the train's throbbing as signifying the "eroticism and sensuality that Adela expects in her marriage but may now be deprived of it on account of Ronny's having become a sahib. Gradually Adela begins displacing her desire from Ronny to

India" (94-97).

The dinner scene at Hamidullah's house is followed by Aziz's being snubbed by the ladies at Major Callendar's house and his subsequent refuge in the mosque away from the nasty British. The scene comes very close to the one in the novel. Even the mosque is a very clever replica of the mosque described in the novel. Here it would be fruitful to point out a certain pattern in the film, which is very compelling, in its use as a device to diffuse any tension which threatens to usurp the ongoing narrative. There is, as mentioned earlier, a recurrence of water images in the film. Lean makes a cut to a water body, either a river or a lake, whenever there is a conflict which threatens to remain unresolved. So that Aziz who is nursing his grievances against the British in the mosque is seen gazing at the stars out of a broken casement. Inside, in the courtyard an ablution tank glistens with fresh water. The whole effect of the setting: the soft moonlight shimmering over the water surface on the tank inside the mosque and on the Ganges outside creates a very harmonious effect as if to nullify the rude behaviour of the British.

Later as Mrs. Moore enters the mosque, she is framed in a medium shot with her scarf covering her head like an "Oriental" woman. As she emerges from the darkness, surrounded with a soft halo around her figure. Henceforth, Mrs. Moore will be seen mostly with her head covered with a scarf. In fact, even when she dies en route to Britain by sea, her head is covered with a scarf. Incidentally, Peggy Ashcroft, who plays Mrs. Moore, also played the role of Barbie in the television serial, *The Jewel in the Crown*. She brings nuances of that character into her role of Mrs. Moore. So that Mrs. Moore often appears as a sequel to Barbie- who too at the time of her death in *Jewel in the Crown* is seen wearing a scarf, with her forefinger frozen in rigor mortis as if in an abstract accusation against the unfortunate British. The British, she feels, having failed in their missionary duties of spreading love and kindness amongst the natives as promised by Queen Victoria (as in the TV serial *Jewel*), the benevolent mother figure, have lost the moral imperative to rule India. The same line of thought continues in Ashcroft's role as Mrs. Moore in *APTI* as well. At one point she says to Ronny,

"God has put us on earth to love one another" (Lean *APTI*).

It is interesting to note the paradox that accompanies the chronology of the publication and release of *APTI* and *Jewel in the Crown* the novels and their films. In that *The Jewel in the Crown*, which was written in 1966 is often considered as continuing the legacy of Forster in taking up the themes left unresolved in *APTI*. But here, in case of their cinematic versions, the situation is a bit reversed in that the television serial on Scott's Quartet was filmed in 1982 and the film on *APTI* made in 1984. The film unsurprisingly often seems imitative of the serial in its settings, the portrayal of the characters, the acting, and even in the music it employs to suggest the mysteriousness of India.

To return to the discussion of the development of the film's plot however, once the visitors are settled in India, the film begins registering the gradual disappointment of both Adela and Mrs. Moore whose desire for the "real India" is subsumed by British India's complete social denial of the natives. The collector nevertheless concedes to giving a "bridge party" for the visitors. The bridge party in the novel serves to function as an indictment of the divide between the two nations and provides a glimpse into the deep chasm between the colonized and the colonizer. It is declared a failure, the guests are treated badly, they stand in one corner huddled together in groups, the party is a farce at Fielding's college house, where a tea party has been arranged for Adela and Mrs. Moore. There, an old man is seen plucking water-chestnuts from the pond. In the novel the water-chestnut gatherer is a splendidly formed young man as is indeed the punkah-walla in the court during the trial scene as against the film. Critics[8] have argued that this is an indication of Lean's undermining the homosexual subtext of the novel. But this interpretation appears flawed because it seems that by replacing the water-chestnut gatherer and the punkah-walla as indistinguishable old men in the film Lean has exempted the British from any homoerotic gaze towards the Indians. Instead, the charge of homoerotic desire is shifted over to Aziz who is more than willing to offer himself as a locus point for such a desire. Though the critics are of the view that the film is about heterosexual tensions one feels that the homosexual theme underlies the heterosexual one, albeit surreptitiously. But the burden of the homoerotic gaze rests with Aziz and not with any of the British characters. Indeed, Aziz in the film is invested with certain popularly circulated and accepted norms of femininity: he is emotional, volatile, child-like, and over-anxious; and in contrast to James Fox who plays Fielding, Victor Banerjee who plays Aziz is of a medium height and of a slight frame. Later towards the end, when Aziz declares to Fielding "he has become an Indian at last", he is seen applying kohl to his eyes like an Indian woman. Dressed in a silk Sherwani and a Mughal cap he bursts out in an emotionally charged tirade against Fielding, accusing him of having an affair with Adela.

Forster has been accused of displacing the homoerotic desire upon Aziz, "which Fielding as a White and English male, will not be caught carrying" (Freedgood 135). Lean, it seems is only carrying this legacy further and absolves the British of any allegations of homoeroticism. Lean removes all the "splendidly formed Indians" from the film and substitutes them with old, "thin hammed, flat chested mediocrities of Chandrapore". Godbole, the Hindu professor at Fielding's college, is another significant character in the novel who is also introduced to the viewer at the tea party. Alec Guiness plays the role of Godbole in the film. This is an instance of what Robyn Weigman refers to as "role stratification" which "reproduces racial hierarchy by denying non-white actors major film roles but also reproduces a form of ethnocentrism whereby white actors may occupy and signify the full range of humanity in a way that non-white actors may not" (164).

What is more, Godbole's character in the film has been reduced to the banal stereotype of the inscrutable Oriental. In the novel too, his character has been caricatured. But Forster invests him with a certain metaphysical understanding of the universe and acknowledges through him that there may indeed be worlds, which may not be understood solely through the intellect and reason. Forster takes care not to confuse Hindu metaphysics with superstition but Lean conflates the two categories and proceeds to create in Godbole a character, who declares the closing of the railway gate as "inauspicious" and calls Mrs. Moore a "very old soul."

Lean establishes a spiritual connection between them through an eye line cut, so that whenever Mrs. Moore looks in the direction of Godbole he looks at her with great reverence. When Mrs. Moore leaves for England, Godbole is seen standing in the dark gateway next to the railway station with folded hands bidding her goodbye. During the tea party itself he mouths a lot of mumbo-jumbo regarding the cycle of birth and death and the theory of karma.

The film till now has been echoing the development of the story in the novel. Hence, immediately after the tea party, Adela on account of Ronny's insularity at the tea party breaks her engagement with him. She announces this decision to Ronny during a polo match. Just as she makes the announcement a rider falls from his pony, the scene is evocative of the state of Ronny who it appears has fallen from grace. But Adela recants her decision after her bicycle-ride in the jungle near Chandrapore.

In the film, in an entirely original sequence, Adela is seen cycling miles outside of Chandrapore until she comes across the ruins of erotic statues scattered around an old Hindu temple. To emphasize the state of mind of Adela there are a series of crosscuts between the statues and Adela's face. The background music during the whole sequence "repeats the overture's opening theme and orchestrates it with reed instruments, which are often the West's musical evocation of the mysteriousness of the east" (Donaldson 98). Here there is a very close similarity between the televised series of *Jewel in the Crown*, and *APTI* in terms of their use of bicycles and music. A similar music plays when Daphne Manners riding on her bicycle goes towards the Bibighar, where she is raped by village hooligans. It wouldn't be far fetched to suggest that the idea of cycle ride in Lean's *APTI* seems to be inspired by Peter Duffel's *Jewel in the Crown*. There is a fetishization and a conspiratory intertexuality in the use of bicycles in the Raj films. Used mostly by British women they come to represent not only their mobility but also their vulnerability to predatory natives, lurking in the shadows of old Bibighars and caves waiting to assault them.

In the case of *APTI* however, first it is the monkeys, who, human like, descend upon Adela and chase her through the labyrinths of her own unacknowledged sensual desires. Later it will be Aziz chasing her down the Marabar Hills. Laura Kipnis in her essay "The Phantom Twitchings of an Amputated Limb" in *Wide Angle* feels this is:

> a moment of epic semiosis that manages to congeal and reconform the elements of pathological sexuality, the landscape, and the unheimlichness of the Orient. These monkeys, human-like but not quite human, transform the bucolic moment of Adela's burgeoning sexual awakening into a scene of screeching animality. (47)

Later during the night, the same reed music is played again as the camera focuses closely on Adela's face as she contemplates the erotic statuary. The addition of this scene in the film is a clear attempt to emphasize Adela's burgeoning sexuality. The same line of thought continues as she embarks upon the cave journey with Aziz and Mrs. Moore. During the train journey there is an instance of Aziz monkeying around the train as it crosses a deep chasm. The scene is also a sequel to the earlier scene of the Bridge party where the Indian ladies applaud the arrival of their British guests (Aziz clowns around to please his guests).

However on reaching the Marabar station a beautifully painted elephant awaits the arrival of Aziz's guests to carry them across to the caves on the mountains. But after the experience in the first cave itself Mrs. Moore collapses and declines to go further into the caves on top of the mountain and advises Aziz and Adela not to take too many people along.

During the climb Aziz and Adela engage in a personal conversation and Adela wants to know if Aziz loved his wife. As he prepares to answer the question, the camera, closes upon his face. He gazes at Adela's face and offers his hand in assistance to her. Adela looks hesitant for a while but extends her hand and returns the gaze of Aziz. The camera then closes up on their clasped hand until they arrive at the caves. Soon after Aziz leaves Adela behind and is seen smoking a cigarette near the entrance of a cave while Adela waits for him at the mouth of another cave and is later seen entering it on her own. Immediately after, Aziz is seen looking for her, calling out her name he comes and stands at the entrance of the cave where Adela is. There is a shift of scene and the camera quickly cuts to show Adela running down the incline, her clothes torn, her skin bloodied. In a rapid editing sequence Aziz is seen running next as if after Adela, the camera cuts again to show Mrs. Moore waking up with a start. Just then Fielding arrives, Aziz joins them and explains what happened looking very guilty.

If the film's text suggests that Adela suffers a hallucination, Aziz too has not been given a clean chit. The editing sequence subtly insinuates that Aziz may not be completely innocent. With the intercut images of his shadow looming at the mouth of the cave in the lowlit cave, and then running after a terrified Adela suggests a connection. Indeed in one of the earlier scenes in the film, when Adela is seen reflecting upon the erotic statues, the film interweaves scenes of Aziz announcing he is sick while leafing through pornographic magazines. In the same scene, he discusses Adela's breasts with Fielding and suggests he might procure a woman "with breasts like Bombay mangoes" for him.

In the novel however the cave episode is treated differently, Aziz loses his composure upon being asked by Adela "if he had one wife or more than one"? "Damn the English even at their best" he says, offended at the insensitivity of Adela and disappears to smoke a cigarette and regain his composure. But what does happen in the cave remains a mystery, as indeed Sharpe has shown that in the deleted section of the manuscript of *APTI*, Forster did attempt an explanation in which Adela is indeed attacked by an assailant but she manages to save herself and cries out:

"Not this time" (126).

There is a similarity in Lean's interpretation of the official text with that of the absent text, and though he doesn't show anyone attacking Adela, the implicit suggestion is that perhaps there was someone in the cave. As Lean admits in his interview with Harlan Kennedy:

> And when the idea is presented that Aziz had attempted whatever he attempted in the cave, I thought, "what?" It didn't work. And I wanted to set it up so that you couldn't argue afterwards, "Did he ? Didn't he?"(30)

Critics like Sharpe, Donaldson and Kipnis all blame Forster and Lean of 'scapegoating' Adela in a bid to creating an "anti-imperialist message". Lean in his film not only legitimizes the popular reading of the sexual repression of Adela, in fact he firmly establishes that her repressed sexuality is responsible for the sexual hysteria, which takes place in the caves. Not just because she is frigid, unattractive and sexually repressed but because India is a place where this can happen. In his interview with Kennedy, Lean says:

> In the book and in the play she was not a believable character on the whole, as far as her sexuality was concerned. I thought that I had to find a way that fills her a little more, to let you see that she is beginning to awaken sexually...because India can do this, you know. (30)

He constructs India as the site of a dangerous sexuality where sensible people lose their balance but it isn't as if Lean is alone in thinking like this. Forster himself exploited the theme, which Said claims is so characteristic of 'orientalism':

> Every European traveler or resident in the Orient has had to protect himself from its unsettling influences...In most cases, the Orient seemed to have offended sexual propriety; everything about the Orient...exuded dangerous sex, threatened hygiene and domestic seemliness with an excessive "freedom of intercourse". (*Orientalism* 166-167)

Forster's own response to the question of what happened in the cave as purposely turning it into an obfuscating incident has already been mentioned before as "a particular trick" he felt justified in trying because "my theme was India" (*APTI* 26). Lean taking his cue from Forster does the same and is not the first one to try and situate an English woman in surroundings where she might lose her balance and experience a sexual hallucination. Lean has in fact not only elaborated upon what might have happened in the caves, but he attempts to explain explicitly Adela's state of mind when she enters the cave.

Later during the trial scene in the film Lean recreates the history of British justice as a traditionally fair system. In the novel the court trial becomes a mockery of British justice and fair play, until Adela withdraws her accusation. But, before this happens, the British make a fuss about seating Adela on the platform, and eventually each one of them except Fielding ends up on the platform. The trial itself is slated to come before Ronny, but the Indians object to it and Ronny is replaced by Das, his assistant. The English convulse with "wrath" that an Indian "should judge over an English girl" in fact some women even "sent a telegram about it to Lady Mellanby, the wife of the Lieutenant-Governor" (*APTI* 201).

In the film the tough issues in the novel are depoliticized so that there is no mention of the English moving their seats on the platform. Lean himself admits in his interview with Kennedy that he removed the scene from the film because:

> I must tell you that one or two people objected that in the trial, which practically rewrote and made a big scene of it...It would look really stupid if you are going to have a trial at which Aziz and eventually the girl are up against the English- they've got to be worthy opponents. And people moving their chairs up and down would be wrong. I am glad I made that change....(31)

The damage control effected by Lean is further consolidated when Ronny announces to Mrs. Turton that he has willingly stepped down in favour of Das because "I am an interested party" and that "Das is a good man". Having established the British as morally and culturally superior, the Indians are portrayed as petty and ungracious - Mahmoud Ali is shown throwing his papers in the air, exhorting people outside the court to shout slogans and chant Mrs. Moore's name. During the trial Adela gets into a detailed explanation of how when she looked through the binoculars at Chandrapore, she realized she "did not love Ronny". In the novel this incident takes place in her mind. The victory, which comes as a result of Adela's withdrawal is not a vindication of the character of Aziz, but of the essential honesty of Adela; of the British character which does not flinch from speaking the truth even at the cost of losing everything.

One of the striking aspects of the film is that in imagining India, Lean manages to keep out the Indians from most of the film except in the scenes where crowds and mobs are required to fill in a frame to evoke an unruly, untamed, chaotic India, bursting at the seams and unable to contain itself except through the force of the policewalla's cane. As it happens during the trial scene, where the Indians are seen crowding all over, a man painted like a monkey is seen being beaten up by the police -- a continuation of "screeching animality" (Kipnis 47).

However, by the end of the trial Fielding and Aziz are estranged and the scene shifts from Chandrapore to Kashmir, where Aziz has a clinic in a houseboat. Fielding comes to visit Aziz there and finally the two friends reconcile under the benign influence of Mrs. Moore. The ending, again like the beginning of any film, is important, it is a privileged moment in the narrative of any film, and merits close attention. The film ends with Aziz writing a conciliatory letter to Adela, asking her to "forgive him", and telling her "it has taken me all this time to appreciate your courage". The film ends with Adela reading Aziz's letter leaning against a window, as the rains fall outside.

Conclusion

Having examined Forster's novel and Lean's film it may be said that where Forster's text is a limit case of Liberal Humanism and admits of failure in forming viable personal relationships between the Indians and the British until a political solution is found to the problem of colonialism, Lean's text exempts the British Empire from many historical wrongdoings and is unabashedly nostalgic for a lost era.

The film's narrative is deeply embedded in racism and Eurocentrism, which both legitimizes the rationale of imperialism and minimizes the oppressive thrust of British Empire by providing a manipulative reading of the novel. But of course the source of the film itself is not free of a Eurocentric consciousness so that there, are at the same time, similarities in the written and the visual texts. Both shift the blame for the failure of the empire to its lower order of officials and to women and do not engage with the question of the oppressive structures of imperialism per se. Nor are there any efforts to engage with the economic, military and other exploitative aspects of colonialism in either the novel or the film. The film, even while departing from the novel in its treatment of the themes of the novel, does not in any significant way distort the discourse of the novel. In fact Forster's novel itself is not entirely free of the criticism leveled against Lean's film.

In fact, the film articulates more prominently the gaps and inconsistencies of the novel. The film nevertheless, in the final analysis is more reductive in its representation of India, and of the colonial situation. And though it is shot in a realist style and produces an illusory reality effect, its goal is not realism. A structured absence of history is conspicuous by its absence throughout the film. The film is shot partly as a tourist brochure where the viewer is lured to travel backwards in time and history into the grand spectacle of the British Raj, refurbished and made vivid to portray a glorious past with the gritty edge of history retouched out of the picture perfect frame.

There is, as Arun Mukherjee says, an attempt in the film to "exorcise the past and to make it appear as though the bad part — the sin and guilt part — never happened". Mukherjee is right in suggesting that such a film is a "cultural re-colonization, an attempt to go back to the place of one's past crime and recreate the past in a way that the crime is displaced, muffled, and washed out"(40). Nevertheless, one crucial difference between the novel and the film is that where the novel is apologetic about colonialism and interrogates its dominant discourse through its style of ironic commentary, the film's overall form is embedded in the triumphalist discourse of the Raj epic and glosses over the debasing experience of historical, cultural, psychological victimization perpetrated by Imperialism.

Notes

1. Chidananda Dasgupta in his "Making Kipling out of Forster," quotes Santha Rama Rau as saying, "Satyajit Ray had asked For-

ster for permission to make a film of the novel. Forster refused on principle, and with great difficulty". *Indian Express.* 30 Sept 1984. (p.4)
2. Dasgupta, in the same article claims that the King's College trustees "succumbed to the blandishments of Lord John Brabourne, whose father had been a Governor of Bombay (and had for a short while, officiated as viceroy of India) and whose father-in-law was Lord Louis Mountbatten. Producer director (David Lean) and script writer (Santha Rama Rau) were all highly acceptable, so why not." (p. 4)
3. To speak of Forster is in a way to speak of a saint. Not a saint of God, certainly, but an anthropocentric apostle—to whom the obscene vocabulary of boys, the indiscrete discretions of Indians, the violence of Italians, the passions of a Maharaja, the awkward straightness of an Englishman, so many faces and despairs, are signs of an internal music, of a pure human truth, aspects of an earthy logos". *The Meaning of India.* (New Delhi: Vision Books, 1996. p. 102).
4. "Forster's *A Passage to India* is an oasis in the desert of Anglo-Indian fiction. It is a refreshing book; refreshing in its candour, sincerity, fairness, and art, and is worth more than the whole of the trash that passes by the name of Anglo-Indian fiction".
5. G.K. Das is of the opinion that the "novel portrays the political conflict and links it mainly with the lapses in the imperial policies of the government in the past" (*E.M. Forster's India.* MacMillan Press Ltd, 1977. p. 3).
6. Michael Gorra makes a similar point in his essay "Rudyard Kipling to Salman Rushdie." Kipling he says, emphasized the knowability of India so as to "subdue the subcontinent to description" but "Forster's India is knowable only in its unknowability...the novel as a whole suggests something else: see India, and realize all we don't understand about this alien land; see it and realize that we have no business here." *The Columbia History of the British Novel.* (New York: Columbia University Press, 1994. p.640-641).
7. Played by Judy Davis. The other actors of the film are James Fox who plays Fielding, Victor Banerjee who is Aziz, Dame Peggy Ashcroft as Mrs. Moore and Alec Guiness as Godbole.

8. Iqbal Masud in his article, "The Lean Legend" published in *The Indian Express*, writes, "Lean deliberately left out one underlying strand of *Passage* - the current of homosexual love... Andrew Robinson, Ray's biographer told me, Lean was so scared he would not touch this theme with a bargepole" (*Indian Express*, 5 May 1991 p.3).

References

A Passage to India. Dir. David Lean. Perf. - Judy Davis, James Fox, Victor Banerjee, Peggy Ashcroft and Alec Guiness. Columbia Pictures, 1984.

Beer, Gillian. "Negation in *A Passage to India*." *A Passage to India: Essays in Interpretation*. Ed. John Beer. London: Macmillan Press Ltd, 1985.

Bhabha, Homi K. *Location of Culture*. London: Routledge, 1994.

Comb, Richard. "David Lean: Riddles of the Sphinx." *Monthly Film Bulletin*. 52. 615 (1985): 102-106.

Das, G.K. "A Passage to India: A Socio-historical Study." Beer. 1-15.

---. *E.M. Forster's India*. London: Macmillan Press Ltd, 1977.

Dasgupta, Chidananda. "Making Kipling out of Forster" *Indian Express*. 30 Sept. 1984. 4.

Dirks, Nicholas B. "Introduction: Colonialism and Culture." *Colonialism and Culture*. Ann Arbor: The University of Michigan Press, 1993. 1-25.

Donaldson, Laura E. *Decolonizing Feminisms: Race, Gender and Empire Building*. London: University of North Carolina Press, 1992.

Forster, E.M. *A Passage to India* (1924) New York: Penguin Books Ltd, 1979.

Freedgood, Elaine. "E.M. Forster's Queer Nation: Taking the Closet to the Colony in *A Passage to India*." *Bodies of Writing, Bodies in Performance*, Eds. Thomas Forster, Carol Seigel, and Ellen E. Berry. Genders 23. New York: New York University Press, 1996. 123-144.

Goodman, W. R. *A History of English Literature*. New Delhi: Lucky Press, 1959.

Gorra, Michael. "Rudyard Kipling to Salman Rushdie: Imperialism to Postcolonialism". *The Columbia History of the British Novel.* Ed. John Richetti. New York: Columbia University Press, 1994. 631-657.

Herz, Judith. "Listening to Language." Beer. 59-70.

Hill, John. *British Cinema in the 1980s.* New York: Oxford University Press, 1999

Kennedy, Harlan. "Brits have gone Nuts." *Film Comment.* 21.4 (1985): 51-55

Kipnis, Laura. "The Phantom Twitchings of an Amputated Limb: Sexual Spectacle in the Post-Colonial Epic" *Wide Angle.* 11. 4(1989): 43-54.

Lean, David. "I'm a Picture Chap" Interview by Harlan Kennedy. *Film Comment.* 21.1(1985): 28-32.

Masud, Iqbal. "The Lean Legend." *The Indian Express.* 5 May 1991. 3

Mukherjee, Arun P. *Oppositional Aesthetics: Reading from a Hyphenated Space.* Toronto: TSAR. 1994.

Parry, Benita."Materiality and Mystification in *A Passage to India.*" Novel. 31. 2 (1998): 174- 194.

Pether, Penelope. "A Passage to India: A Passage to the Patria?" *New Casebooks: E.M. Forster.* Ed. Jeremy Tambling. London: McMillan Press Ltd, 1995. 195-212.

Rao, Raja. *The Meaning of India.* New Delhi: Vision Books, 1996.

Said, Edward. *Orientalism.* New York: Vintage Books, 1978.

—. *Culture and Imperialism.* London: Vintage Books, 1994.

Sharpe, Jenny. *Allegories of Empire: The Figure of Woman in the Colonial Text.* Minneapolis: University of Minnesota Press, 1993.

Shohat Ella and Robert Stam. *Unthinking Eurocentrism: Multiculturalism and the Media.* New York: Routledge, 1994.

Singh, K. Natwar. "Only Connect...: Forster and India." *Aspects of E.M. Forster.* Ed. Oliver Stallybrass. London: Edward Arnold Ltd, 1969. 37-50.

Stam, Robert and Louise Spense. "Colonialism, Racism and Representation: An Introduction." *Film Theory and Criticism: Introductory Readings.* Ed. Leo Braudy and Marshall Cohen. 1999ed. New York: Oxford University Press, 1974. 235-250.

Stone, Wilfred. *The Cave and the Mountain: A Study of E..M. Forster.* London: Oxford University Press, 1966.

Suleri, Sara. "Forster's Imperial Erotic." *Tambling.* 151- 170.

Tambling, Jeremy. ed. *New Casebooks: E. M. Forster.* London: McMillan Press Ltd., 1995.

Trivedi, Harish. *Colonial Transactions: English Literature in India.* Calcutta: Papyrus, 1993.

Wiegman, Robyn. "Race, Ethnicity and Film", *The Oxford Guide to Film Studies.* Eds. John Hill and Pamela Church Gibson. Oxford: Oxford University Press, 1998.

24

Postcoloniality after 1947: The Split Identity of the Nation

Veena Singh

Postcolonialism, a complex term in itself, has acquired some dominant meanings as its trademark. Critics have moved from their early disputes about the beginning of postcolonialism to identifying its major tropes as resistance to the imperial other and reconstruction of a new national identity. If one was to follow the argument put forward in *The Empire Writes Back* and look at the first point of the encounter between the imperial power and the natives, one could trace the beginning of postcolonialism to the Battle of Plassey, 1757. Nearly two centuries later, the imperial rule, which began then, and was formally constituted into an Empire by the government of India Act, 1858, ended on August 15, 1947.

The period between 1757 and 1858 was one kind of an exercise at self-definition on part of the Indians, and the post 1857 period was an exercise of a different kind. The early admiration for western ideas yielded to a resistance to the British rule. The basic premise of the postcolonial impulse and the effort to reconstruct a national identity was the relationship between the 'self' and the 'other'. The white races needed the coloured 'savages' to build the myth of the white man's burden and the whole civilizing discourse. The idea of 'nationhood' was a 'united India', in which religion was not the basis of division. 'Difference' itself was never cause enough for the two-nation theory. But then happened partition. And the literature of the partition shows us a nation divided, it reflects the agony of a split consciousness. Postcoloniality, apparently had converted itself into a narrow nationalism. Hindus and Muslims who had lived together in reasonable harmony and nurtured dreams of freedom, were suddenly enemies.

Since time immemorial if the Indian mind has been influenced by the Vedas and the philosophical ideas of Vedanta, it has also assimilated the Sufi tradition. The Bhakti saints like Amir Khusru and Kabir in the 14th century had taught that Ram and Rahim, Ishwar and Allah are the names of the same God. It was in this atmosphere of 'Ganga Jamuni Tehzeeb' that the values of humanism and composite culture of India bloomed and manifested and articulated itself in the life of the people.

Alok Bhalla in 'Introduction' to *Stories About the Partition of India*, Vol. I, asserts if, "there had been irreconcilable hatred or non-negotiable aversion between the Hindus and the Muslims, it would have been reflected in the cultural and social practices of the two groups. The pain of living together would have been extensively recorded ...(viii)." He further states, "It is perhaps the fact that the daily life of the Hindus and the Muslims, at the ordinary and the local levels, even as late as 1946, was so richly interwoven as to have formed a rich archive of customs and practices...(Bhalla, ix)."

Till the Independence of India in 1947 if there was any 'other' it was the British—the colonizer. The resistance movement was against Imperialism. The people of United India, as one nation, questioned the imperial position and redefined self and identity.

But with the declaration of the independence of the country the issue changed. The concepts of the 'self' and the 'other' changed. The attention from the 'outsider' shifted to 'home'. Allegiance to a particular religion made one 'the other'. Community became one's identity. In fact, the idea of resistance to the 'other' was turned inwards.

This sort of upheaval left both the Hindus and the Muslims confused and bewildered. With the ultimate division of the country a new nation was born but it put a question mark on the question of nationhood and home.

Timothy Brennan in his essay, "The National Longing For Form", with reference to 'postcolonial responsibility' while citing the case of Salman Rushdie writes: "In fact, the central irony of his novels is that independence has damaged Indian spirits by proving that 'India' can act as abominably as the British did" (Brennan, 174). The entire partition literature irrespective of who the writer is—whether Muslim writers who migrated to Pakistan like Intizar Husain and Manto, or Hindus who migrated to India like Bhisham Sahani and Chaman Nahal—brings out the appalling savagery during the partition time. The writers address themselves to questions of 'nation', 'belonging' and 'self'. They also underline the artificiality of the division, which was induced by an external agency—the outgoing colonizer.

Asgar Wajahat's play, *Jis Lahore Nahin Dekhya O Jamyai Nahin* (He who has not seen Lahore, has not been born), is an important play which has captured the subtle nuances of this division, which in actuality has no clear cut boundaries, is not a division of faith but of power. Wajahat's play has long been in circulation, at least for two decades of more, and has been staged in different places—in India, Pakistan and Western countries—has been translated into several languages and subjected to a variety of directorial interpretations.[1] It has also been prohibited from performance on ideological grounds.[2] This play narrates the story of a Hindu woman who refuses to leave her home in Pakistan and, after an initial struggle, the Muslim family which has been allotted this supposedly evacuee property, finally accepts her as a member of the family. The woman becomes an archetypal 'Mai' (mother) and one begins to sense a coming together of opposites, a resurfacing of human bonds and a gradual obliteration of division.

Divided into sixteen scenes, the play begins with a frenzied procession raising slogans demanding Pakistan and abusing Khijir Hayat Khan, who is not a member of the Muslim League, thus by inference who is opposing the demand for the partition. Very soon the news that Khijir has joined the League makes him, who a little while ago was "son of a bitch", "our brother". This oscillation between 'ours' and 'the other', 'a friend' and 'a foe' continues as the rumours spread (9-11). The first scene concludes with the partition, which is the central event of the play. The two processions in this scene, one at the very beginning is that of strife, agitation and action, the supporters of Muslim League adamant on the creation of Pakistan and the other procession at the end of the scene that of exodus and resignation though juxtaposed are linked and interdependent. The second procession is a natural consequence of the first procession. If the first procession brings out the theme of fundamentalism the second focuses on the theme humanism. At the end of the scene (as in all other scenes), there is the authorial intervention in the form of a short sensitive poem, used as a background voice. It says, 'as a result Hindustan is divided, the earth is divided, the sky is divided, the styles and expressions of writing and thought are divided, the dreams that we dreamt were different, the Punjab that we see is different'.[3]

After scene i the focus of the play is on Mirza and his family, who woebegone and weather beaten migrate from Lucknow to Lahore and after a few miserable months in the camp are allotted a 22-room haveli, originally belonging to a Hindu jeweller. The possession of the haveli gives the family a feeling of relief which comes with the sense of stability and survival. It is their new 'home' where they hope to grow roots for the sake of their children. But very soon the family discovers there is another owner—an old Hindu woman, Ratan's mother—still living in the house. The 'place' and haveli become a very powerful metaphor.

Though the Mirza asks the old woman to go, she on the contrary asserts her right and stakes her claim to the haveli. The Mirza says that Lahore is in Pakistan and there is no place for Hindus ('you people') in Pakistan (15). But ironically the Muslim refugees from India were also considered outsiders in Pakistan. In the haveli the old woman occupies the first floor. The ground floor of the haveli is occupied by Mirza's family. Mirza's restricted movement in his legally allotted house is a symbolic reflection of the refugees' unwelcome guest status in Pakistan. The Mirza and his family, Hamid Husain and his family, the poet Nasir Kazmi though Muslims are Mohajirs in Pakistan.

Mohajirs, the Urdu speaking Muslims from Uttar Pradesh and other northern areas (the poet is from Ambala), who migrated to what they thought was the land of promise, found it very difficult to integrate themselves with the society over there. These migrants were subjected to all kinds of discriminations. Intizar Husain's stories, 'An Unwritten Epic' and 'A Letter from India' also depict that assimilation into the local culture and acceptance by the local people was in itself a difficult process. In the play the family of Mirza and that of Husain have no fuel for cooking. Mirza's family is bullied by the Pahalwan, who even tries to grab the upper storey of the haveli. The Pahalwan angrily retorts, "What do these coming from outside know" (62). Alim, the local tea stall owner, also refers to them as, "those who have come from the other side."

On the other hand Ratan's mother is a native of Lahore, she does not want to be sent to India. In her words, "there is no place like Lahore" and there can be no substitute for one's own land (50). Lahore is her land. Though a Hindu she has no affinity with India. Her son and his family lived here and died here. Her memories are here in Lahore and of Lahore. For her the division on the basis of religion into two nation states and each country becoming a one-nation dispensation after the partition has no meaning. For her Lahore is her homeland.

Unlike the old woman, the Mirza's family and the poet have come to Pakistan but the memories of the past haunt them. The Mirza is nostalgic about Lucknow and for him there is no other place like Lucknow. He thinks of his 'chikan' work factory and the house, which some Indian migrant from Pakistan, must be occupying. The poet's eyes search for the bird Shyama as his thoughts turn to the flowering mustard fields, monsoon showers and the dancing peacocks and the colour of the sky during the spring in India (64). The question then is which is one' country? The country one emotionally belongs to? Or the country of one's religion or the one is born into? Who are the old woman's own people? Who is the 'other'? For the Pahalwan, the old woman does not belong to Lahore and must not live in Lahore as she is a Hindu. Ironically the Pahalwan and the old Hindu woman both speak the same language, Punjabi, which the UP Muslims do not.

The initial antagonism between the family of Mirza and the old woman gradually melts into a family bond. She reaches out to them. Soon she is Tanoo's and Javed's 'dadi', 'Maji' for Hamida Begam and ultimately Mirza's 'Mai.' In Tanoo she sees her grand daughter Radha. The Mirza urges her to stay on, "you ought to stay with your son, daughter-in-law and grandchildren" (69). The 'you people' of scene ii by scene XIV become an integral part of the family. Though the memory of her missing son and his family is there but the old woman emotionally rehabilitates herself and sees the Mirza's family as her own. The old woman who in scene ii was asserting her claim to the haveli even at the cost of her life by the end of the play is ready to leave the haveli and Lahore and go to Delhi for the sake of the welfare and safety of Mirza's family. Each is now more concerned for the other. The boundaries have been crossed. The Mirza feels that if the Mai goes they would not be able to look themselves in the face. It would be a failure at the human level (69).

The old woman spends her time working and helping the other families out of love. Religious differences or the disparity between the communities does not exist. For the old woman, the fact that she is a Hindu and the others Muslims does not alienate them. They are her very own. Mirza's earlier statement that a rootless tree cannot survive and that the old woman's relative, neighbours have all gone to India and since India is her country how long will she live in Pakistan (sc. iv, 25) sounds ironical. The old woman's roots are struck deep in Pakistan. It is the uprooted who have to grow roots and begin afresh.

The celebration of Diwali by Ratan's mother and the participation of the Mirza and his family, the poet and Hamid in this become very meaningful. The festival is celebrated as a family. The boundary between India and Pakistan blurs and Lucknow and Lahore merge into each other. Tanoo's questions, "Why did all this happen?" "Why did we come to Pakistan?" "If Mai and we can live together in one house why couldn't the Hindus and Muslims live together in Hindustan?" are cryptic questions. The mother has no answers to any of these (54). For Hamid, the old woman is his connection and continuity with the past—a united country, a unified people.

The final test comes with the death of the old woman. Faced by the fact of human mortality, existential questions as to the faith one has grown up in and the funeral rites to be observed acquire importance. As the neighbourhood and Dadi's family of adoption get together, even the Maulvi, for once, stands outside the narrow framework of a single religion. He is the one who holds the opinion that Dadi, having lived the life of a Hindu, should be cremated according to Hindu rites. As they probe their memories and place their observations together, practices of a once-familiar-now-distanced religion are remembered and put together in some kind of order. They all acquire Hindu roles, procure the 'samagri' (the material) required and thus reciting "Ram Naam Sat Hai" (The name of God is Truth), they carry her body to the banks of the river Ravi, and perform the funeral rites.

This penultimate scene—extremely poignant and meaningful—is followed by the climax, the surfacing of narrow hatred once again with the Pahalwan and his group turning their anger upon the Maulvi—the man of faith—in their desire to arrest their Pakistani identity.

Who is the 'other'? The artificiality of the division of the country on religious basis appears a mockery. Juxtaposed to this homogeneous group is the narrow religious fanaticism of the Pahalwan and his friends. They profess that Pakistan is for Muslims alone and therefore they resent the idea of religious tolerance. They look upon themselves as the servants of the faith but their fanaticism leads them to kill the Maulvi in the mosque—a sacrilegious act committed in the name of religion. Can there be a bigger irony than this! In fact he represents hatred, hooliganism and brawn power, which puts on a garb of religion for an ulterior motive.

The play has two endings—one is the funeral procession of 'Mai', which is a substitution for the earlier exodus of the refugees rendered homeless, and driven away from their homes. This procession, in contrast, is a welding together of opposites, and surpasses the quality of passive tolerance. It is an active participation in the life of the 'other'. The narrative is one of a coming together across all kinds of boundaries, a forgetting of hostilities and othernesses, a merging across language, memory and history. Then there is a second ending, just when the audience has been purged of its hatred and ambiguities, just when a catharsis has taken place and human dignity has been honoured and reinstated, at that point comes a resurfacing of greed, materiality and a power struggle which does not recognize the code of civilized behaviour. In the very act of prayer, the Maulvi is killed—murdered stealthily in the mosque by the Pahalwan and his group, a reassertion of the naked struggle of power, which is ruthless and inhuman. The Pahalwan's act is a reassertion of the 'native' inhabitant and a struggle for ownership.

The two endings woven so intricately into each other send out a message, which weaves itself from two opposite strands. There is the humanist discourse, which binds and enhances the quality of life and there is the discourse of aggression, which destroys and annihilates. Both of them are, if one looks at them closely enough, outside religion. One transcends religious ritual; the other hardens it into fanaticism.

Partition, when it came in 1947 was not a sudden happening. The split had occurred earlier. Historians have offered several explanations and traced the beginnings back to 1930s. The differences were political rather than religious. The 1942 Quit India Movement widened the rift between the two dominant political parties. Historical interpretations despite all their documentation do not necessarily try to explain this split in colonial/post colonial terms. But it was, at one level, postcolonialism turned inwards, where the forces of resistance which had aligned to resist the outsider, created the 'other' the outsider, the enemy within the territorial bounds of the state.

Notes

1. In the preface 'Teen Shabd' (Three Words), the playwright mentions how Habib Tanveer in collaboration with the Sri Ram Centre staged the play in his own lyrical style. He then goes onto say that this no doubt added charm to the play but introduction of humour, theatricality and excessive emotionality adversely affected the basic thesis of the play.
2. The writer mentions in the preface that this play was successfully staged in Washington. But with reference to the staging of the play in Pakistan, the playwright recollects the ideological battle that Khalid Ahmed had to fight. He was denied permission by the police to stage the play. The reasons given were one, the killing of the Maulvi in the play is against Islam, two, the characterization of the old Hindu woman 'Mai' was not how the police wanted it to be. Then the play was staged in Karachi at the Goethe German Information Center. Not only was each show 'houseful' but there were people climbing up the trees to see the play.
3. *Aur nateeje mein Hindustan bat gaya*
   Yeh zameen bat gayi aasman bat gaya
   Tarze tehreer, tarze bayaa bat gaya
   Shakhe gul bat gayi, aashiyan bat gaya
   Hamne dekha tha jo khwab hi aur tha
   Ab jo dekha to Punjab hi aur tha. (11)

References

Ashcroft, Bill, Gareth Griffiths and Helen Tiffin. *The Empire Writes Back: Theory and Practice in Post-colonial Literatures*. London: Routledge, 1989.

—, eds, *The Post-colonial Studies Reader*. London: Routledge, 1995.

Bhalla, Alok. (ed.) *Stories About the Partition of India* (3 vols.). New Delhi: Harper Collins Publishers, 1994.

Brennan, Timothy. 'The National Longing For Form' *Nation and Narration*, Homi K. Bhabha (ed.). London: Routledge, 1990.

Wajahat, Asgar. *Jis Lahore Nahin Dekhya O Jamyai Nahin*. New Delhi: Vani Prakashan, 2001.

(References to the play are from this edition. The English translations wherever used are mine.)

25

Moving Beyond Postcolonial Frameworks: Home Concerns

Jasbir Jain

I

Postcolonialism, in itself, a difficult term to define, has however, successfully been used to define almost everything under the sun. For more than three decades the term has ruled the roost, unhesitatingly expanding its hold to all acts of oppression and resistance. Under its umbrella there have been many a temporal and spatial shifts. It has moved back in time to include all modern colonisations, and is now being used for internal schisms and resistance. Right from being a political marker and a literary framework, it has gone on to include gender and psychology. The time has come to put it back on a more rational footing, to make specific distinctions whether it is a category associated with power struggles, the resistance to exploitative power, or to discriminatory practices rooted in patriarchy and racism. Is it possible to extend the concept of postcoloniality to all revolutionary movements and class struggles within a society? And if it is not, then, obviously the nation-state, a community of people and territorial boundaries play a role in the concept of postcolonialism. If it is to be interpreted as a resistance to injustice and aggression, a reconstruction of identities, then its scope becomes unlimited. Ania Loomba has defined colonialism as a reshaping, often violently, of physical territories, social terrains as well as human identities (Loomba 185). Consequently postcolonialism, in its various hues, sets itself the task of constructing a different self, recovering lost histories and cultures and shaping a new identity—national, collective and individual.

Given the above premise, a whole lot of configurations would have to change and whole lot of reevaluations undertaken. First, what happens to the individual consciousness in this collective realization? All evolutionary (and revolutionary) struggles are also identity constructions. In fact, postcolonialism moves simultaneously in two opposite directions. On the one hand it is an assertion of identity (and nationhood), and on the other it is a term which tries to bring all kinds of heterogeneous groups into a homogenous situation by describing them in similar categories. Similarly, the basic impulse of working towards independent identities, aesthetics, epistemological frameworks is overlaid by shifting it to the First World and merging it in terms like ethnicity and multiculturalism. The defining parameters are subtly transformed and once again it remains a power relationship, this time not necessarily on native soil but on foreign soil.

In recent years there has been an extension of the term to literatures of languages other than English. Some of us persisted in including writing from other Indian languages, which to begin with was a welcome step for it prevented a split on the basis of language. It also linked them with the enterprise of modernity and stressed the connections between society and literature. But, at the same time, this visibility placed them within the time-lag theory and subjected them to a single dominant perspective, that of postcoloniality, and subtracted both from their strengths and relevance. It needs be recognised that postcoloniality is primarily other-directed, it remains subordinated to the other as it is constantly in some kind of a relationship with external, 'colonising' forces.

Perhaps, as several critics have observed, it did serve a useful purpose in enabling the process of 'visibility' of the erstwhile colonies in the First World, in forcing a recognition on them. But even this visibility has several dimensions. Arun Mukherjee in *Oppositional Aesthetics* resents the clubbing together of very different cultures and literatures in a single group and insists upon the rootedness of literatures in the cultural environment and mythical inheritance. There is an element of cultural density, which is not always accessible through linguistic structures.

The propagation of a critical grid which renders interpretation easy, but perhaps equally meaningless, is detrimental to the interpretation of any literature. Whatever does not specifically come under that approach gets marginalized. The other-directed, postcolonial approach has a tendency towards unidimensionality and begins to cater to the politics of publication. It needs to be recognised first, that all resistance is not postcolonial and secondly, there is much in literature that is not resistance. To narrow it down to protest and resistance is to falsify the situation. The primary feature which characterises postcolonialism is a resentment against an unequal cultural equation and within this dominant trope, identity and nationhood play a role. An extension of this trope to all power relations dislocates all other kinds of literature—romantic, realistic, dystopian and futuristic, autobiographical and existential writing—all are brushed aside.

Works which immediately come to mind as falling outside the postcolonial metaphor are a whole range of writing by Indian writers—those writing in English as well as in other languages. Salman Rushdie's *The Ground Beneath her Feet*, Vikram Seth's *An Equal Music*, all of Shashi Deshpande's writing U.R. Anantha Murthy's works, specially *Sanskara* and *Bhav*, Krishna Sobti's novels, Shivarama Karanth's *The Woman of Basrur*—all of them deal with personal struggles, questionings of tradition, relationships, kinship patterns, dreams, reinterpretation of myths, making sense of the world, reframing and reorganizing it. They are ways of findings out how to live and as they do so, alternative traditions and patterns emerge, some parallel others different, and still others similar. They reveal an intimate knowledge of specific societies and resist any kind of lumping together. And they refuse to be contained by the term 'postcolonial'.

U.R. Anantha Murthy in his essay "The Search for an Identity: A Kannada Writer's Viewpoint", narrates the experience of a painter. In order to photograph the stone which a peasant worshipped, the painter requested permission to shift the stone and photograph it. Later he apologised if he had in any way polluted it. The peasant's reply was, "It doesn't matter ... I will have to bring another stone and anoint *kumkum* on it". Anantha Murthy's comment on this is:

> what mattered was his faith, not the stone. Do we understand the manner in which the peasant's mind worked? ... Can we understand the essentially mythical and metaphorical imagination which directed his inner life? Will Lukacs and Russell, who influence the structure of our thinking now, help us see instinctively the way the peasant's mind worked? (150)

It is the 'subject', the 'inward-look', the concept of a self-rooted identity of self, generated through one's faith which is important. The significance and the importance of the stone, the 'object' of worship in this case, is important and created by the 'self' thus this is a reversal of the self's dependence on the other. Anantha Murthy's observation also stresses the fact that there is much in India which has not been changed or affected by colonialism, which falls outside its impact and has a meaning and relevance of its own.

The idea of a 'self' still remains a central issue both in society and in literature. Both terrorism and fundamentalism are different ways of responding to this issue, the former believing in action and resistance, the latter in insistence on tradition and religion. They are tools and methods in a larger power-game, that of globalisation. Thus simultaneously they work at several levels, in concentric circles, beginning with the individual in the family (patriarchy, gender, hierarchy), moving on to the community (caste, race, religion), and then to a negotiation with cultural parameters working in a spatio-temporal framework, to enter into conflict with other cultures, other identities, other power structures.

In literature the rewriting of history is not necessarily other directed, it is not always a questioning or displacement of the western version of facts but a search for answers to our current problems. The reworking on historical ground is an attempt to look within, to find out answers to the question: what went wrong? where are we accountable?

This return to the past is not only an attempt to construct a new identity, but also a desire to establish continuities and cease being a vulnerable 'postcolonial subject'. The new historical novel is both interpretative and investigative; in it the boundaries between history and politics are blurred and done away with. And even as it bases itself on earlier knowledge, it is a questioning of that knowledge. Foucault has viewed history as archaeology, a search which brings about a displacement. He observes that an event "is not a decision, a treaty, a reign or a battle, but the reversal of relationship of forces... the entry of a masked other" (Foucault 40), history thus is the 'mother of all sciences.' Man is a 'historical' being in the sense that he is placed in a temporal reality. It is against this background/framework that I wish to locate the contemporary fictional presentations of history of India and explore the meaning of these rewritings and reinterpretations. A majority of these novels are, and acquire importance as, documents concerned with the first half the twentieth century, the period of the freedom struggle, its conflicting ideological forces, Hindu-Muslim relationships, the Partition and its aftermath. How does the contemporary Indian writer view this phase of the nation's past? I propose to focus on Mukul Kesavan's *Looking Through Glass*, Nayantara Sahgal's *Lesser Breeds* and Shashi Tharoor's *Riot*, to find some kind of answer to the above question.

II

Amnesia had its rules and I kept to them. Once 1942 became undeniable, I chose to lose my memory.

(*Looking Through Glass* 14)

Mukul Kesavan's 1995 novel is about the Quit India Movement of 1942 and its aftermath, Kesavan is a working historian and the novel can safely be taken as an account of his reading of the past. It takes its title not only from Lewis Carroll's novels, as has been pointed out often enough, but also from another senior fellow historian, Sir Penderel Moon's, book *Divide and Quit*, and more specifically to his "empathic yet hard-headed narrative of the holocaust as it was experienced in one part of the Panjab, the princely state called Bahawalpur" (Raychaudhuri 188). The passage runs as follows:

> ...I found myself in a 'through the looking glass' world of normal conventions. There was a complete breakdown, or rather reversal of the ordinary moral values. (p. 177, qtd by Raychaudhuri 197)

Looking Through Glass is a total reversal of everything -- time, identities and emotions. The young nameless protagonist falls into the river of time, is caught in a time warp in the forties, is given protection by a Muslim family, takes on a Muslim name and later, in Delhi, lives simultaneously in a double consciousness. As he walks through the streets of Delhi, he is aware of the changes which the inbetween forty years, from the mid-forties to the mid-eighties, have made, he knows which buildings have been demolished and which handed over for other purposes. And as he lives through these changing roles, he undergoes a circumcision and joins the Muslim refugees in the Purana Qila Refugee Camp. Thus the basic premise is one of empathy working through the basic trope of guilt. The one essential fact on which the novel rests itself is the disappearance of Masroor on the morning of August 9, 1942, signifying the wiping away of the nationalist Muslim identity. What went wrong? In what way was the Congress declaration of the Quit India Movement responsible for the aftermath? Kesavan's interpretation of history is reflected in the novel even as he uses unrealistic modes to make his statement. In this connection, Mumtaz Shah Nawaz's 1948 novel, *The Heart Divided* (FP 1957 rpt. 2004) provides a very useful perspective on the politics of the forties. Krishna Kumar, the noted educationist, in his 'Foreword' to the novel observes:

> I first read *The Heart Divided* a few years ago, when I was trying to make sense of the 1930s. I was in the midst of an ambitious project, analysing the rival accounts of the freedom struggle fed to

present day Indian and Pakistani children through school textbooks. The two grand narratives follow predictable nationalist tracts, coming close at times, diverging at others, but they stay within the reach of interpretative imagination except when they cover the late 1930s. Something apparently strange happened in that decade, so strange that it continues to render even scholarly political history rather thin and unsatisfying.

And as I read the novel, soon after a rereading of Attia Hosain's *Sunlight on a Broken Column*, the pre-Pakistan situation, with all its regional differences, became abundantly clear. The novel reads like a slow motion film of the thirties, but the political history, documented through the generational, cultural and religious differences comes, through in a heart rending manner. Tapan Raychaudhuri's essay "Rereading *Divide and Quit*", is an insightful juxtaposition of two different kinds of reflections on the 1942 movement and its aftermath, one contemporary and the other retrospective, separated from each other by a time gap of fifty years, and cultural and national backgrounds. The two together reach similar conclusions: it is not faith, not religion which divided the nation, but a struggle for power and dominance.

A persistent concern that the contemporary historical novel works with is the events which divided the national subject, foregrounded this power struggle and have subsequently spilled over into the present, across national boundaries. The Hindu-Muslim relationship is a crucial factor in India's present political reality and ideology. Raychaudhuri is one of the few writers to refer to the violence of 1947 as 'holocaust'. (I have not come across many writers who refer to it as such because the word is so strongly etched in our memories as the 'label' for the Nazi persecution of the Jews, it seems strange to bring it home, so close to us in time and memory.)

It is worth noting that Raychaudhuri put together his essays after a ten-month stay in Germany (1999 or thereabouts, while the essays included in the volume have been written between 1992-1997), where the "liberal intellectual is obsessed with the national sense of guilt" (Preface x). It is a similar sense of guilt which can be seen working through the protagonist of *Looking Through Glass*.

There has to be some kind of an identification, a moving across to the other. One the most crude ways of identifying the victim, is through external appearances—dress, beard, marks of superficial identification like a 'bindi' or a 'tilak' and a bodily one like a circumcision. Time and again, all pretence to civilized behaviour has crumbled at these barriers. The act of circumcision, literally chopping of a bit of one's body, is an attempt at reducing the external difference, and moving into the enemy camp to share his vulnerability. Kesavan's novel does not only reassess the 1942 movement, it goes further than that to suggest alternative ways of coping with division. The family which adopts him does so whole heartedly, identities are mixed and exchangeable. Masroor's father was a Kashmiri Hindu, Kalidas Ganjoo; Ammi refuses to move to Pakistan, she stands outside religious divisions; Haasan, a close friend of the family, is a non-Muslim with a name which labels him as one. Thus the outward labels need not bear any correspondence to the reality, indicators can be misleading, and identities mistaken: the unreliability of this kind of slot labelling is pointed out over and over again, and additionally it is also stressed that identities can be falsely constructed by society. In *Looking Through Glass*, there are a number of crossing overs, Masroor's father, Kalidas Ganjoo crosses over through conversion, ('Urdu verse which keeps nibbling at his soul', 24). Haasan, through the act of naming belongs, to two different camps, the village which claims him as do the Muslims because of this sharing. Haasan is mistaken to be a Muslim, because the perception of the observers are guided by their own limited experience. Food is another way of crossing over, and circumcision yet another. Finally, the act of 'belonging', of 'owning' a kinship is also important. The anonymous hero of the novel works towards his own rehabilitation through the trope of guilt. And all the markers of identity like name, language, kinship, location and politics are seen to be unreliable.

Nayantara Sahgal's preoccupation with history has been an ongoing concern, and more specifically so in the four novels beginning with *Rich Like Us*. Beginning in the 70s, when the Emergency was declared, the narrative moves backwards through diaries, letters and newspaper cuttings right back to the early 19th century, takes up the 'sati' motif as it surfaces in various forms again and again and repeatedly asks the question as to where does the responsibility lie for all that is happening to us. The attempt is to come out of the victim syndrome and face the responsibility for one's own failures. The seeds of the emergency, the power hunger, the succumbing of the weak and the tyranny of the strong are part in the nation's own past. No outsider can be blamed for it. The novel is about India, and not about any one single character, yet the questions asked are about the nature of the human character which, in this case, happens to be dominantly Indian. There is a crossing over through marriage, friendship and business relationships.

Plans of Departure works through the 1910s and 1920s and links up Tilak's character with that of Tulsidas. The genealogical inheritance of attitudes is traceable across time and generations. But as Sahgal moves to *Mistaken Identity* and *Lesser Breeds*, she shifts her focus to more specific events. *Mistaken Identity* covers a period of roughly three years, 1929 to 1931, and Bhushan's imprisonment runs parallel to Bhagat Singh's. The prison cell, occupied by ten prisoners, is a miniscule representation of the nation. Both reality and identity show a tendency of changing right before one's eyes. The trial frames Bhushan as a communist revolutionary, a setter-off of Hindu-Muslim riots, and an anti-British poet and protester, a framing which is very different from the 'reality' of Bhushan's playboy nature and love affair with Razia. The personal becomes political. Bhushan's identity is a fuzzy one with his affiliations with Urdu poetry and Hindu origins. He defies a narrow confining sense of identity and finally there is crossover when he marries Comrade Yusuf's daughter, and his mother comrade Yusuf himself, and symbolically enough, together they try to grow a garden in a desert. The end may seem romantic and unrealistic but it reveals the subconscious of the nation and symbolises a non-recognition of artificial boundaries which have been created for political purposes.

The new historical novel does not attempt to record details or to portray history in its external manifestations and encounters but prefers to look at the various ways in which these events can be interpreted and explores the gaps between the appearance of what seems real and the individual's own comprehension of that reality. It also questions all kinds of conventional markers of identity. Bhushan's compulsive meaningful relationship to a Muslim woman is the central thrust of the novel. The Bhushan-Razia affair constitutes the main strand of the narrative and has a natural culmination in his marriage to Comrade Yusuf's daughter.

Lesser Breeds takes its title from Kipling's poem and the novel takes up the story of India from the point where *Mistaken Identity* had left it. It spans a period of about thirty five years, right from the revolutionary agitation in the 30s to freedom and its aftermath. Once again the narrative is a reflection on the meaning of reality and more specifically of historical reality as it is presented and understood. Nurullah, the observer participant, is significantly a Muslim orphan, a bastard, son of a woman who had been raped and he comes to Bhai's house to observe the 'movement', that is the Gandhian movement, and learn about it. A non-believer to begin with, he is soon neckdeep in it, what with tutoring the seven year old Shan (Bhai's daughter), escorting Bhai's mother and daughter to visit him in jail and cultivating 'another way of seeing', to counter teach the lessons she learns at school (23), in short, to provide alternative ways of looking at the past, to turn facts around, to shift perspectives, to become the subject rather then remain an object. As the young man struggles to evolve a new epistemology, he himself is reeducated and weaned away from the European perspective.

As the narrative progresses, from 1932 onwards, it is divided into three parts. Of these the first "Company Bagh" covers both the non-violent movement and the revolutionary phase. The second section is titled "An Island called America", and comments upon the insularity of the powerful. India does not matter to the Western World. The third section is the shortest, in the nature of an epilogue, and titled "Trade Winds". It clearly reveals the new face of imperialism. The chase is now for 'oil and allied treasure' and Nurullah realises that this would exact a 'more terrifying price than pepper, gold and nutmeg, or teak and diamond did' (369). Shan, who is now a minister, dies in an air crash, which apparently has been engineered, as this sane voice of a newly independent country has to be silenced in the interests of capital gains.

Lesser Breeds works through contrasts, juxtapositions, personal relationships and love attractions across racial, religious and national boundaries. It functions through cartography. There is a map in Mr. Jenners's (the publisher) office which labels the non-western world as 'peopled by Monsters' (220), another map is in Bhai's study which identifies the large mineral resources in the colonies (79-80). Earlier Mukul Kesavan had also worked through maps. Masroor, who had disappeared on the fateful August day, is seen by the narrator selling a jigsaw puzzle on the roadside which is a map of India (228-230) and indicates the foolishness of first cutting up "your own country into pieces with your own hands and then trying to put it together piece by piece to understand how complex Indian unity is, how hard to build" (230). Sahgal's *Lesser Breeds* is concerned with the replay of imperialism, and its persistence in cornering the erstwhile colonies. It is a power struggle whether within or outside national boundaries.

These historical novels are concerned with the nation state as well as with the nation space—with identities and relationships. In *Riot*, Shashi Tharoor, narrows down to Ayodha, which suddenly becomes a temple town, the birthplace of 'Ram lalla, the child Ram', a new addition to Hindu mythology, and the war cry is "*Mandir wahin baneyage*", where the mosque stands, that is, 'It is here that the temple will be constructed'. In more than one sense it is a resurrection of anti-nationalism, of the hidden forces of Hindutva as they surface again to push aside the humanistic discourse. Shashi Tharoor has consistently concerned himself with history. First in 1989 in *The Great Indian Novel*, than in 1997 he turned to nonfiction where he comments on the dualism present in the distinction between 'Bharat' and 'India'. Referring to the excessive violence in the country, he writes, "As an Indian I ask myself what this daily haemorrhage is doing to the quality of the national blood. Why do the death of Indians, not result in more changes of policy of procedure, or of personnel?" (*From Midnight to Millenium* 289). The native obsession with the personal self has to be transcended to reach out to the other. Solutions, if any, lie in involvement and in crossing over.

The anxiety manifested in *From Midnight to Millenium* is carried over to the *Riot* (2001), which is about the needless violence which is artificially stoked to sustain political power. Language, class, caste, religion, (divisive factors in themselves) are not cause enough to divide India and it is still possible to nourish a dream of an extraordinary, 'polyglot, polychrome, polyconfessional country', until militant Hinduism arises to challenge the 'very basis of this Indianness' (*Riot* 44-45).

Riot is a contrapuntal narrative with multiple narrations: Lakshman, Gurinder Singh, Priscilla Hart, her parents, Ram Charan Gupta, the Hindu chauvinist, and Mohammed Sarwar, a history professor. These are all people from different religions, communities, politics and nationalities, converging on this contested space. History and mythology merge and at times are indistinguishable, furthermore history is not only about events, it is also about geography, and as memories of an earlier massacre surface – the 1984 riots – it is also about memory. History, it needs to be understood, is not merely a perspective or a selection of events, or location in the power relationships, or about remembering. It is also about forgetting. Like Kesavan's nameless protagonist of *Looking Through Glass*, a meaningful amnesia has to be willed in which forgiveness and forgetting of wrongs done have to merge in order to sustain humanistic discourse. Those who want revenge from history, do not realize that 'history has its own revenge' (14).

These novels go back to the past in search of solutions and to the 'emotional logic' of togetherness which even defies a sense of linear continuity and exposes the multilayers of reality. 'Emotional logic' may seem a contradiction in terms but it expresses a logicality based on compassion and intelligence, where the solutions looked for are human in their assumptions. Their engagement with the past is a self reflexive exercise, undertaken partly in guilt and partly in sorrow. They seek to probe the psyche of the nation and the forces of instigation which are at work. Tanika Sarkar in *Hindu Wife, Hindu Nation* (2000), has traced the history of the emotional exploitation of the people worked through *Vande Mataram* for political reasons, and Advani's first Rath Yatra, the serialization of the *Mahabharata* and *Ramayana* on the TV, all continued efforts in one direction, and Tapan Raychauduri has traced the history of the RSS's role in the construction of this new Hindutva, which reflects a power struggle, a construction of a *Hindu Rashtra*. These writers turn to the past to trace the genesis of these divisions, they turn to the past to examine the solutions which men of earlier generations had posited, they reexamine the wrong turns taken and the wasted opportunities and attempt to build up a new humanistic discourse, untainted by any civilizational discourse of the imperialist variety, one which can sustain itself through empathy, a crossing over and a sharing. The writing of history is a process of self-questioning and nation building, it looks both to the past and the future. The past always connects up with the future: the intellectual proceeds to meet it half way. These novels present a counter discourse to the tirades of hatred and anger, to the ideas of revenge, and prod our narrowing memories and shrinking humanity. They constitute both dissent and warning. One of the epigraphs which Sahgal uses in *Lesser Breeds* speaks volumes for the whole enterprises:

"*Vaishnava jan to tehne re kahiye je pid parayi jaane re*"
(Him we call a Vaishnav who knows the pain of others)

This engagement with history is not passive, not objective, not distant, not even an expression of one's views but a getting into the skin of the 'other', the so called target of one's hatred, and of reaching across to the mind of the instigator, in order to assess the chess game he is engaged in.

References

Anantha Murthy, U.R. "A Search for an Identity: A Kannada Writer's Viewpoint", *Creating Theory: Writer on Writing*. Ed. Jasbir Jain. Delhi: Pencraft International, 2000.

Foucault, Michel. *The Order of Things* (1966), English translation 1970. London: Routledge Classics, 2002.

Hasan, Mushirul, "Rewriting the Histories of India's Partition", *Economic and Political Weekly*. Oct. 10-16, 1998.

Hosain, Attia. *Sunlight on a Broken Column* (1961). New Delhi: Arnold Heinemann, 1979.

Kesavan, Mukul. *Looking Through Glass.* Delhi: Ravi Dayal Publisher, 1995.

Loomba, Ania. *Colonialism / Postcolonialism.* London: Routledge, 1998.

Raychauduri, Tapan. *Perceptions, Emotions, Sensibilities.* New Delhi: Oxford University Press, 1999.

Sahgal, Nayantara. *Lesser Breeds.* New Delhi: Harper Collins, 2003.

—. *Mistaken Identity.* London: Heinemann, 1988.

—. *Plans for Departure.* London: Heinemann, 1986.

—. *Rich Like Us.* London: Heinemann, 1985.

Shah Nawaz, Mumtaz. *The Heart Divided* (FP 1957). New Delhi: Penguin, 2004.

Tharoor, Shashi. *India From Midnight to Millennium* (1997). New Delhi: Penguin, 2000.

—. *Riot.* New Delhi: Viking (Penguin), 2001.

—. *The Great Indian Novel.* New Delhi: Penguin, 1989.

Contributors

Supriya *Agarwal* teaches at Khandelwal College, Jaipur. Her doctoral work was on *Orphan Women Characters of the Mid-Victorian Novel*.

Amina *Amin*, was formerly on the faculty of English at Gujarat University, Ahmedabad. Dr. Amin is currently engaged in translation from Gujarati to English.

Meenu *Bhambhani* worked for her doctoral degree on the *Experimentation in the Early Plays of Osborne* and is currently in the U.S. on a Ford Foundation Fellowship.

Jyoti *Bhatia* has worked for her doctoral degree on the *Female Comic Tradition from Burney to Eliot*. She teaches English at Government College, Chittorgarh.

Santosh *Gupta*, Professor, University of Rajasthan is interested in postmodernist and postcolonial writing and has published in these areas.

Meghraj *Khatri* is on the faculty of English, in BJS Rampuria College, Bikaner. Dr. Khatri has worked on *Contemporary Interpretation of Shakespeare* for his doctoral work.

Jasbir *Jain* is currently working on the Postindependence Novel in India. She has published extensively on contemporary literature.

Veena *Jain* is posted at Government College, Alwar. She has worked on Jean Rhys and has interest in feminist studies.

R.K. *Kaul*, formerly professor University of Rajasthan and Professor Emeritus, has published work in several areas. His recent publication is a collection of essays being brought out posthumously.

Seema *Malik* is on the faculty of English at Mohanlal Sukhadia University at Udaipur, and has worked for her doctoral thesis on novels of the partition.

Tanuja *Mathur* teaches English at the University of Rajasthan, she has worked on *The Plays of O'Neill* for her doctoral degree. She is specially interested in Indian poetry in English and drama.

Purabi *Panwar* teaches English in Delhi. She contributes book reviews, literary interviews and literary articles regularly to newspapers and magazines and has published *India in the Writings of Kipling, Forster and Naipaul*.

Neelam *Raisinghani* teaches English at Dungar College, Bikaner. She has worked on the novels of Fanny Burney. Dr. Raisinghani has also translated short stories from Hindi to English.

Krishna *Sharma* has worked an Indian writers and has published in this area. A qualified lawyer she has given up her legal practice in favour of teaching. Dr. Sharma teaches at Government College, Dausa.

Avadhesh Kumar *Singh* is Professor of English at Saurastra University, Rajkot and has a deep interest in narrative structures and language literatures and has written extensively in these areas.

Veena *Singh*, Professor at the University of Rajasthan, is interested in the novels of the Empire and has also worked on Paul Scott. Dr. Singh has edited *Literature and Ideology*.

Vijaya *Singh* worked for her thesis as Forster's Novel into Films. Interested in films, she is researching in this area.

Urmil *Talwar* teaches English at Government Girls' College, Shahpura and has worked on the writers of the thirties. Dr. Talwar is also interested in translation.

Pradeep *Trikha* teaches English at Dayanand College, Ajmer. His specialisation is in Australian literature. Dr. Trikha has interest in translation.

Index

Abbé Dubois 15, 62, 64ff.95
Abhigyanshakuntalam 15, 43ff., 55
"About Chinese Women" 76
Abrams, M.H. 133
Achebe, Chenua 161ff, 169ff 176ff
After Amnesia 37
Ahmad, Aijaz 10, 16, 23, 37, 59, 82ff, 99ff., 103ff., 183, 239, 245
allegory 107ff.
Allegories of the Empire: The Figure of Woman in Colonial Text 267
Allegory: The Theory of a Symbolic Mode 110
Alphonso-Karkala J.B. 150
An Area of Darkness 18, 187, 190

Anand Math 34
Anand, Mulk Raj 93, 151, 265
Anantha Murthy 63, 93, 301, 302
Andrews, C.F. 94
Arya Samaj 34, 114
Ashcroft 10, 164
Ashcroft, Griffiths and Tiffin 10, 12, 23, 41, 112
Attila the Hun 91
Atwood, Margaret 10
Aurobindo, Sri 27, 34, 90, 96

Bandung Conference 105
Between Tradition and Modernity 36
Beyond Belief 186

Bhabha, Homi K. 10, 23, 37, 71, 79, 239, 244ff., 266
Bharatipura 63
Bhatnagar, Manmohan K. 150
Bhattarcharya, P.C. 139, 150
Bhave, Vinoba 200
Biographia Literaria 109
Boehmer, Elleke 25
Borges 107, 251
Bose, Jagdish Chandra 97
Bose, Subhas 118
Brahma 124, 128
Braithwaite 231
Brennan, Timothy 183, 291
British Imperialism 264
Butalia, Urvashi 21
Byron 60

Caliban 56
Carroll, Lewis 303
Cave and the Mountain 264
Césaire, Aimé 23, 34
Chandra, Vikram 32
Chatterjee, Sarat Chandra 30
Chatterjee, Suniti Kumar 110
Chattopadhaya, Bankim Chandra 29, 34, 42
Chaudhary, Nirad 94, 96
Chaudhuri, Tapan Roy 22
Chiplunkar, Vishnu Shashtri 42
Chomsky, Noam 60
Chronicles of Wasted Time 25
Chronicle of Higher Education 21
Cixous, Helene 78
Clive, Robert 61
Coleridge 91, 109

colonialism 54, 100, 103
Colonialism and Filmic Representation 274
Communist block 103, communist countries 106
"Conflict in Cultures" 30
Conrad, Joseph 30
Coomaraswaamy, Ananda 96
"Coping with Postcolonialism" 21
Cornwallis 61
"Crisis in Civilization" 30, 36
Crow 251
Crucible 220
Culture and Imperialism 59, 270

Dalai Lama 91
Dallmayr, Fred and Devy Ganesh 36
Dalpat 42
Dalton, Dennis 29ff., 36
Dance of the Forests 218, 219
Dandi March 120
"Dangerous Art Form" 245
Daruwalla, Keki 10, 240
Darwinism 93
Das, G.K., 265, 267
Das, Kamala 10
Das, Sisir Kumar 110
Dasenbrook, Reed Way 132, 134
Dasgupta, Chidananda 261
Davidson, Harriet 157
Death and the King's Horseman 18, 203ff, 210ff, 214ff., 219
Deb, Amiya 110
decolonisation 102

Decolonizing Feminisms: Race, Gender and Empire Building 274
Decolonizing the Mind 24, 204
Derrida 31, 70, 77ff
Derridean 37
Desai, Mahadev 35
Desai, Morarji 200
Devi, Mahasweta 31
Devy, Ganesh 31
Dhar, T.N. 183
Dharma Sastra 63
Dhingra, Madanlal 27
Dickens, Charles 261ff
Dirlik, Arif 24, 110
Discourse 25
Discovery of India 192ff
Donaldson, Laura 272, 274
Do Ser Dhan 110
Dostoevsky 250
"Drama and the African World View" 211, 218

Eisenstein, Sergei 251
Elaide, Mircea 213, 219
Eliot, T.S. 56, 122, 156ff
Elizabethan and Metaphysical Imagery 110
Empire Writes Back 11, 13, 22, 34, 41, 113, 289
Enigma of Arrival 193
Enlightenment 26, 35, 57, 60
Europe Reconsidered 23
"Explanation and Culture: Marginalia" 70ff
Ezekiel, Nissim 10, 240

Fanon, Frantz 10, 23, 34, 114, 176
Fantastic 248
fantasy 18, 247ff.
Fantasy: The Literature of Subversion 248
Far Pavilions 262
feminisms 75ff
Feminist Theory 75ff
Fictions 251
"Fire Sermon" 156
Fletcher, Angus 110
Forster 261, 263
"Forster's Imperial Erotic 266
Foucauldian 33, 101
Foucault 31, 37, 303
Frankenstein 259
"French Feminism in an International Frame" 76
French Feminism 69ff., 77ff
From Midnight to Millenium 309
"From Ritual to Theatre" 218
Frye, Northrop 108

"Gandhi's Theory of Society and Our Times" 36
Gandhi 10, 15, 26ff, 34ff., 42, 94ff., 113ff, 123ff, 125ff, 133, 138ff, 145, 198, 200
Gandhi, Indira 186, 191, 199, 200
Gandhi, Leela 12
Gandhi, Sanjay 191
Gandhi-Irwin pact 112
Gandhian 31, 94
Gandhian ideology 114ff.
Gandhian movement 112
Gates, Henry Louis 25, 35

Ghose, Sisir Kumar 30
Ghosh, Amitava 32
Gokak, V.K. 110
"Goodbye to Enlightenment" 57
Gora 29, 35
Graff, Gerald 260
Grain of wheat 55
Grass, Gunter 251, 259
Great Indian Middle Class 102
Great Indian Novel, The 309
Griffiths 10, 22, 34
Grimus 250

Habib, Irfan 35, 110
Harding, D.W. 232
Harishchandra, Bhartendu 42
Hastings, Warren 61
Heart Divided, The 304
Heart of Darkness 182
Heat and Dust 262
heteroglossia 73
Hind Swaraj or Indian Home Rule 15, 27, 28ff, 30, 34, 42, 95, 114
Hindu Manners, Customs and Ceremonies 16, 62, 95
Hindu Rashtra 29
Hindu-Muslim relationship 305ff
Hindu Wife, Hindu Nation 310
Hinduism 118ff
"Historiographic Contest and the Postcolonial Theory" 183
History 302
History of India 61
History-Fiction Interface in Indian English Fiction 67

Hitler 91, 193, Hitler's Germany 192
Hodge, Bob 41
Hoff, James 247, 259
Hosain, Attia 305
Hughes, Ted 251
Huizanga, Johan 211, 218
120 Days of Sodom 259
Hyder, Qurratulain 32

Illegitimacy of Nationalism 29, 34, 35
Imagining India 35
Imperial Eyes: Travel Writing and Transculturation 25
Imperialism 14, 53, connection with psotcolonialism 53
In Theory 82, 99ff, 108ff
Inden, Ronald 35
India: A Million Mutinies Now 192, 193ff, 201ff
India: A Wounded Civilization 17ff., 28, 186ff, 190ff, 194ff., 197ff, 202
Indian Opinion 27
Indian Struggle, The 118
Intimate Enemy 13, 16, 31, 36ff, 89ff, 229
Irigaray 78
Iyengar, K.R.S. 124ff., 132, 150

Jackson, Rosemary 248
Jain, Jasbir 131, 205, 229, 236, 237
Jallianwala massacre 56, 252
Jameson, Fredric 24, 32, 101ff, 105, 107

320 • Index

JanMohammed, Abdul 161
Jasmine 235
Jawahar Lal (also see Nehru) 120ff
Jejuri 222ff.
Jewel in the Crown 262, 275ff, 278
Jhabuala, Ruth 262
Jis Lahore Nahin Dekheya, O Jamyai Nahin 291ff
Jones, William Sir 44, 59
Joyce, James 32
Justine of the Misfortunes of Virtue 259

Kachru, Braj 143
Kafka 107
Kalhana 94
Kalidasa 15, 43ff., 52, 64
Kamleshwar 32
Kanthapura 17, 112ff, 122ff., 131ff.
karma 27, 64
Kaye, M.M. 262
Kelkar, Ashok 31
Kesavan, Mukul 32, 303ff, 309
Khomeini, Ayatullah 94
Kundera, Milan 251
King, Bruce 239
Kipling, Rudyard 94, 95ff, 265, 269, 308
Kipnis, Laura 279
Kirpal, Viney 105, 183, 239
Kolatkar, Arun 18, 222ff, 243
Kongi's Harvest 218
Kosambi, D.D. 96
Krishna 128, 139
Krishnaswamy, Revathi 183
Kristeva, Julia 16, 31, 76ff
Kumar, Krishna 304

Larson, Charles R. 133
Last Man 259
"Laugh of the Medusa" 78ff
Laws of Manu 63
Lean, David 261ff, 271ff, 277, 280ff
Lener Breeds 307ff
Lewis, M.G. 248
Lion and the Jewel 218
Literature and Ideology 183
Location of Culture 245
Looking Through Glass 303ff, 306, 310

Macaulay 61, 113
Madmen and Specialists 205
Mahabharata 15, 45, 85, 123
Maini, D.S. 131, 150
Maley 12
Manichean code 161; discourse 79
Manu 50, 64
Mao 91
"Marginality in the Teaching Machine" 73
Marquez, Garcia 74, 251
Marx 102ff
Marxist Feminist 69ff
Marxist 74, 80, 100ff., 104ff, 110
Materialist Feminists 69
Max Muller 59, 66
Maxwell, Anne 79
Mazzini 60

McSweeney, Kerry 189
McClintock 43
Mehrotra, Arvind K. 244
Midnight's Children 18, 191, 250ff., 252
Mill, James 61
Mill, John Stuart 60, 61
Mills, Sara 25ff
Mishra, Vijay 41
Mistaken Identity 307
Mitchell, W.J.T. 21
modernist elements in *APTI* 264
Mohanty, Gopinath 109
Moon, Sir Penderel 304
Moore-Gilbert, Bart 12
Muggeridge, Malcolm 25
Mukherjee, Arun 23, 34, 284, 301
Mukherjee, Bharati 229, 235
Mukherjee, Meenakshi 23, 129
Mukherjee, Sujit 110
Muslim identity 304
My Story 230
"Myth of the Postmodern Breakthrough" 260

Nadir Shah 91
Naik, M.K. 149
Naipaul, V.S. 17, 18, 28, 185ff., 196ff., 240
Nandy, Ashis 10, 13, 16, 29, 31, 34, 35ff., 89ff., 94ff., 229
Naoroji, Dadabhai 27
Napoleon 61
Narasimhaiah, C.D. 110
Narayan, Jai Prakash 200
Narayan, R.K. 97, 121, 151, 197, 265

Narmad 42
Nath, Suresh 132, 150
"National Longing for Form" 291
Nativism 37
Nauriya, Anil 29
Nehru 192, Nehruvian 118ff., 125ff
Nelson, Cecil 143, 50
Nemade, Bhalchandra 31
Neruda, Pablo 74
New French Feminism: An Anthology 76
Newton, Judith 69

Of Grammatology 69
One Hundred Years of Solitude 251
Opera Wonyosi 205
Oppositional Aesthetics 301
Orient 59, 62ff, 99
Orientalism 13, 37, 59ff, 99, 105, 229
Orientalists 16, 59, 62ff, 64ff; English 61
Orwell 94
Other Side of Postcolonialism 11
Outside in the Teaching Machine 245
Overcrowded Barracoon and other Articles 187, 191

Pacification of the Primitive Tribes of Lower Niger 182
Paraja 110
Paranjape, Makarand 21, 37, 41

Parry, Benita 78ff
Parthasarthy, R. 18, 222, 227, 228ff, 230ff, 233ff, 236, 238, 240ff
partition 289ff, 296
Parvati 126
Passage to India 261ff, 271ff (the film)
Pather Dabi 30
Patil, V.T. 150
Perushek, Darshan 21
Peter, Penelope 266
Phelps, Gilbert 178
Picture of Dorian Gray 259
Pillai, Thakazi Shiva Shankar 109
Plans for Departure 307
Poetry From Leeds 230
Postcolonial Studies Reader 12, 113
Postcolonial Criticism 12
Postcolonial Theory 12
Postcolonial World 263
Postcolonial 12, enterprise 33, identity 24, 23
Postcolonialism/s 9, 10, 12ff, 19, 24, 31, 40ff, 238ff, 289ff, 296, 299ff
Postcoloniality 15, 19, 20
Power relationship 20
Prakash, Prem 150
Pratt, Mary Louise 25
Private Memories and Confessions of a Justified Sinner 259
Prospero 56, 188
Proust 32

Radha Krishnan 96

Raghuvansa 94
Raizada, Harish 150
Ram 120, 123, 124, 128, 139, 236
Ramanujan 97, 222, 230, 243
Ramayana 28, 88, 123
Ramrajya 28
Rangra, Ranavir 133
Rao, Raja 17, 112ff, 122ff, 131ff, 148ff, 265
Ravana Raj 139
Ravana 120, 123, 124, 139
Ray, Niharranjan 110
Ray, Satyajit 261
Raychaudhuri, Tapan 395, 310ff. "Rereading *Divide and Quit*" 310ff.
Raza, Rahi Masoom 32
Renu, Phaneshwar Nath 32
resistance 300
Rhys, Jean 79
Rich Like Us 306ff
Richards, David 215
Riot 309ff
"Road" 218
Rosenfelt, Deborah 69
Rough Passage 18, 222ff, 228ff, 230f, 240, 244
Rousseau 92
Roy, Ram Mohan 92
Rushdie, Salman 18, 32, 33, 102, 183, 191, 239, 245, 250ff., 252ff, 262, 301

Sade 247, 259
Sahgal, Nayantara 32, 33, 229, 235, 303, 306
Sahni, Bhisham 32

Said, Edward 10, 15, 23, 54, 59ff., 66, 71, 89ff., 99ff, 103ff, 183, 229, 265, 270
Samskara 93
Saran, A.K. 36
Saraswati Swami Dayanand 26, 113
Sarkar, Tanika 310
Sartre 182ff
Satanic Verse 250
satyagraha 27
Schorer, Mark 168, 196
Scott, Paul 262
"Search for an Identity: A Kannada Writer's View" 302
secular concept 28
Seth, Vikram 301
Shah Nawaz, Mumtaz 304
Shahane, V.A. 265
Shakespeare 44, 56
Shame 250
Sharma, Atma Ram 150
Sharma, K.K. 150
Sharma, L.K. 194
Sharpe, Jenny 267, 268
Shelley 60
Shelley, Mary 247, 259
Shohat and stam 263
Singh, Khushwant 32
Singh, Namvar 110
Sita 139
Siva 126, 128
Slemon 41
Sobti, Krishna 32, 301
Sontag, Susan 60
Soyinka 18, 162, 203ff, 210ff, 217ff, 218
Spence, Louis 263

Spivak, Gayatri 10, 16, 23, 31, 37, 42, 68ff, 70ff., 73ff, 78, 239, 245
Srivastava, Ramesh 150
Stam, Robert 263
Stanton 12
Stevenson, R.L. 247, 259
Stone, Wilfred 264
Strange Case of Dr. Jekyll and Mr. Hyde 259
structuralism 100
Studies in William Jones 66
Suleri, Sara 266
Sunlight on a Broken Column 305
Swaraj 27
Synge, John Millington 218

Tagore, Rabindranath 29ff., 35, 36
Taine, Hippolyte 60
Tainenmin Square 94
Tharoor, Shashi 303, 309ff
"Technique as Discovery" 168
Ten Twentieth Century Poets 230
Tempest 15, 24, 43, 56
The Film Sense 251
The Tin Drum 251
The World, The Text and the Critic 59, 101
Thiang'o, Ngugi wa 23, 24, 204
Things Falls Apart 17, 55, 161ff, 168ff, 176ff
Thoreau 60
Tiffin, Helen 166
Tilak, Bal Gangadhar 27
Tipu Sultan 62
To Sir, With Love 231

Todorov 248
Tolstoy 60
Trails of Brother Jero 218
Tree of Man 182
Trevelyan, George Otto 185
Trinh-Minh ha 80
Tristam Shandy 251
Trivedi, Harish 21, 43
Tuve, Rosamund 110
Twice Born Fiction 129
"Typists in a Phoenix Building" 156ff

Ulysses 236
Unthanking Eurocentrism: Multiculturalism and Media 263

Ved Vyas 15, 45ff
Vietnam, Vietnamese 60

Vivekanand 27, 29, 34

Waiting for the Mahatma 121
Wajahat, Asgar 291ff
Walker, Shirley 155
Waste Land 122, 156, 159
Wellesley 61
Wide Sargasso Sea 79
Wilde, Oscar 247, 259
Wilkins, Charles 61
Williams, Monier 63
Wilson, Edmund 75
Woman to Man, "Woman to Man" 153ff, 156ff, 159
Wordsworth 92
Wretched of the Earth 10, 13, 182, 183
Wright, Judith 17, 153ff

Xiaoping, Deng 91

$32